3rd Workshop on Threat, Aggression and Cyberbullying (TRAC 2022)

Gyeongju, South Korea
12-17 October 2022

ISBN: 978-1-7138-6197-3

Printed from e-media with permission by:

Curran Associates, Inc.
57 Morehouse Lane
Red Hook, NY 12571

Printed with permission by Curran Associates, Inc. (2023)

For permission requests, please contact the Association for Computational Linguistics at the address below.

Association for Computational Linguistics
209 N. Eighth Street
Stroudsburg, Pennsylvania 18360

Phone: 1-570-476-8006
Fax: 1-570-476-0860

acl@aclweb.org

Additional copies of this publication are available from:

Curran Associates, Inc.
57 Morehouse Lane
Red Hook, NY 12571 USA
Phone: 845-758-0400
Fax: 845-758-2633
Email: curran@proceedings.com
Web: www.proceedings.com

COLING

International Conference on Computational Linguistics

Proceedings of the Conference and Workshops

COLING

Volume 29 (2022), No. 12

Proceedings of the Third Workshop on Threat, Aggression and Cyberbullying (TRAC 2022)

The 29th International Conference on Computational Linguistics

October 12 - 17, 2022
Gyeongju, Republic of Korea

Introduction

As the number of users and their web-based interaction has increased, incidents of a verbal threats, aggression and related behaviour like trolling, cyberbullying, and hate speech have also increased manifold globally. The reach and extent of the Internet have given such incidents unprecedented power and influence to affect the lives of billions of people. Such incidents of online abuse have not only resulted in mental health and psychological issues for users, but they have manifested in other ways, spanning from deactivating social media accounts to instances of self-harm and suicide.

To mitigate these issues, researchers have begun to explore the use of computational methods for identifying such toxic interactions online. In particular, Natural Language Processing (NLP) and ML-based methods have shown great promise in dealing with such abusive behaviour through early detection of inflammatory content.

In fact, we have observed an explosion of NLP-based research on offensive content in the last few years. This growth has been accompanied by the creation of new venues such as the WOAH and the TRAC workshop series. Community-based competitions, like tasks 5/6 at SemEval-2019, task 12 at SemEval-2020, and task 5/7 at SemEval-2021 have also proven to be extremely popular. In fact, because of the huge community interest, multiple workshops are being held on the topic in a single year. For example, in 2018 ACL hosted both the Abusive Language Online workshop (EMNLP) as well as TRAC-1 (COLING). Both venues achieved healthy participation with 21 and 24 papers, respectively. Interest in the topic has continued to grow since then and given its immense popularity, we are proposing a new edition of the workshop to support the community and further research in this area.

As in the earlier editions, TRAC focuses on the applications of NLP, ML and pragmatic studies on aggression and impoliteness to tackle these issues. As such the workshop also includes shared tasks on 'Aggression Identification. The task consisted of two sub-tasks - (1) Bias, Threat and Aggression Identification in Context and (2) Generalising across domains - COVID-19. For task 1, the participants were provided with a "thread" of comments with information about the presence of different kinds of biases and threats (viz. gender bias, gendered threat and none, etc) and its discursive relationship to the previous comment as well as the original post (viz. attack, abet, defend, counter-speech and gaslighting). In a series/thread of comments, participants were required to predict the presence of aggression and bias in each comment, possibly making use of the context. In this task, a total dataset of approximately 60k comments (approximately 180k annotation samples) in Meitei, Bangla and Hindi, compiled in the ComMA Project, were provided for training and testing.

Both the workshop and the shared task received a very encouraging response from the community. The proceedings include 4 oral, 3 posters, and 2 system description papers. In addition to this, the workshop also includes 1 Demo to be presented in the workshop.
We would like to thank all the authors for their submissions and members of the Program Committee for their invaluable efforts in reviewing and providing feedback to all the papers. We would also like to thank all the members of the Organising Committee who have helped immensely in various aspects of the organisation of the workshop and the shared task.

Workshop Chairs

Workshop Chairs

Ritesh Kumar, Dr. Bhimrao Ambedkar University, India
Atul Kr. Ojha, University of Galway, Ireland & Panlingua Language Processing LLP, India
Marcos Zampieri, George Mason University, USA
Shervin Malmasi, Amazon Inc., USA
Daniel Kadar, Research Institute for Linguistics, Hungarian Academy of Sciences, Hungary

Assistant Organisers

Siddharth Singh, Dr. Bhimrao Ambedkar University, India
Shyam Ratan, Dr. Bhimrao Ambedkar University, India

Shared Task Organising Committee

Shervin Malmasi, Amazon Inc., USA
Siddharth Singh, Dr. Bhimrao Ambedkar University, India
Shyam Ratan, Dr. Bhimrao Ambedkar University, India
Ritesh Kumar, Dr. Bhimrao Ambedkar University, India
Atul Kr. Ojha, University of Galway, Ireland & Panlingua Language Processing LLP, India
Bharathi Raja Chakravarthi, University of Galway

Programme Committee

Atul Kr. Ojha, University of Galway, Ireland & Panlingua Language Processing LLP, India
Bharathi Raja Chakravarthi, University of Galway
Bornini Lahiri, Indian Institute of Technology-Kharagpur, India
Bruno Emanuel Martins, IST and INESC-ID
Cheng-Te Li, National Cheng Kung University, Taiwan
Chuan-Jie Lin, National Taiwan Ocean University, Taiwan
David Jurgens, University of Michigan
Denis Gordeev, The Russian Presidential Academy of National Economy and Public Administration under the President of the Russian Federation
Dennis Tenen, Columbia University, USA
Dhairya Dalal, University of Galway
Els Lefever, LT3, Ghent University, Belgium
Faneva Ramiandrisoa, IRIT
Han Liu, Cardiff University
Hugo Jair Escalante, INAOE, Mexico
Koustava Goswami, University of Galway
Liang-Chih Yu, Yuan Ze University, Taiwan
Lun-Wei Ku, Academia Sinica, Taiwan
Lütfiye Seda Mut Altın, Pompeu Fabra University Mainack Mondal, University of Chicago, USA
Manuel Montes-y-Gómez, INAOE, Mexico
Marco Guerini, Fondazione Bruno Kessler, Trento
Ming-Feng Tsai, National Chengchi University, Taiwan
Monojit Choudhury, Microsoft Turing
Nemanja Djuric, Aurora Innovation
Parth Patwa, Indian Institute of Information Technology, Sri City
Preslav Nakov, Qatar Computing Research Institute, Qatar
Priya Rani, University of Galway

Ritesh Kumar, Dr. B. R. Ambedakar University, India
Roman Klinger, University of Stuttgart, Germany
Ruifeng Xu, Harbin Institute of Technology, China
Saja Tawalbeh, University of Antwerp
Sara E. Garza, Universidad Autónoma de Nuevo León (UANL), Mexico
Shardul Suryawanshi, University of Galway
Shubhanshu Mishra, Twitter Inc.
Valerio Basile, University of Turin
Veronique Hoste, LT3, Ghent University, Belgium
Xavier Tannier, Université Paris-Sud, LIMSI, CNRS, France
Zeerak Waseem, University of Sheffield, UK

Invited Speaker

Valerio Basile, University of Turin, Italy

Valerio Basile is an Assistant Professor at the Computer Science Department of the University of Turin, Italy, member of the Content-centered Computing group and the Hate Speech Monitoring lab. His work spans across several areas such as: formal representations of meaning, linguistic annotation, natural language generation, commonsense knowledge, semantic parsing, sentiment analysis, and hate speech detection, perspectives and bias in supervised machine learning, from data creation to system evaluation. He is currently PI of the project BREAKhateDOWN "Toxic Language Understanding in Online Communication", and among the main proponents of the Perspectivist Data Manifesto: https://pdai.info

Title: The Evaluation of Language Models for Undesirable Language Analysis

Abstract:

In the past five years, the field of Natural Language Processing has seen several important changes and paradigm shifts. Methodologically, large neural language models have taken the spotlight as the new state of the art for most classification (and other kinds of) tasks. At the same time, the focus of research has opened up more and more to the study of pragmatics phenomena in natural language. Among these, toxic, abusive, offensive language, hate speech, and other undesirable phenomena have been subject of the development of specialized models, language resources, and evaluation campaigns.

In this talk, he will give a partial overview of the design and the results of large-scale evaluation efforts, in a multilingual perspective. Quantitative results on such subjective and hard-to-define phenomena should not be taken at a face value. Rather, the quality of benchmarks, and the annotated data behind them, should be carefully analysed. Finally, he will briefly introduce the perspectivist framework and its potential impact on the evaluation of models for undesirable language analysis.

Panelists: Amitava Das (Wipro AI), Stavros Assimakopoulos (University of Malta), Pilar G. Blitvich (University of North Carolina) and Bertie Vidgen (The Alan Turing Institute)

Table of Contents

Conference Program

Monday, October 17, 2022 (GMT+9)

09:00–09:15 **Inaugural Session**
Chair: Workshop Chairs

09:00–09:15 *Welcome*
Workshop Chairs

09:15–10:30 **Q&A Session 1**

09:15–09:30 *L3Cube-MahaHate: A Tweet-based Marathi Hate Speech Detection Dataset and BERT Models*
Hrushikesh Patil, Abhishek Velankar and Raviraj Joshi

09:30–09:45 *Which One Is More Toxic? Findings from Jigsaw Rate Severity of Toxic Comments*
Millon Das, Punyajoy Saha and Mithun Das

09:45–10:00 *Can Attention-based Transformers Explain or Interpret Cyberbullying Detection?*
Kanishk Verma, Tijana Milosevic and Brian Davis

10:00–10:15 *Bias, Threat and Aggression Identification Using Machine Learning Techniques on Multilingual Comments*
Kirti Kumari, Shaury Srivastav and Rajiv Ranjan Suman

10:15–10:30 *The Role of Context in Detecting the Target of Hate Speech*
Ilia Markov and Walter Daelemans

10:30–11:00 ***COFEE BREAK***

Monday, October 17, 2022 (GMT+9) (continued)

11:00–12:30 Q&A Session 2

11:00–11:25 *Annotating Targets of Toxic Language at the Span Level*
Baran Barbarestani, Isa Maks and Piek Vossen

11:25–11:50 *Is More Data Better? Re-thinking the Importance of Efficiency in Abusive Language Detection with Transformers-Based Active Learning*
Hannah Kirk, Bertie Vidgen and Scott Hale

11:50–12:15 *A Lightweight Yet Robust Approach to Textual Anomaly Detection*
Leslie Barrett, Robert Kingan, Alexandra Ortan and Madhavan Seshadri

14:00–15:00 Keynote Talk

14:00–15:00 *The Evaluation of Language Models for Undesirable Language Analysis*
Valerio Basile, University of Turin

15:00–16:00 *COFEE BREAK*

16:00–17:00 Panel Discussion

16:00–17:00 *The Role of Pragmatics in Offensive and Aggressive Language Identification Research*
Amitava Das (Wipro AI), Stavros Assimakopoulos (University of Malta), Pilar G. Blitvich (University of North Carolina) and Bertie Vidgen (The Alan Turing Institute)

17:00–17:50 Q&A Session 3

17:00–17:25 *Detection of Negative Campaign in Israeli Municipal Elections*
Marina Litvak, Natalia Vanetik, Sagiv Talker and Or Machlouf

17:25–17:50 *Hypothesis Engineering for Zero-Shot Hate Speech Detection*
Janis Goldzycher and Gerold Schneider

17:50–18:00 Closing

17:50–18:00 *Vote of Thanks*
Workshop Chairs

L3Cube-MahaHate: A Tweet-based Marathi Hate Speech Detection Dataset and BERT models

Abhishek Velankar[1,3], **Hrushikesh Patil**[1,3], and **Raviraj Joshi**[2,3]
[1]Pune Institute of Computer Technology, Pune
[2]Indian Institute of Technology Madras, Chennai
[3]L3Cube, Pune
{velankarabhishek,hrushi2900}@gmail.com
ravirajoshi@gmail.com

Abstract

Social media platforms are used by a large number of people prominently to express their thoughts and opinions. However, these platforms have contributed to a substantial amount of hateful and abusive content as well. Therefore, it is important to curb the spread of hate speech on these platforms. In India, Marathi is one of the most popular languages used by a wide audience. In this work, we present L3Cube-MahaHate, the first major Hate Speech Dataset in Marathi. The dataset is curated from Twitter and annotated manually. Our dataset consists of over 25000 distinct tweets labeled into four major classes i.e hate, offensive, profane, and not. We present the approaches used for collecting and annotating the data and the challenges faced during the process. Finally, we present baseline classification results using deep learning models based on CNN, LSTM, and Transformers. We explore mono-lingual and multi-lingual variants of BERT like MahaBERT, IndicBERT, mBERT, and xlm-RoBERTa and show that mono-lingual models perform better than their multi-lingual counterparts. The MahaBERT model provides the best results on L3Cube-MahaHate Corpus. The data and models are available at https://github.com/l3cube-pune/MarathiNLP .

Keywords: Natural Language Processing, Convolutional Neural Networks, Long Short Term Memory, FastText, BERT, Hate Speech Detection.

1 Introduction

In the past decade, there has been an expeditious rise in the popularity of online social media platforms all over the globe. People have become more open to sharing their opinions without thinking excessively. This often leads to the spread of hate or offensive speech thereby causing violence and cyberbullying. Hate speech is a kind of abusive language directed towards a community that is underprivileged in terms of race, gender, ethnic origin, disability, etc., or can be an insult or threat to an individual (MacAvaney et al., 2019; Matamoros-Fernández and Farkas, 2021). The users often defy the boundaries of freedom of speech without even realizing it by posting harmful messages and comments (Waseem and Hovy, 2016). Therefore it is today's need to neutralize these activities from proliferating further.

In this work, we consider hate speech detection in the Marathi language, a regional language in India, spoken by over 83 million people across the country (Joshi, 2022). Despite being one of the popular languages in India, work in the area of hate speech detection in Marathi is extremely limited (Mandl et al., 2021; Velankar et al., 2021; Glazkova et al., 2021; Bhatia et al., 2021) as compared to other languages (Del Vigna12 et al., 2017; Romim et al., 2021; Corazza et al., 2020; Schmidt and Wiegand, 2019). Even general text classification in Marathi has received limited attention (Kulkarni et al., 2022, 2021). In this paper, we present, L3Cube-MahaHate Corpus, the largest publicly available hate speech dataset in Marathi. The dataset is collected from Twitter, tagged with four fine-grained labels which are defined as follows-

Hate (HATE): A Twitter post abusing a specific group of people or community based on their religion, race, ethnic origin, gender, geographical location, etc. stimulating violent behaviors.

Proceedings of the 29th International Conference on Computational Linguistic, pages 1–9
October 12–17, 2022.

Offensive (OFFN): A tweet containing harmful language leading to insulting or dehumanizing, at times threatening a particular individual.

Profane (PRFN): A tweet including the use of typical swear words or profane, cursing language which is ordinarily insupportable.

Not (NOT): A post that does not contain any insulting or abusive content or profane words in the language used.

The dataset consists of over 25000 samples tagged manually with the classes explained above. We further provide an extensive study of the data collection approaches, different policies used, and challenges faced during the annotation process as well. We also provide the statistical analysis of our dataset along with the distribution of train, test, and validation data. Lastly, we perform multiple experiments to evaluate state-of-the-art deep learning models on the dataset and provide the baseline results to the community. All the resources will be publicly shared on Github.

The MahaBERT model fined-tuned on L3Cube-MahaHate is termed as MahaHate-BERT[1][2] and is shared publicly on model hub. All the resources are publicly shared on github[3].

2 Related Work

Hate speech detection is considered to be a highly critical problem and a lot of attempts have been made to control it. A significant amount of work can be seen in English text analysis. But recently, efforts have been made towards widening the research in regional languages like Marathi as well.

Gaikwad et al. (2021) presented the Marathi Offensive Language Dataset (MOLD), with nearly 2,500 annotated tweets labeled as offensive and not offensive. It is considered the first dataset for offensive language identification in Marathi. Also, they evaluated the performance of several traditional machine learning models and deep learning models (e.g. LSTM) trained on MOLD.

Bhardwaj et al. (2020) collected over 8200 hostile and non-hostile Hindi text samples from multiple social media platforms like Twitter, Facebook, WhatsApp. Hostile posts were further extended into fake, defamation, hate, and offensive. A total of 8192 posts were collected and tested on various machine learning models using mBERT encoding.

A Hindi-English code-mixed corpus was constructed in Bohra et al. (2018) using the tweets posted online for the duration of five years. Tweets were scrapped using Twitter python API by selecting certain hashtags and keywords from political events, public protests, riots, etc. After removing noisy samples a dataset of 4575 code-mixed tweets was created. The experiments were performed with SVM and Random Forest algorithms along with character and word N-gram features.

In Kulkarni et al. (2021) authors presented a dataset containing over 16000 Marathi tweets, manually tagged in three classes namely positive, negative and neutral. They also provided a policy for tagging sentences by their sentiment. Analysis was performed on CNN, BiLSTM, and BERT models.

Davidson et al. (2017) collected hate phrases identified by Hatebase.org and then used those phrases to collect English tweets from Twitter using Twitter API. The final set of 25k tweets was annotated by CrowdFlower workers with labels hate, offensive and neither. This dataset was then tested on Logistic Regression, Naive Bayes, Decision Trees, random forests, and linear SVMs.

In Geet D'Sa et al. (2021), the authors evaluated the effect of filtering the generated data used for Data Augmentation (DA). This demonstrates up to 7.3% and up to 25% of relative improvements on macro-averaged F1

[1]https://huggingface.co/l3cube-pune/mahahate-bert

[2]https://huggingface.co/l3cube-pune/mahahate-multi-roberta

[3]https://github.com/l3cube-pune/MarathiNLP

on two widely used hate speech corpora.

Ajao et al. (2019) proposed a hypothesis that there exists a relation between fake messages or rumors and sentiments of the texts posted online. The experiments were performed on the standard Twitter fake news dataset and showed good improvement on the same.

Gao and Huang (2018) provided an annotated corpus of hate speech with the context information. This evaluates by using logistic regression and neural network models for hate speech detection around 3% and 4%, and it improves to 7% by combining these two models together.

Mathur et al. (2018) presented MIMCT to detect offensive(Hate or Abusive) Hinglish tweets from the proposed Hinglish Offensive Tweet dataset. Demonstrated the use of the multi-channel CNN-LSTM model for sentiment analysis.

3 Dataset Creation

3.1 Collection

We created the Hate Speech dataset using the tweets posted online by different users across the Maharashtra region considering the period of over the last 5 years. There are plenty of different python libraries available such as Twint[4], GetOldTweets[5], Snscrape[6], etc. which can be used to collect Twitter posts. Twitter provides its own API as well. We used the Twint python library for scraping the tweets.

To obtain the hateful tweets, firstly, we created a list of over 150 bad words in Marathi which are predominantly used by online users to spread hostility. Some of these are typical swear words in Marathi and other offensive words. These words were in Marathi Devanagari script as we are not concerned about Roman or code-mixed text in this work. We will be publishing the final list on GitHub. These words were used as a search query to obtain hate, offensive, and profane tweets. The majority of the tweets that we obtained are related to political and social issues. We also made a note of controversial events with their time frame happening in India in the last couple of years which particularly triggered violence on social media. To avoid bias towards certain words or phrases, we have limited the tweets for a particular search query to a number less than 150. Also, while collecting the tweets, we have not included any reference to the author of the tweet thereby eliminating the bias towards that author.

In our publicly available version of the dataset, we have kept all the hashtags, symbols, emojis, and URLs for anyone to experiment on. However, we have removed all of these while performing the baseline experiments. Furthermore, we will be removing the user mentions from the public dataset to maintain complete user anonymity.

3.2 Annotation

The entire dataset has been labelled manually by the 4 annotators considering four major classes viz. hate, offensive, profane, and not. All the annotators were native Marathi speakers and were fluent in reading and writing in Marathi. The annotation guidelines were set before the tagging exercise. The first 200 sentences were tagged together to further improve the consistency post which sentences were tagged in parallel except for ambiguous sentences. The tweets which were targeted at a single individual thereby criticizing or dehumanizing the individual are tagged as offensive. These tweets were mainly attributed to an individual politician, celebrity, or any random person with the use of singular phrases. The tweets which were targeted at a group of people describing the deficiencies towards race, political opinion, sexual orientation, gender, etc. are tagged as hate. These tweets were majorly concentrated towards political parties or the ruling government. Also, a few samples belong to negative comments on minority groups and gender bias. The tweets which contain swear or profane words are strictly tagged as profane,

[4]https://pypi.org/project/twint/

[5]https://pypi.org/project/GetOldTweets3/

[6]https://github.com/JustAnotherArchivist/snscrape

even if they describe the offensive or hateful category. The tweets that do not satisfy any of the above criteria are simply tagged as NOT. Congratulatory and thanking tweets are tagged as NOT as well. Some sample tweets for the above classes are given in Table 3.

In some cases, the intention of the user behind a tweet cannot be suitably identified. In such cases, the tweets were reviewed again and voting among 4 annotators was used to decide on the labels. Also, we encountered a few tweets where hateful comments were quoted by a news handle. As these posts may indirectly promote violence, we tagged them in the hateful category. To collect the NOT tweets, we selected many Marathi Twitter handles and scraped their tweets, which gave us unbiased data.

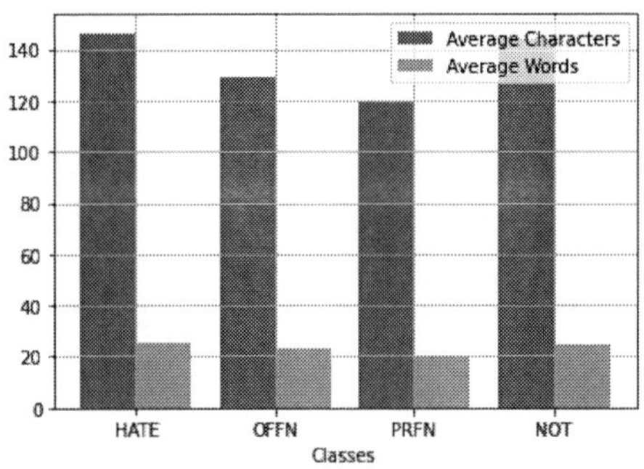

Figure 1: Average characters and words per label

3.3 Dataset Details

Initially, we collected over 40k tweets in Marathi. Among these, we annotated ~28000 samples. After removing over 3k noisy tweets which particularly included poorly written text i.e. the text with the use of regional words which are not commonly spoken in Marathi or a large number of grammatical mistakes, we randomly selected 6250 samples from each of the 4 classes giving the total count of 25000 tweets. Although this uniform distribution of tweets does not represent the true distribution it makes the model building easier and does not require imbalance handling. We analyzed a few statistics on the dataset. The average number of words per tweet in an entire dataset is 21 and the average number of characters is 113. The label-wise distribution is given in Figure 1. The length of samples varies in the range of 2 to 93. The distribution of the length of tweets and the number of characters per tweet is given in Figures 2 and 3 respectively. The dataset can be used for binary classification as well. To match the number of hateful samples viz. Hate, Offensive, Profane all included, we collected over 12500 extra NOT samples apart from that of 4-class corpus giving an equal distribution of 18750 samples in hateful and non-hateful categories. This binary corpus of 37.5k will also be provided along with the original dataset. The binary dataset is distributed into train, test and validation sets in the ratio of 80:10:10 percent of the total dataset. Table 1 shows the 4-class dataset distribution in training, testing and validation samples.

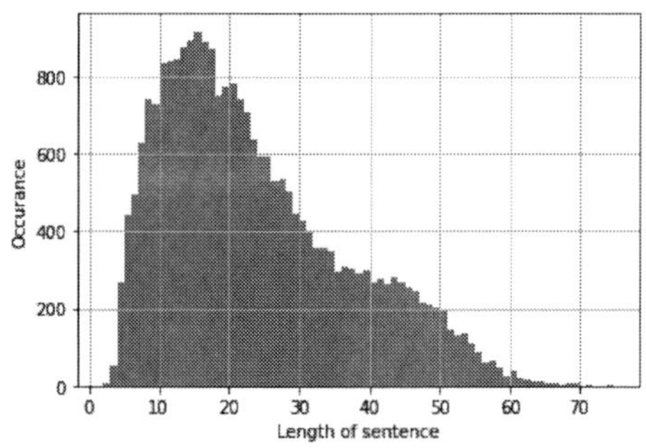

Figure 2: Distribution of the length of a tweet

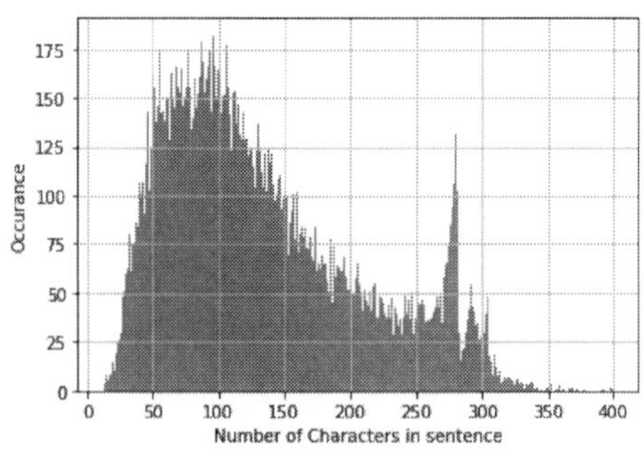

Figure 3: Distribution of the number of characters in a tweet

Split	HATE	OFFN	PRFN	NOT	TOTAL
Train	5375	5375	5375	5375	21500
Test	500	500	500	500	2000
Validation	375	375	375	375	1500

Table 1: Dataset label distribution

Model	Variant	2-Class Accuracy	4-Class Accuracy
CNN	Random	**0.880**	0.703
	Trainable	0.866	0.710
	Non-Trainable	0.870	**0.751**
LSTM	Random	0.857	0.681
	Trainable	0.860	0.691
	Non-Trainable	**0.869**	**0.751**
BiLSTM	Random	0.858	0.699
	Trainable	0.860	0.664
	Non-Trainable	**0.870**	**0.761**
BERT	IndicBERT	0.865	0.711
	mBERT	0.903	0.783
	xlm-RoBERTa	0.894	0.787
	MahaALBERT	0.883	0.764
	MahaBERT	**0.909**	**0.803**
	MahaRoBERTa	0.902	0.803

Table 2: Classification results on different architectures

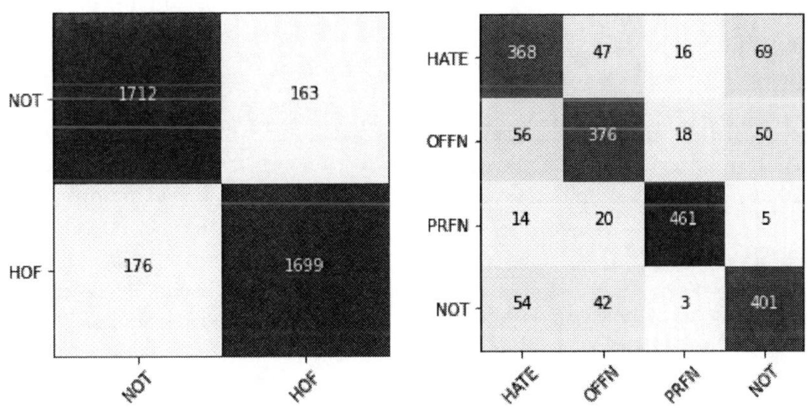

(a) 2-class classification

(b) 4-class classification

Figure 4: Confusion matrices for the best models

4 Experiments

4.1 Model architectures

We have used multiple state-of-the-art deep learning architectures (Velankar et al., 2021), (Joshi et al., 2021), (Joshi et al., 2019) to obtain the baseline results on 2-class as well as 4-class classification. Before training the models, we have cleaned the data by removing unwanted symbols, user mentions, hashtags. Following algorithms are used for the evaluation of results:

CNN: The CNN model has a 1D convolution layer with a filter of size 300 and a kernel of size 3. It used ReLU activation, followed by max-pooling with pool size 2. the same layers were added again which is followed by a dense layer of size 50 and ReLU activation. Lastly, the layer with softmax activation and 2 nodes was used. A dropout of 0.3 was used after the 1D max-pooling layer.

LSTM: The LSTM layer with 32 nodes was used. It was followed by a 1D global max-pooling. The dense layer with 16 nodes along with ReLU activation was used, followed by 0.2 dropout. A dense layer with 2 nodes and softmax activation was used as a final layer of the model.

BiLSTM: Bi-LSTM layer with 300 nodes followed by a 1D global max-pooling layer was used. The dense layer was used with 100 nodes and ReLU activation was used with it. This was followed by a dropout of 0.2. At last, the final layer with 2 nodes with activation softmax was used.

BERT: BERT is a bi-directional transformer-based model (Devlin et al., 2019) pre-trained over large textual data to learn language representations. It can be fine-tuned for specific machine learning tasks. We used the following variations of BERT to obtain baseline results:

- Multilingual-BERT (mBERT) - trained on and usable with 104 languages with Wikipedia using a masked language modeling (MLM) objective (Devlin et al., 2018).
- IndicBERT - a multilingual ALBERT model released by Ai4Bharat, trained on large-scale corpora (Kakwani et al., 2020), covering 12 major Indian languages: Assamese, Bengali, English, Gujarati, Hindi, Kannada, Malayalam, Marathi, Oriya, Punjabi, Tamil, Telugu.
- XLM-RoBERTa - a multilingual version of RoBERTa (Conneau et al., 2019). It is pre-trained on 2.5TB of filtered CommonCrawl data containing 100 languages with the Masked language modeling (MLM) objective and can be used for downstream tasks.
- MahaBERT - a multilingual BERT model (Joshi, 2022) fine-tuned on L3Cube-MahaCorpus and other publicly available Marathi monolingual datasets containing a total of 752M tokens.

4.2 Results

We performed our experiments on CNN, LSTM, and Transformer based models. For CNN and LSTM models, we have used random and fast text initialization for the word embeddings. The pre-trained embeddings were used in both trainable and non-trainable modes. The former means it was used by letting the embedding layer adapt to the training data and the latter by preventing it from being updated during training. Additionally, we used pre-trained language models, particularly the variations of BERT such as IndicBERT, Multilingual BERT, XLM-RoBERTa, and a few custom BERT models to obtain the results. All the 2-class and 4-class accuracies are displayed in Table 2.

In CNN and LSTM based models, non-trainable fast text mode is outperforming other configurations in both the binary and 4-class results. All the monolingual Marathi BERT models are surpassing the multilingual versions of BERT models i.e IndicBERT, mBERT, and xlm-RoBERTa. It was observed that the non-trainable fast text setting for CNN and LSTM based models is performing competitively with the BERT models even surpassing the indicBERT for both classes. The MahaBERT model gives the best binary classification results whereas MahaRoBERTa gives the best 4-class accuracy. The confusion matrices for respective best results are shown in figures 4a and 4b.

5 Conclusion

In this paper, we have presented L3CubeMahaHate - a hate speech dataset containing 25000 distinct samples equally distributed in 4 classes. This is the first major dataset in the domain of hate speech. We also provide the binary version of the dataset of over 37500 samples. We further perform experiments to obtain baseline results on various deep learning models like CNN, LSTM, BiLSTM, and transformer-based BERT models such as IndicBERT,

S.No.	Tweet	English Translation	Tag
1	अशा प्रकारे खोडसाळ बातम्या देणाऱ्या या वृत्तसंस्थाना जोडयाने मारले पाहिजे.	In this way, the news agencies which spread vicious news should be beaten up by the pair of shoes.	HATE
2	स्वतःचे खिसे भरत आहेत. यांना सामान्य जनता मेली तरीही काही फरक पडत न्हाई. स्वार्थी राजकारण नीच वृत्ती ह्या लोकांची.	They are filling their own pockets. Even if the general public dies, it makes no difference to them. Selfish politics, and the mischievous attitude of these people.	HATE
3	काहीही माहिती नसताना दुसर्यांना नालायक म्हणतोस म्हणजे तुझं खुपचं शिक्षण झालं आहे असं वाटते. मुर्खा कुठंही तोंड घालत जाऊ नकोस बेअक्कल.	Calling others incompetent when you don't know anything means you seem to have a lot of education. Idiot, don't put your mouth everywhere, stupid.	OFFN
4	तुझी लायकी काय तू बोलतो कोणा बद्दल काय लाज लज्जा आहे की नाही.	What are your qualifications? Who are you talking about? Do you have any shame or not?	OFFN
5	या मा**द ला वेळीच आवरा नायतर परिणाम भोगायला तयार राहा.	Restraint this m*f*ker on time, otherwise be prepared to suffer the consequences.	PRFN
6	लोकांना असेच चु**या बनवा तुम्ही.. सरसकट आरक्षण काढून टाका आणि सर्वांना जिल्हा परिषद शाळेत शिकवा.	You make people moron like that.. Remove all reservations and teach everyone in Zilla Parishad schools..	PRFN
7	सरकारला आता उत्तर द्यावं लागेल, सामान्य जनतेचा विचार करावा लागेल आता.	The government has to answer now, need to think now of the general public.	NOT
8	तुमचं प्रेम आणि आशीर्वाद यामुळे माझी वाटचाल व्यवस्थित सुरू आहे. अशीच साथ कायम राहू द्या. त्यातूनच मला मातीतल्या माणसांचे प्रश्न, त्यांच्या प्रेरणादायी गोष्टी सांगायचं बळ मिळतं.	Thanks to your love and blessings, my journey is going smoothly. Always keep up this support. It gives me strength to tell the questions of the people of the soil, their inspiring stories.	NOT

Table 3: Sample tweets for each of the 4 classes with English translation .

mBERT and RoBERTa. The dataset is also evaluated on monolingual Marathi BERT models like MahaBERT, MahaALBERT, and MahaRoBERTa. For CNN and LSTM based models, the non-trainable fast text mode outperforms its trainable counterpart in both binary and 4-class classification. In transformer-based models, MahaBERT and MahaRoBERTa give the best results in binary and 4-class classification respectively.

Acknowledgements

This work was done under the L3Cube Pune mentorship program. We would like to express our gratitude towards our mentors at L3Cube for their continuous support and encouragement.

References

Oluwaseun Ajao, Deepayan Bhowmik, and Shahrzad Zargari. 2019. Sentiment aware fake news detection on online social networks. In *ICASSP 2019 - 2019 IEEE International Conference on Acoustics, Speech and Signal Processing (ICASSP)*, pages 2507–2511.

Mohit Bhardwaj, Md Shad Akhtar, Asif Ekbal, Amitava Das, and Tanmoy Chakraborty. 2020. Hostility detection dataset in hindi.

Mehar Bhatia, Tenzin Singhay Bhotia, Akshat Agarwal, Prakash Ramesh, Shubham Gupta, Kumar Shridhar, Felix Laumann, and Ayushman Dash. 2021. One to rule them all: Towards joint indic language hate speech detection. *arXiv preprint arXiv:2109.13711*.

Aditya Bohra, Deepanshu Vijay, Vinay Singh, Syed Sarfaraz Akhtar, and Manish Shrivastava. 2018. A dataset of hindi-english code-mixed social media text for hate speech detection. In *Proceedings of the second workshop on computational modeling of people's opinions, personality, and emotions in social media*, pages 36–41.

Alexis Conneau, Kartikay Khandelwal, Naman Goyal, Vishrav Chaudhary, Guillaume Wenzek, Francisco Guzmán, Edouard Grave, Myle Ott, Luke Zettlemoyer, and Veselin Stoyanov. 2019. Unsupervised cross-lingual representation learning at scale. *CoRR*, abs/1911.02116.

Michele Corazza, Stefano Menini, Elena Cabrio, Sara Tonelli, and Serena Villata. 2020. A multilingual evaluation for online hate speech detection. *ACM Transactions on Internet Technology (TOIT)*, 20(2):1–22.

Thomas Davidson, Dana Warmsley, Michael Macy, and Ingmar Weber. 2017. Automated hate speech detection and the problem of offensive language.

Fabio Del Vigna12, Andrea Cimino23, Felice Dell'Orletta, Marinella Petrocchi, and Maurizio Tesconi. 2017. Hate me, hate me not: Hate speech detection on facebook. In *Proceedings of the First Italian Conference on Cybersecurity (ITASEC17)*, pages 86–95.

Jacob Devlin, Ming-Wei Chang, Kenton Lee, and Kristina Toutanova. 2018. BERT: pre-training of deep bidirectional transformers for language understanding. *CoRR*, abs/1810.04805.

Jacob Devlin, Ming-Wei Chang, Kenton Lee, and Kristina Toutanova. 2019. Bert: Pre-training of deep bidirectional transformers for language understanding.

Saurabh Gaikwad, Tharindu Ranasinghe, Marcos Zampieri, and Christopher M. Homan. 2021. Cross-lingual offensive language identification for low resource languages: The case of marathi.

Lei Gao and Ruihong Huang. 2018. Detecting online hate speech using context aware models.

Ashwin Geet D'Sa, Irina Illina, Dominique Fohr, Dietrich Klakow, and Dana Ruiter. 2021. Exploring Conditional Language Model Based Data Augmentation Approaches For Hate Speech Classification. In *TSD 2021 - 24th International Conference on Text, Speech and Dialogue*, Olomouc, Czech Republic.

Anna Glazkova, Michael Kadantsev, and Maksim Glazkov. 2021. Fine-tuning of pre-trained transformers for hate, offensive, and profane content detection in english and marathi. *arXiv preprint arXiv:2110.12687*.

Ramchandra Joshi, Purvi Goel, and Raviraj Joshi. 2019. Deep learning for hindi text classification: A comparison. In *International Conference on Intelligent Human Computer Interaction*, pages 94–101. Springer.

Ramchandra Joshi, Rushabh Karnavat, Kaustubh Jirapure, and Ravirai Joshi. 2021. Evaluation of deep learning models for hostility detection in hindi text. *2021 6th International Conference for Convergence in Technology (I2CT)*.

Raviraj Joshi. 2022. L3cube-mahacorpus and mahabert: Marathi monolingual corpus, marathi bert language models, and resources. *arXiv preprint arXiv:2202.01159*.

Divyanshu Kakwani, Anoop Kunchukuttan, Satish Golla, Gokul N.C., Avik Bhattacharyya, Mitesh M. Khapra, and Pratyush Kumar. 2020. IndicNLPSuite: Monolingual Corpora, Evaluation Benchmarks and Pre-trained Multilingual

Language Models for Indian Languages. In *Findings of EMNLP*.

Atharva Kulkarni, Meet Mandhane, Manali Likhitkar, Gayatri Kshirsagar, Jayashree Jagdale, and Raviraj Joshi. 2022. Experimental evaluation of deep learning models for marathi text classification. In *Proceedings of the 2nd International Conference on Recent Trends in Machine Learning, IoT, Smart Cities and Applications*, pages 605–613. Springer.

Atharva Kulkarni, Meet Mandhane, Manali Likhitkar, Gayatri Kshirsagar, and Raviraj Joshi. 2021. L3cubemahasent: A marathi tweet-based sentiment analysis dataset.

Sean MacAvaney, Hao-Ren Yao, Eugene Yang, Katina Russell, Nazli Goharian, and Ophir Frieder. 2019. Hate speech detection: Challenges and solutions. *PloS one*, 14(8):e0221152.

Thomas Mandl, Sandip Modha, Gautam Kishore Shahi, Hiren Madhu, Shrey Satapara, Prasenjit Majumder, Johannes Schaefer, Tharindu Ranasinghe, Marcos Zampieri, Durgesh Nandini, and Amit Kumar Jaiswal. 2021. Overview of the hasoc subtrack at fire 2021: Hate speech and offensive content identification in english and indo-aryan languages.

Ariadna Matamoros-Fernández and Johan Farkas. 2021. Racism, hate speech, and social media: A systematic review and critique. *Television & New Media*, 22(2):205–224.

Puneet Mathur, Ramit Sawhney, Meghna Ayyar, and Rajiv Shah. 2018. Did you offend me? classification of offensive tweets in hinglish language. In *Proceedings of the 2nd Workshop on Abusive Language Online (ALW2)*, pages 138–148.

Nauros Romim, Mosahed Ahmed, Hriteshwar Talukder, Saiful Islam, et al. 2021. Hate speech detection in the bengali language: A dataset and its baseline evaluation. In *Proceedings of International Joint Conference on Advances in Computational Intelligence*, pages 457–468. Springer.

Anna Schmidt and Michael Wiegand. 2019. A survey on hate speech detection using natural language processing. In *Proceedings of the Fifth International Workshop on Natural Language Processing for Social Media, April 3, 2017, Valencia, Spain*, pages 1–10. Association for Computational Linguistics.

Abhishek Velankar, Hrushikesh Patil, Amol Gore, Shubham Salunke, and Raviraj Joshi. 2021. Hate and offensive speech detection in hindi and marathi.

Zeerak Waseem and Dirk Hovy. 2016. Hateful symbols or hateful people? predictive features for hate speech detection on twitter. In *Proceedings of the NAACL student research workshop*, pages 88–93.

Which one is more toxic? Findings from Jigsaw Rate Severity of Toxic Comments

Millon Madhur Das, Punyajoy Saha, Mithun Das
Indian Institute of Technology, Kharagpur, India
millonmadhurdas@kgpian.iitkgp.ac.in, {punyajoys, mithundas}@iitkgp.ac.in

Abstract

The proliferation of online hate speech has necessitated the creation of algorithms which can detect toxicity. Most of the past research focuses on this detection as a classification task, but assigning an absolute toxicity label is often tricky. Hence, few of the past works transform the same task into a regression. This paper shows the comparative evaluation of different transformers and traditional machine learning models on a recently released toxicity severity measurement dataset by Jigsaw. We further demonstrate the issues with the model predictions using explainability analysis.

Note: *This paper contains examples of toxic posts. But owing to the nature of work, we cannot avoid them.*

1 Introduction

In social media, toxic language denotes a text containing inappropriate language in a post or a comment. The presence of toxic language on social media hampers the fabric of communication in the social media posts; e.g., toxic posts targeting some community might silence members of the community (Das et al., 2020). Subsequently, social media platforms like Facebook (Facebook, 2022) and Twitter (Twitter, 2022) have laid down moderation guidelines. They also employ various automatic and manual detection techniques to detect such forms of language and apply appropriate moderation (Schroepfer, 2021). Henceforth, researchers have started looking into this direction (Das et al., 2021b; Banerjee et al., 2021; Das et al., 2021a). Most of the past research focused on developing a classification task which again varies based on the classification labels the researchers choose, i.e., abusive/non-abusive, hate speech/offensive/normal, troll/non-troll etc. (Nobata et al., 2016; Mathew et al., 2021; Saha et al., 2021; Das et al., 2022a,b) This variation in the classification labels makes transferring models across different datasets tricky. Secondly, assigning a label to a post in terms of toxicity labels is complicated as many of the posts can be subjective (Aroyo et al., 2019). Finally, a further challenge is that after encountering several highly toxic comments, an annotator might find subsequent moderately toxic comments as not toxic (Kurrek et al., 2020).

Research is currently trying to situate the toxicity detection tasks as regression tasks. In its simplest form, an annotator is provided two samples, and they have to decide which one is more toxic. Eventually, these annotated comparisons are converted to a scalar value which denotes the level of the toxicity of the post. Hada et al. (2021) uses best-worst scaling (Kiritchenko and Mohammad, 2017) to assign toxicity scores to a post based on the comparison annotated by annotators. Besides, another study (Kennedy et al., 2020) used Rasch measurement theory for converting the comparisons to scalar values.

In this shared task, Jigsaw released a new dataset for understanding the severity of toxic language. The organizers select a set of 14,000 datapoints. They used these datapoints to create multiple pairs, which were then annotated by some annotator. The annotators marked one of the comments as toxic based on their notion of toxicity. These comparisons were compared with the ones received from models, and average agreement was used as the final score.

Jigsaw is a unit within Google that explores threats to open societies, and builds technology that inspires scalable solutions. They forecast emerging threats like Disinformation, Censorship, Toxicity and Violent Extremism and explore how technology can protect individuals and societies.

In this paper, we focus on developing models for this task. Since the shared task did not provide any training dataset, we utilized different classification-based toxic language datasets and converted their labels to a scalar value based on various strategies.

Proceedings of the 29th International Conference on Computational Linguistic, pages 10–15
October 12–17, 2022.

Finally, we use simple models like TF-IDF to complex models like Transformers. We conclude the paper with a detailed error analysis to understand the behavior of the models.

2 Datasets

In this section, we illustrate the datasets used for this task. The first section 2.1 describes the task dataset, and the second section 2.2 exhibits the dataset used for training the models since we don't have any training dataset associated with this task.

2.1 Task dataset

In the task dataset [1], pairs of comments were presented to expert raters, who marked one of two comments more harmful – each according to their notion of toxicity. The final label for each pair is decided with a majority vote. The validation dataset contains $\sim$ 30k data points where each datapoint was a pair of toxic posts with the annotation mentioning which one is more toxic. However, this data cannot be used to train the models as they do not contain a toxicity score value for each comment. Apart from this we were provided with 5% of the test dataset for validating our models. The rest, 95%, is private and was used as hidden test data. Our results are discussed for the validation dataset and entire test dataset (150k posts).

2.2 External datasets

2.2.1 Ruddit

This dataset (Hada et al., 2021) contains English language Reddit comments that have fine-grained, real-valued scores between -1 (maximally supportive) and 1 (maximally offensive). The annotators were given a set of 4 comments and asked to arrange them in order of their toxicity/abusiveness. These were converted to scalar scores using best-worst scaling (Kiritchenko and Mohammad, 2017). We transformed these scores to a value between 0 and 1 to keep the distribution of values uniform to other datasets. This dataset contains $\sim$ 16k data points.

2.2.2 Jigsaw Toxic Comment Dataset(JTC)

This dataset contains a large number of Wikipedia comments labeled by human raters for toxic behavior. The types of toxicity are toxic, severe toxic, obscene, threat, insult, and identity hate. Each comment can have any one or more of these labels. It contains $\sim$230k data points. This dataset is a part of the Toxic Comment Classification Challenge hosted on Kaggle [2]. We converted the labels into a single score. The different toxicity categories were given different weights, and the final toxicity score was the sum of weights for each example. Our final weighing scheme was, severe toxic:12, identity hate:9, threat:8, insult:6, obscene:5, toxic:4

2.2.3 Jigsaw Unintended Bias Dataset

This dataset is part of a Kaggle Competition, Jigsaw Unintended Bias in Toxicity Classification [3]. Each comment has a toxicity label that lies between 0 and 1. It has $\sim$ 2 million samples. This attribute (and all others) are fractional values representing the fraction of human raters who believed the attribute applied to the given comment. For evaluation, test set examples with a target >= 0.5 will be considered to be in a positive class (toxic).

The data also has several toxicity sub-type attributes like severe toxicity, obscene, threat, insult, identity attack, and sexually explicit. We have used mapping similar to that used for the Jigsaw Toxic Comment dataset for assigning the toxicity score.

2.2.4 Davidson

The dataset is sourced from (Davidson et al., 2017). The data is compiled using a hate speech lexicon, and all the instances are from Twitter. A minimum of 3 coders labeled tweets into classes Hate speech, Offensive, and Neither. The final sample consisted of $\sim$ 24,000 examples, and only about 5% fell into the Hate Speech class. We map the toxicity score using the formula - (3∗(# hate speech annotations)+2∗(# offensive annotations)+(# neither annotations))/No.of labelers. We then normalise this value between 0 and 1.

2.2.5 Founta

Similar to the previous dataset, (Founta et al., 2018) analyzed comments from Twitter and published a dataset with $\sim$ 80k examples. It has three labels (0, 1, 2) with an increasing level of toxicity. We scaled it between 0 and 1 by normalizing it.

3 Methodology

We preprocessed the datasets using standard techniques like stemming, lemmatization, removing contractions, and hyperlinks. For the toxic severity rating, we first tried traditional techniques

[1] https://www.kaggle.com/c/jigsaw-toxic-severity-rating

[2] `https://tinyurl.com/2p85bsnj`

[3] `https://tinyurl.com/9cbyp3ry`

like TF-IDF (Rajaraman and Ullman, 2011) and doc2vec (Le and Mikolov, 2014) based regressors to set the baseline. We further add other deep learning setups based on Transformers (Vaswani et al., 2017) to check if the scores improve further.

3.1 Baselines

Initially, we used TF-IDF and Doc2Vec as feature extractors. **TFIDF** is a method to find the importance of a word to a document in a text corpus (Rajaraman and Ullman, 2011). Doc2Vec is an unsupervised method to represent a document as a vector. To train using these features, we use ridge regression, which enhances linear regression by adding L2 regularization.

We used a hyperparameter optimization framework, Optuna, to automate the hyperparameter search for TFIDF. We found the Tfidf vectorizer to work best with the 'charwb' analyzer, n-gram range (3,5) & vocabulary of $\sim$ 30k most frequent words. The ridge regressor had a regularization strength of $\sim$ 1.

Doc2Vec was trained with a feature vector of size 300, learning rate α of 0.025. Both distributed memory and distributed bag of words methods were tested. As the performance was unsatisfactory, we did not conduct hyperparameter tuning for doc2vec.

3.2 Transformers

We take a pre-trained transformers model (Vaswani et al., 2017) that outputs a 768-dimensional vector representation of an input sentence. As this output cannot be directly used as a score for toxicity, we added a single linear layer on top of the encoder to get a single value for toxicity. As we feed input data, the entire pre-trained transformers model and the additional untrained regression layer is trained on our specific task. We focused on tuning hyperparameters manually instead of using any hyperparameter search library due to resource constraints. All the transformers were trained for three epochs with a batch size of 16.

In the following section, we discuss the specifics of the pre-trained models used in detail.

3.2.1 bert-base-multilingual-cased (M-BERT)

This language representation model is a modification of BERT, introduced by (Devlin et al., 2018). It was pretrained on a large corpus of multilingual data from Wikipedia with the objective of Masked language modeling(MLM) in a self-supervised setting. In the masked language model pre-training, the model learns using predicting some of the mask tokens in the text, and it should also be noted that this model is case sensitive.

3.2.2 bert-base-uncased (BERT)

Similar to the above model, this was also pretrained using MLM objective, except this model was trained only on English text corpus, specifically on the BookCorpus, and is not case sensitive.

3.2.3 Hate-speech-CNERG/dehatebert-mono-English(dehateBERT)

(Aluru et al., 2020) benchmarked hate speech classification models for 9 different languages and 16 datasets. All their models are based on the multilingual BERT model. We used their model that was finetuned on an English text corpus.

3.2.4 cardiffnlp/twitter-roberta-base-hate(HRoBERTa)

This model is derived from the RoBERTa-base model (Liu et al., 2019) trained on $\sim$ 58M tweets and finetuned on for hate speech detection with the TweetEval benchmark (Barbieri et al., 2020). Unlike the previous two models, this is an end-to-end regression model, meaning given a sentence, it directly outputs a number between 0 and 1.

3.2.5 GroNLP/hateBERT

This is a re-trained BERT model for abusive language detection in English by (Caselli et al., 2020). It was trained using MLM objective on RAL-E, a large-scale dataset of Reddit comments in English.

3.2.6 sentence-transformer/mpnet-base-v2(mpnet)

This is a sentence embedding model introduced by (Reimers and Gurevych, 2019) trained using a self-supervised contrastive learning objective. It is trained on 1 billion sentence pairs and is based on the pretrained Masked and Permuted Network introduced by (Song et al., 2020). It solves the problems of MLM in BERT and PLM (permuted language modeling) in XLNet and achieves better accuracy.

3.3 Ensembles

Finally, we experimented with ensembles of the models described in the previous sections. To do the ensembling, we predict the scores for a typical post using various models and then combine the

Less Toxic Sentence	More Toxic Sentence
real encyclopedia So F**k you f**king all f*g f**ks	vandalism will you please stop vandalizing my talk page ? it very irritating and borderlining outright harassment
Hey F*ck you c*nt bag ! you dont own wikpedia and please report my i want to close my account any way you creep	Please stop your disruptive editing If your vandalism continues you will be blocked from editing Wikipedia andemu
i said F**S OFF YOU GEEKY LITTLE S**T	And yes people should recognize that but they usually do not One of the first objections you hear directed at someone who says he favors free markets is invariably There no such thing as a free market Ridiculously trivial
F**k up.	Wikinfo, and purge devils from here. Muzemike damned for being enemy of God: I was banned for this: So be damned, MuZemike, daemon in human skin.
Why don't you go s*rew Why don't you go s*rew instead of harassing me?	I also think ... For example i can say that Muslims go to mosques, pray, beat, up their wives, blow, up, etc, what do atheists do?.

Table 1: Samples mislabeled by human labeler (top 3) and model misclassifications (bottom 2). The highlighted text denotes how words affect the model predictions. Darker highlight denotes that the model is paying more attention to that words.

scores using a weighted average. The weights are decided based on the performance of the validation dataset. We used the weights as a variable using the Limited-memory BFGS (LM-BFGS) method, which is an optimization function in the family of quasi-Newton methods that approximates the Broyden–Fletcher–Goldfarb–Shanno algorithm (BFGS) using a limited amount of computer memory. It is a popular algorithm for parameter estimation in machine learning. The algorithm's target problem is to minimize $f(x)$ over unconstrained values of the real-vector x where f is a differentiable scalar function.

Dataset	Models	Val. Acc.	Test Acc.
Ruddit	TF-IDF	57.54	69.38
	M-BERT	59.83	74.71
	BERT	60.71	78.41
	HRoBERTa (A)	**61.06**	**79.47**
	hateBERT	60.69	78.46
	dehateBERT	58.52	71.28
JTC	TF-IDF	61.01	78.57
	doc2vec	59.87	68.80
	M-BERT (B)	61.31	79.17
	BERT (C)	61.32	78.79
	HRoBERTa (D)	**61.53**	**80.16**
	hateBERT (E)	61.25	78.90
	dehateBERT	59.81	74.95
Founta	TF-IDF	64.58	72.66
	BERT	51.50	75.67
Toxic Unintended	TF-IDF	62.64	72.47
	BERT	59.92	77.70
Davidson	TF-IDF	62.64	72.47
	BERT	52.38	76.64
A+B+C+D+E		**76**	**80.74**

Table 2: Performance on Jigsaw Rate Severity of Toxic Comment Dataset for the validation and entire test dataset.

4 Results and Inference

In this section, we present a detailed analysis of the performance of our models.

4.1 Comparative study of performance

Table 2 shows the performance of our model on the validation dataset and total test dataset. As expected, the transformer-based approaches outperform the traditional approaches like TF-IDF/doc2vec. We found that HRoBERTa model performed the best among the transformers models. It is interesting to note that BERT & M-BERT give comparable results to language models already pre-trained for detecting toxicity(hateBERT & dehateBERT). Experiments on the transformed Founta, Davidson, and Toxic unintended did not give good scores; hence we did not perform further experiments on them.

Our team secured a rank of 145 out of 2301 in the Kaggle Jigsaw Rate Severity of Toxic Comments Competition with an accuracy of 79.84% in the private leaderboard. However, one of our ensembles which was not part of our final submission, performed even better. We achieved an accuracy of 80.74% in the final standings (Table 2). It is also worth mentioning that our approach was quite similar to the winning approach(accuracy of 81.39%), except they used Genetic Algorithm (Xu) to find weights for their ensemble. Our method using an ensemble of 5 models performs half a percent worse than their 15 ensemble model.

4.2 LIME

We also conducted local interpretable model-agnostic explanations extensively on our best model (HRoBERTa) to identify potential issues with model predictions on the validation dataset. The validation set contains pairs of sentences labeled as less toxic and more toxic.

We ranked the model predictions and checked the top 100 wrong predictions manually. The top 100 wrong predictions were found by ranking the difference between the score assigned to less toxic to more toxic sentence. For most of the cases, it was not the model but the human annotator who was at fault. There were several cases where we found difficult to select the more toxic comment. We found 68 samples where the annotator was wrong, 3 samples where our model was wrong and found 29 samples to be equally toxic. We add some of the samples from each category in Table 1.

The top 100 worst predictions were selected on the following basis. At first, for each sample we compared the scores generated by our model. The samples where the more toxic sentence had a lower score than less toxic sentence(similarly, less toxic with higher score than more toxic sentence) were marked as incorrectly classified samples. For all the incorrect classifications, the difference between the scores generated for less toxic and more toxic comment was computed. This list was sorted in descending order according to the difference. The top 100 samples were selected for LIME analysis. Hence, the samples where the model is more confident about the prediction yet wrong are selected. We believe that this method captures the worst errors of the model.

5 Conclusion

We present a detailed analysis of both the traditional and modern machine learning algorithms for toxicity detection. Instead of a binary classification, a relatively new notion of toxic speech rating is explored. The existing toxicity classification datasets are modified to train the models to output a toxicity score in a continuous range. We test our models on a new dataset proposed by Jigsaw. Additionally we present the LIME analysis to understand the model predictions.

References

Sai Saketh Aluru, Binny Mathew, Punyajoy Saha, and Animesh Mukherjee. 2020. Deep learning models for multilingual hate speech detection. *arXiv preprint arXiv:2004.06465*.

Lora Aroyo, Lucas Dixon, Nithum Thain, Olivia Redfield, and Rachel Rosen. 2019. Crowdsourcing subjective tasks: the case study of understanding toxicity in online discussions. In *Companion proceedings of the 2019 world wide web conference*, pages 1100–1105.

Somnath Banerjee, Maulindu Sarkar, Nancy Agrawal, Punyajoy Saha, and Mithun Das. 2021. Exploring transformer based models to identify hate speech and offensive content in english and indo-aryan languages. *arXiv preprint arXiv:2111.13974*.

Francesco Barbieri, Jose Camacho-Collados, Leonardo Neves, and Luis Espinosa-Anke. 2020. Tweeteval: Unified benchmark and comparative evaluation for tweet classification. *arXiv preprint arXiv:2010.12421*.

Tommaso Caselli, Valerio Basile, Jelena Mitrović, and Michael Granitzer. 2020. Hatebert: Retraining bert for abusive language detection in english. *arXiv preprint arXiv:2010.12472*.

Mithun Das, Somnath Banerjee, and Animesh Mukherjee. 2022a. Data bootstrapping approaches to improve low resource abusive language detection for indic languages. pages 32–42.

Mithun Das, Somnath Banerjee, and Animesh Mukherjee. 2022b. hate-alert@ dravidianlangtech-acl2022: Ensembling multi-modalities for tamil trollmeme classification. In *Proceedings of the Second Workshop on Speech and Language Technologies for Dravidian Languages*, pages 51–57.

Mithun Das, Somnath Banerjee, and Punyajoy Saha. 2021a. Abusive and threatening language detection in urdu using boosting based and bert based models: A comparative approach. *arXiv preprint arXiv:2111.14830*.

Mithun Das, Binny Mathew, Punyajoy Saha, Pawan Goyal, and Animesh Mukherjee. 2020. Hate speech in online social media. *ACM SIGWEB Newsletter*, (Autumn):1–8.

Mithun Das, Punyajoy Saha, Ritam Dutt, Pawan Goyal, Animesh Mukherjee, and Binny Mathew. 2021b. You too brutus! trapping hateful users in social media: Challenges, solutions & insights. In *Proceedings of the 32nd ACM Conference on Hypertext and Social Media*, pages 79–89.

Thomas Davidson, Dana Warmsley, Michael Macy, and Ingmar Weber. 2017. Automated hate speech detection and the problem of offensive language. In *Proceedings of the International AAAI Conference on Web and Social Media*, volume 11, pages 512–515.

Jacob Devlin, Ming-Wei Chang, Kenton Lee, and Kristina Toutanova. 2018. Bert: Pre-training of deep bidirectional transformers for language understanding. *arXiv preprint arXiv:1810.04805*.

Facebook. 2022. Facebook community standards. (Accessed on 04/15/2022).

Antigoni Maria Founta, Constantinos Djouvas, Despoina Chatzakou, Ilias Leontiadis, Jeremy Blackburn, Gianluca Stringhini, Athena Vakali, Michael Sirivianos, and Nicolas Kourtellis. 2018. Large scale crowdsourcing and characterization of twitter abusive behavior. In *Twelfth International AAAI Conference on Web and Social Media*.

Rishav Hada, Sohi Sudhir, Pushkar Mishra, Helen Yannakoudakis, Saif M. Mohammad, and Ekaterina Shutova. 2021. Ruddit: Norms of offensiveness for English Reddit comments. In *Proceedings of the 59th*

Annual Meeting of the Association for Computational Linguistics and the 11th International Joint Conference on Natural Language Processing (Volume 1: Long Papers), pages 2700–2717, Online. Association for Computational Linguistics.

Chris J Kennedy, Geoff Bacon, Alexander Sahn, and Claudia von Vacano. 2020. Constructing interval variables via faceted rasch measurement and multitask deep learning: a hate speech application. *arXiv preprint arXiv:2009.10277*.

Svetlana Kiritchenko and Saif Mohammad. 2017. Best-worst scaling more reliable than rating scales: A case study on sentiment intensity annotation. In *Proceedings of the 55th Annual Meeting of the Association for Computational Linguistics (Volume 2: Short Papers)*, pages 465–470, Vancouver, Canada. Association for Computational Linguistics.

Jana Kurrek, Haji Mohammad Saleem, and Derek Ruths. 2020. Towards a comprehensive taxonomy and large-scale annotated corpus for online slur usage. In *Proceedings of the Fourth Workshop on Online Abuse and Harms*, pages 138–149, Online. Association for Computational Linguistics.

Quoc Le and Tomas Mikolov. 2014. Distributed representations of sentences and documents. In *International conference on machine learning*, pages 1188–1196. PMLR.

Yinhan Liu, Myle Ott, Naman Goyal, Jingfei Du, Mandar Joshi, Danqi Chen, Omer Levy, Mike Lewis, Luke Zettlemoyer, and Veselin Stoyanov. 2019. Roberta: A robustly optimized bert pretraining approach. *arXiv preprint arXiv:1907.11692*.

Binny Mathew, Punyajoy Saha, Seid Muhie Yimam, Chris Biemann, Pawan Goyal, and Animesh Mukherjee. 2021. Hatexplain: A benchmark dataset for explainable hate speech detection. In *Proceedings of the AAAI Conference on Artificial Intelligence*, volume 35, pages 14867–14875.

Chikashi Nobata, Joel Tetreault, Achint Thomas, Yashar Mehdad, and Yi Chang. 2016. Abusive language detection in online user content. In *Proceedings of the 25th international conference on world wide web*, pages 145–153.

Anand Rajaraman and Jeffrey David Ullman. 2011. *Data Mining*, page 1–17. Cambridge University Press.

Nils Reimers and Iryna Gurevych. 2019. Sentence-bert: Sentence embeddings using siamese bert-networks. *arXiv preprint arXiv:1908.10084*.

Punyajoy Saha, Binny Mathew, Kiran Garimella, and Animesh Mukherjee. 2021. "short is the road that leads from fear to hate": Fear speech in indian whatsapp groups. In *Proceedings of the Web Conference 2021*, pages 1110–1121.

Mike Schroepfer. 2021. Update on our progress on ai and hate speech detection. (Accessed on 04/16/2022).

Kaitao Song, Xu Tan, Tao Qin, Jianfeng Lu, and Tie-Yan Liu. 2020. Mpnet: Masked and permuted pre-training for language understanding. *Advances in Neural Information Processing Systems*, 33:16857–16867.

Twitter. 2022. Twitter's policy on hateful conduct | twitter help. (Accessed on 04/15/2022).

Ashish Vaswani, Noam Shazeer, Niki Parmar, Jakob Uszkoreit, Llion Jones, Aidan N Gomez, Łukasz Kaiser, and Illia Polosukhin. 2017. Attention is all you need. *Advances in neural information processing systems*, 30.

Guanshuo Xu. Jigsaw rate severity of toxic comments winner's approach. (Accessed on 04/16/2022).

Can attention-based transformers explain or interpret cyberbullying detection?

Kanishk Verma[1,2], **Tijana Milosevic**[1,2], **Brian Davis**[1]
ADAPT Centre[1], DCU Anti Bullying Centre[2],
Dublin City University, Ireland
kanishk.verma@adaptcentre.ie

Abstract

Automated textual cyberbullying detection is known to be a challenging task. It is sometimes expected that messages associated with bullying will either be a) abusive, b) targeted at a specific individual or group, or c) have a negative sentiment. Transfer learning by fine-tuning pre-trained attention-based transformer language models (LMs) has achieved near state-of-the-art (SOA) precision in identifying textual fragments as being bullying-related or not. This study looks closely at two SOA LMs, BERT and HateBERT, fine-tuned on real-life cyberbullying datasets from multiple social networking platforms. We intend to determine whether these finely calibrated pre-trained LMs learn textual cyberbullying attributes or syntactical features in the text. The results of our comprehensive experiments show that despite the fact that attention weights are drawn more strongly to syntactical features of the text at every layer, attention weights cannot completely account for the decision-making of such attention-based transformers.

1 Introduction

Repeated hostile and aggressive online behaviour to **intentionally** hurt or embarrass someone through digital communication technologies are generally understood as **Cyberbullying**. (Patchin and Hinduja, 2006). Recent research findings by (B et al., 2021) and (Milosevic, 2021), indicate that 44% children in 11 European countries and nearly 50% children in Ireland have reported an increase in cyberbullying during the COVID-19 lockdown restrictions across multiple social networking sites (SNS) and multiplayer online gaming (MOG) platforms. This growing amount of cyberbullying content emerging across multiple SNS and MOG platforms is alarming and necessitates more effective content moderation, as earlier studied by (Gillespie et al., 2020; Milosevic, 2018; Gillespie, 2018). Therefore, one crucial step toward efficient and effective content moderation is the ability to recognize and define the basis for automated cyberbullying detection systems to classify a textual expression or phrase as cyberbullying.

Recent computational cyberbullying research claim to have outstanding accuracy and precision in automating the identification of cyberbullying using state-of-the-art (SOA) deep learning algorithms like attention-based Transformers, Gated Recurrent Units (GRUs), Long-Short Term Memory (LSTMs). However, upon close examination of such research, including those by (Paul and Saha, 2020; Yadav et al., 2020; Behzadi et al., 2021; Tripathy et al., 2020; Pradhan et al., 2020; Fang et al., 2021) among others, reveal that they rely on datasets for *hate-speech* or *personal-attacks* by (Founta et al., 2018; Waseem and Hovy, 2016; Wulczyn et al., 2017) for cyberbullying identification. In reality, despite their inventive attempts, these studies can only determine whether a text is abusive or hateful. We consider it a poor decision to detect cyberbullying using such out-of-domain datasets.

Additionally, work by (Ruder et al., 2019; Howard and Ruder, 2018; Dodge et al., 2020) has demonstrated the efficacy of transfer learning by fine-tuning pre-trained deep layered language models (LMs) for a variety of natural language processing (NLP) tasks, such as text classification, thereby yielding impressive results. (Verma et al., 2022), have demonstrated that fine-tuning LMs like $BERT_{base-uncased}$ by (Devlin et al., 2018), and $Hate-BERT_{base-uncased}$ by (Caselli et al., 2020) outperform traditional machine learning algorithms and aid in more accurate detection of textual cyberbullying across multiple SNS platforms. Research by (Vaswani et al., 2017; Devlin et al., 2018) demonstrates that the attention-based mechanisms within the deeply layered architecture of such pre-trained LMs can display dependencies between input and output. High attention weights for

Proceedings of the 29th International Conference on Computational Linguistic, pages 16–29
October 12–17, 2022.

inputs (such as words) are frequently referred to be accountable for the output, which provides the model's interpretability (Mullenbach et al., 2018; Xie et al., 2017; Martins and Astudillo, 2016; Lei et al., 2017; Choi et al., 2016; Xu et al., 2015). To our knowledge, these assertions and presumptions have not undergone a formal evaluation for user-generated content (UGC) datasets collected from various SNS and MOG platforms categorically labelled for cyberbullying.

(Kitchin, 2017; Ananny and Crawford, 2018; Katzenbach and Ulbricht, 2019) question the existing opaqueness of automated algorithmic content moderation and decision-making practices by SNS and MOG platforms. It has thus become necessary to design and develop transparent and equitable algorithms for moderation and regulation. To that effect, we attempt to extend the work by (Verma et al., 2022) on multiple platform cyberbullying detection, by addressing the following research question,

- **RQ.1** Can attention-weights of attention-based LMs fine-tuned on real-life cyberbullying datasets be relied upon to detect and explain cyberbullying in an interpretable and understandable way?

Hence, we hypothesize that if attention-based LMs fine-tuned on real-life cyberbullying datasets learn textual cyberbullying traits for detecting cyberbullying; they would have higher attention weights for a) Parts-of-speech (POS) tags like adjectives, nouns, proper nouns, pronouns, and b) words with more negative sentiment. We also hypothesize that this assumption will be valid for text samples categorically annotated as cyberbullying across different datasets sourced from varied SNS and MOG platforms.

Content Warning: This article contains examples of abusive language in Section 5.4. All examples are taken from existing datasets (Section 3) to illustrate its composition.

2 Related Work

2.1 Cyberbullying Detection on Multiple platforms

There has been research on cross-platform cyberbullying detection, but they have had a narrow focus. (Edwards et al., 2020) devise a dataset from direct messages (SMS) shared between participants across multiple SNS platforms, social media posts collected from now-defunct Formspring.me [1] and tweets from Twitter[2] focusing only on one topic (2016 USA elections). However, despite their novel attempts at developing a cross-platform cyberbullying dataset and devising supervised machine learning classifiers to identify cyberbullying, their focus on a specific type of text-based communication like SMS and only on two types of SNS platforms, of which one is now defunct. On the other hand, (Nikhila et al., 2020; Yi and Zubiaga, 2022) also devise novel techniques to identify textual cyberbullying using adversarial neural network algorithms. Nevertheless, for training the classifiers, they rely on datasets by (Waseem and Hovy, 2016; Wulczyn et al., 2017) marked for either personal attacks or hate speech. On the contrary, work by (Van Bruwaene et al., 2020) is both novel and apt for cyberbullying research. They devise a high-quality dataset and experiment with Support Vector Machines (SVM), Convolutional neural networks (CNNs), and XGBOOST algorithms to develop a cross-platform cyberbullying detection system. To our knowledge, the work by (Van Bruwaene et al., 2020) is the only one that leverages real-life cyberbullying datasets. However, due to proprietary reasons, it is not yet made publicly available. (Verma et al., 2022) leverage real-life cyberbullying datasets collected by computational researchers from multiple SNS and MOG platforms such as Instagram[3], Twitter, ASK.fm[4], now-defunct SNS platforms Formspring.me, and Vine[5]. On training multiple binary cyberbullying classifiers on single platforms and benchmarking their efficacy on different platforms, they found that attention-based LMs could achieve better precision and recall than traditional machine learning algorithms at classifying cyberbullying samples as cyberbullying. However (Verma et al., 2022) were unable to determine why these phenomena occur, and were also unable to establish whether the attention-based LMs were dependent on any textual cyberbullying traits (eg. profanities or negative sentiment words).

[1] an anonymous question-answering SNS

[2] https://twitter.com

[3] `https://www.instagram.com`

[4] ASK.fm - `https://ask.fm`; is an anonymous question-answering SNS platform

[5] Video-sharing platform like TikTok `https://en.wikipedia.org/wiki/Vine_(service)`

2.2 Analysing Attention in attention-based language models

Attention-based transformer LMs developed by (Devlin et al., 2018; Yang et al., 2019; Caselli et al., 2020) consists of a deep architecture with many hidden layers stacked on top of one another. Within these layers are many attention-heads or sub-layers that assign attention-weights to a token (word) for learning the importance of the token. Substantial research conducted by (Zhang et al., 2019; Adadi and Berrada, 2018; Sundararajan et al., 2017) and others have demonstrated frameworks for explaining and interpreting these deep-layered LMs by analyzing these attention-weights at every layer. Moreover, (Vig, 2019a; Vig and Belinkov, 2019) have developed tools and resources that aid in visualizing the attention weights. This allows human users to comprehend and trust the results of such deep-layered LMs. However, studies by (Jain and Wallace, 2019; Serrano and Smith, 2019; Sun and Lu, 2020; Vashishth et al., 2019) have demonstrated that these attention-based mechanisms solely cannot be relied upon for interpreting and explaining the intricate workings of LMs. The work by (Elsafoury et al., 2021) for interpreting the attention mechanism of BERT for cyberbullying is closest to our research. We thank the authors (Elsafoury et al., 2021) for their contributions and for making the code repository reproducible. However, they a) rely on out-of-domain datasets like hate speech and personal attack datasets and b) lack in-depth analysis of LMs decision-making for both textual cyberbullying and non-cyber bullying samples. Moreover, they do not report the attention-based LM(s) interpretation for real-world binary instances of cyberbullying in text.

3 Datasets

To overcome current dataset-related gaps in cyberbullying research, we select datasets that are a) annotated by either cyberbullying domain experts or b) clear and precise annotation guidelines aided the annotation for cyberbullying. To our knowledge, there are only *seven* real-life datasets in English language that have been devised for cyberbullying markers with such annotations. We categorise the seven datasets into four groups based on a) type of SNS or MOG platform and b) average length of tokens observed from each of the seven platforms (See Figure 1). These groups include,

- **Question-answering SNS**: Question-answering SNS are both anonymous and non-anonymous platforms like ASK.fm, Reddit[6], and Quora[7] that allow platform users to respond to questions posted by other users. Dataset devised by (Van Hee et al., 2018) from the ASK.fm platform is available in both English and Dutch. Annotations in this dataset are both binary and fine-grained, i.e., it is annotated for different cyberbullying forms and varied cyberbullying participant roles. (Reynolds et al., 2011) collected English language dataset from now-defunct Formspring.me. Annotations in this dataset are binary, i.e., textual samples are labelled as cyberbullying and non-cyber bullying.

- **Twitter SNS**: (Xu et al., 2012) formulated a dataset by collecting tweets[8] from Twitter in the English language. Their dataset annotations are annotated as binary textual cyberbullying samples and for varied author roles such as victim, bully, reporter, and others. (Salawu et al., 2020) formulated a dataset from tweets in the English language. They have various labels such as profanity, insult, spam, sarcasm, threat, exclusion, and bullying.

- **User-comment SNS**: User-comment SNS are platforms that allow users to comment on images or videos posted by other platform users. Such platforms include but are not limited to Instagram, Facebook, TikTok, Vine, etc. (Hosseinmardi et al., 2015) collected multi-modal data (inclusive of images and textual comments) from Instagram. The annotations in this dataset are for both cyberbullying and cyber aggression. (Rafiq et al., 2015) also collected multi-modal data (inclusive of videos and textual comments) from now-defunct Vine platform. The annotation in this dataset includes both cyberbullying and cyber-aggression.

- **MOG platforms**: On MOG platforms, players communicate on forums, in-game chats, or via voice (either in-built or by plug-in voice-call platforms like Discord). (Bretschneider and Peters, 2016) collected text from fo-

[6]https://www.reddit.com

[7]https://www.quora.com

[8]https://help.twitter.com/en/resources/twitter-guide/topics/how-to-join-the-conversation-on-twitter/how-to-tweet

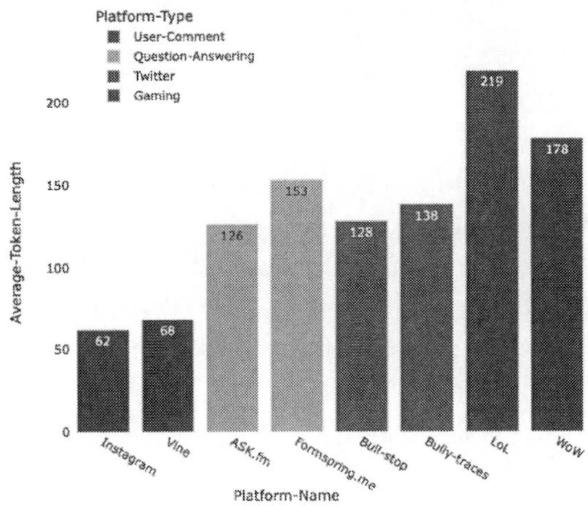

Figure 1: Length of tokens in every dataset

rums of highly popular MOG platforms like like World-of-Warcraft (WoW)[9] and League-of-Legends (LoL)[10]. The annotations in this dataset are of two types a) role-based binary annotations, i.e., bully and victim, and b) binary labels for cyberbullying for each text sample.

As seen in Table 1, number of sentences for cyberbullying content is very low across all seven datasets. Each of the four grouped datasets were split into training, validation, and test sets. The training set makes up 80% for each of the grouped dataset, while the validation set and test set each make up for 10% of the datasets. The test set was further broken into two parts a) 90% was used to evaluate performance of fine-tuned LMs performed, and b) 10% was used to analyze attention weights and gradient-based feature importance scores for each layer and head in the architecture of the LMs.

4 Experiment Setup

Tasks depicted in the first block of Figure 7 (See Appendix A.3) are described in detail in sections 4.1 and 4.3. As depicted in other two blocks of the Figure 7, we discuss the strategies for fine-tuning, hyper-parameter optimization strategies, and the attention-weight and gradient-based feature importance score at each layer for both bullying and non-bullying sentences in Sections 4.2 and 4.4. The code repository for reproducing this study can be found online[11].

4.1 Data anonymization, pre-processing and handling data imbalance

4.1.1 Data Anonymization

Adhering to General Data Protection Regulation (GDPR) directive (Council of European Union, 2016), we fully anonymised and normalised the datasets for any Personally Identifiable Information (PII) data. Such data included but was not limited to email-address, user names, geographical locations, and user-profile details, among others. Using GATE Cloud (Tablan et al., 2013) and the TwitIE API (K. Bontcheva, 2013), PII data was de-identified by masking and replacing the original words with masked value. For example, the sentence *"mary@gmail.com is based in London"*, was masked as *"email-address is based in location"*.

4.1.2 Pre-processing

Due to the abundance of non-standard language in the datasets, including lexical variants like *supa* → *super*, and acronyms, e.g., *tbh* → *to be honest*, and spelling errors, we applied several normalization heuristics for spelling and slang corrections. We removed a) URLs, user mentions, and non-ASCII characters for all datasets, b) retweet (RT) markers in text for *twitter* datasets, and c) lower-cased all text, and d) converted contractions to formal format. We also gathered a list of slang words and acronyms with their standardized forms from an online website[12]. Finally, we developed an algorithm (See Appendix A.1 for details) to fix spelling errors with the most accurate semantic corrections.

4.1.3 Data Imbalance

The percentage of cyberbullying content in Table 1 shows a high imbalance skewed towards the non-bullying class. Handling the imbalance was paramount to avoid learning the *bias* towards the majority class in imbalanced datasets. Due to the limited nature of the dataset and to avoid the risk of losing context and sequence of words in a sentence, we leveraged the simple random over-sampling technique (Moreo et al., 2016) over Synthetic Minority Oversampling Technique (SMOTE) (Bunkhumpornpat et al., 2009). It is worth noting

[9] `https://us.forums.blizzard.com/en/wow/`

[10] `https://www.leagueoflegends.com/en-us/news/community/`

[11] `https://gitlab.computing.dcu.ie/vermak3/xai-cyberbullying-attention`

[12] https://www.webopedia.com/reference/text-abbreviations/

Platform-Type	Study	% Cyberbullying Content	# of Sentences
Question-Answering	(Van Hee et al., 2018)	4.73	113,698
	(Reynolds et al., 2011)	9.42	25,802
User-Comment	(Hosseinmardi et al., 2015)	41.28	32,074
	(Rafiq et al., 2015)	34.58	78,249
Twitter	(Xu et al., 2012)*	5.99	9,965
	(Salawu et al., 2020)*	4.67	4,009
Gaming	(Bretschneider and Peters, 2016)	2.3	34,229

Table 1: Dataset Description.
"*" Numbers vary to original dataset, as the tweet is unavailable due to deletion by tweet authors.

that the random oversampling was done in only one training set, and data imbalance was not handled in the validation and test set to match real-life scenarios. Also, to verify if over-sampling techniques affect the classification models' accuracy, we run experiments with imbalanced and over-sampled datasets.

4.2 Language Models and Hyper-parameters

To ascertain which SOA LMs is able to a) better capture dependencies and b) learn better representation of cyberbullying text from noisy UGC data, we leverage pre-trained $\text{BERT}_{base-uncased}$ by (Devlin et al., 2018), and Hate-$\text{BERT}_{base-uncased}$ by (Caselli et al., 2020). $\text{BERT}_{base-uncased}$ is a bi-directional auto-encoding attention-based transformer with twelve layered transformer blocks, with each block containing twelve self-attention layers and a total of 768 hidden layers, resulting in approximately 110 M parameters. Hate-$\text{BERT}_{base-uncased}$ is a BERT LM re-trained on hateful comments from RAL-E Reddit's banned communities (Chandrasekharan et al., 2017). We utilized the implementation provided by HuggingFace's Transformer Library (Wolf et al., 2019) and by (Caselli et al., 2020), and follow (Verma et al., 2022) experiments to fine-tune the pre-trained LMs. To find optimal hyper-parameters, we used the Weights & Biases (Biewald, 2020) plug-ins to conduct multiple grid-based experiments with a varied range of hyper-parameters and optimized it to achieve maximum validation accuracy. The range of hyper-parameters includes,

- Maximum Token Length(s): `[128, 256]`
- Batch-size(s): `[8, 16, 32]`
- Epochs: `[2, 3, 4]`
- Loss Function: *Binary Cross Entropy*
- Optimizer Function: *Adam Weighted*
- Learning Rate(s): $1e^{-5}$, $2e^{-5}$, $3e^{-5}$, $4e^{-5}$, $5e^{-5}$

4.3 Collecting Parts-of-speech (POS) Tags & Sentiment Scores

To formally evaluate our hypothesis and assumptions addressed in Section 1. As the datasets leveraged in this study are a) sourced from SNS and MOG platforms, b) are not in formal language, and c) do not include POS tags or sentiment scores, we leveraged Spacy's POS tagger [13] (Honnibal and Montani, 2017) to collect POS tags and VADER by (Hutto and Gilbert, 2014) to collect sentiment scores. Please note that both POS tags and sentiment scores were collected only for 10% of the test-set, (See Table 4 in Appendix A.2).

4.4 Attention-weights and gradient-based importance scores

To address our **RQ.1** and compare with other experiments (Jain and Wallace, 2019; Serrano and Smith, 2019; Sun and Lu, 2020; Vashishth et al., 2019), we extract attention-weights of the fine-tuned LM(s) on 10 % of test-set reserved for attention analysis. Many experiments on transformer-based attention-analysis refer to gradient-based feature importance scores as a measure for providing importance of individual features with known semantics (Clark et al., 2019; Serrano and Smith, 2019; Sun and Lu, 2020). We leveraged the *Integrated Gradients* algorithm by (Sundararajan et al., 2017) for pytorch[14] to model interpretability by (Kokhlikyan et al., 2020) to compute the gradient-based feature importance scores on 10% of the test-set reserved for attention analysis. As the pre-trained LMs used

[13] https://spacy.io/usage/linguistic-features#pos-tagging

[14] A python language framework for deep learning https://pytorch.org/

in this study have 12 transformer block layers and 12 attention heads, we computed the mean attention weights for each head of every layer. Extending (Jain and Wallace, 2019)'s work, we use Pearson's correlation coefficient (PCC) to measure the linear correlation between mean importance scores and mean attention weights. Moreover, we also a) compute mean-attention weights and gradient-based feature importance scores for every token for every POS tag of the reserved test-set and b) observe both mean-attention weights and gradient-based feature importance scores for tokens in the reserved test-set that have a greater negative sentiment.

5 Results

5.1 Impact of Data Imbalance

To assess if our simple oversampling strategy on training data referred to in Section 4.1.3 yields any significant improvement over the no-sampling strategy on training data, we check the model's validation accuracy on the non-sampled validation dataset. As depicted in Table 5 (See Appendix A.4) , we find no significant differences in the performance of either oversampling or no-sampling when both BERT and HateBERT LMs are fine-tuned on *user-comment, twitter*, and *question-answering* datasets, except for the *gaming* dataset. Both LMs fine-tuned on over-sampled *gaming* dataset perform better than fine-tuning on no-sampled datasets. We believe this is because, as seen in Table 1, there are only 2.3% bullying samples in the *gaming* dataset, and it is highly skewed towards non-bullying samples.

5.2 Hyper-parameters Finetuning

As discussed in Section 4.2, we experiment with different combinations of hyper-parameters with the help of the Weights & Biases plug-in for grid-based experiments. Table 2 represents the results of optimal hyper-parameters on validation-set for both fine-tuned LMs on each of the four datasets. We find that hyper-parameters vary for each model on every dataset. Overall, optimal hyper-parameters include, token-length of 128, batch-sizes ranging from 8 to 32, learning-rates between 1e-5, 2e-5, 3e-5, and 5e-5, and with 2 Epochs. With the help of these hyper-parameters, maximum accuracy can be achieved on validation sets.

5.3 Cyberbullying Detection

After training and validating both $BERT_{base-uncased}$ and $HateBERT_{base-uncased}$ with the optimal hyper-parameters (See Table 2) for every dataset, we assessed both LMs performance for their F1-scores for a) bullying, and b) non-bullying samples. In cyberbullying detection, false negatives and false positives are crucial, especially in cases of imbalanced data. We believe that F1 scores for each class are an apt metric for evaluating classifiers. As depicted in the Table 3 fine-tuning the HateBERT LM for each of the four platform datasets, does perform better than just fine-tuning the BERT LM. Moreover, these generalized LMs perform better with the grouped Twitter datasets.

5.4 Attention-weights & Gradient-based feature analysis

5.4.1 Correlation between attention-weights & gradient-based feature importance scores

As observed in the Figure 2, the Pearson's correlation coefficient (PCC) between attention-weights and gradient-based feature importance scores for fine-tuned HateBERT ranges from *0.0129* for bullying-samples in *user-comment* dataset to *0.1202* for bullying-samples in *gaming* datasets. Whereas, for fine-tuned BERT the PCC between attention-weights and gradient-based feature importance scores ranges from 0.0042 for bullying-samples in *question-answering* datasets to 0.19 in *twitter dataset.* Overall, as depicted in the Figure 2, this PCC is close to zero for both BERT and HateBERT LMs fine-tuned on *user-comment* dataset. For BERT LM fine-tuned on *twitter* and *gaming* datasets, the PCC between attention-weights and gradient-based feature importance scores is in the range of 0.08 to 0.19. However, for HateBERT LM fine-tuned on *twitter* datasets, this is not the case; the PCC between attention-weights and gradient-based feature importance for this data is nearly zero (0.070-0.078).

From Table 3, we can deduce that HateBERT LM fine-tuned on *twitter* datasets has better F-scores than BERT LM fine-tuning on the same dataset. The near zero-correlation observed between mean attention-weights and gradient-based importance scores for both generalized LMs, especially for better performing HateBERT LM fine-tuned on *twitter* datasets, helps us substantiate

Model	Dataset	Token length	Batch-size	Learning Rate	Epochs	Val-Accuracy
BERT+	Gaming	128	8	$5e^{-5}$	4	0.7746
	UC	128	32	$3e^{-5}$	2	0.7476
	QA	128	8	$5e^{-5}$	2	0.9496
	Twitter	128	32	$2e^{-5}$	2	0.94
HateBERT+	Gaming	128	8	$1e^{-5}$	2	0.7478
	UC	128	16	$3e^{-5}$	2	0.7497
	QA	128	16	$1e^{-5}$	2	0.9498
	Twitter	128	32	$5e^{-5}$	2	0.939

Table 2: Optimal Hyper-parameters for every model with every dataset
Note: UC → user-comment; QA → question-answering

Model	Dataset	Bullying F1	Non-Bullying F1	Average F1
BERT+	QA	0.62	0.68	0.65
	UC	0.65	0.77	0.71
	Twitter	0.75	0.79	0.77
	Gaming	0.68	0.79	0.72
HateBERT+	QA	0.73	0.73	0.73
	UC	0.68	0.84	0.76
	Twitter	0.78	0.84	0.81
	Gaming	0.74	0.78	0.76

Table 3: Cyberbullying Classification Results
Note: UC → user-comment; QA → question-answering

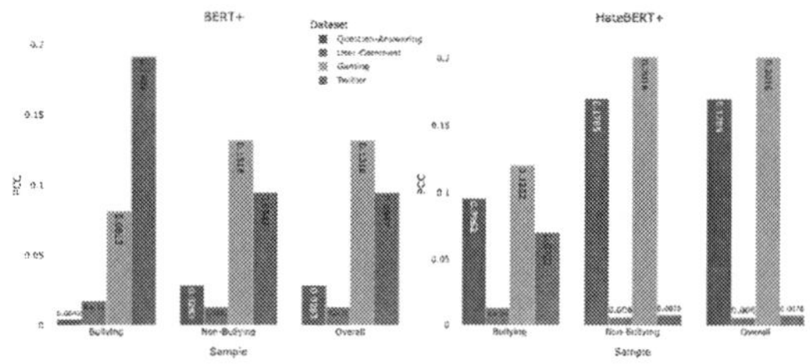

Figure 2: Pearson's Correlation between Mean Attention Weights and Mean Gradient-Importance Score for all LMs and Datasets

the claims by (Jain and Wallace, 2019; Serrano and Smith, 2019; Sun and Lu, 2020; Vashishth et al., 2019). They claim that while attention-mechanisms improve classification performance, *relying on attention-weights for interpretation is questionable at best*, holds true even for real-life SNS and MOG cyberbullying datasets.

5.4.2 Layer-wise attention Analysis

In this section, we examine the mean-attention weights at each layer for each POS tag as well as sentences with both stronger negative & positive sentiment that were taken from fine-tuned LMs that had a) a higher positive correlation between the mean attention weights and the mean gradient-based feature importance scores and b) a higher classification F-1 score. These models are BERT$+_{t}witter$ and HateBERT$+_{gaming}$ as depicted in the Table 3 and the Figure 2. So, using data from both Twitter and gaming datasets, we provide layer-wise analysis as follows,

- **Layer-wise Attention for Parts-of-speech Tags &**
  In Figures 3 and 4, we represent mean-attention attention weights at each layer for every POS tag in the *twitter* and *gaming* datasets. For adjectives in both bullying and non-bullying samples in these datasets, fine-tuned BERT and HateBERT models have mean attention weights ranging from 0.051 to 0.062. For verbs in bullying samples, fine-tuned BERT has 0.1 mean attention weight at layer 6, and at the end of layer 12, it drops to 0.09, whereas in the fine-tuned HateBERT model for bullying samples, the mean attention weight is as low as it is for adjectives. For nouns in bullying samples, fine-tuned BERT has a mean attention weight of 0.051, and fine-tuned HateBERT has a mean attention weight of 0.14 at the starting layers, but by layers 11 and 12, it drops down to 0.074. For proper nouns, fine-tuned BERT and HateBERT have a much higher mean attention weight for bullying samples. However, in non-bullying samples, fine-tuned HateBERT has a lower mean attention weight of 0.051 throughout all layers. This, in a way, disproves our hypothesis that words that are adjectives, verbs, nouns, and proper nouns will have higher mean attention weights. As depicted in Figures 3 and 4, mean

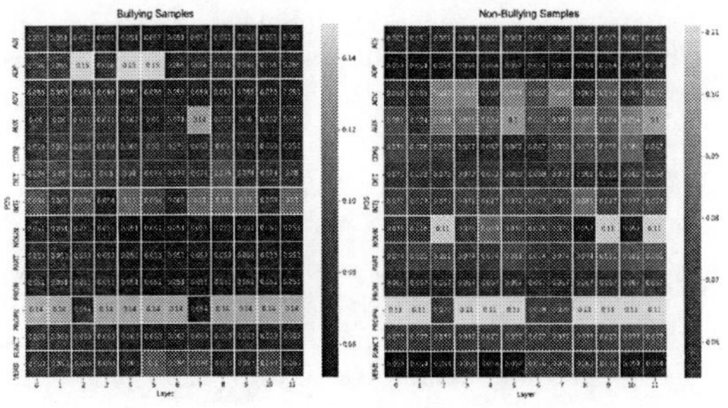

Figure 3: BERT+ Mean-attention weights per Layer POS-tag wise

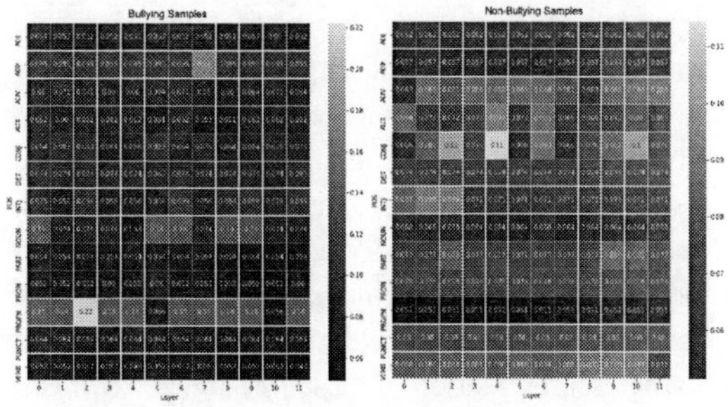

Figure 4: HateBERT+ Mean-attention weights per Layer POS-tag wise

attention weights for auxiliaries, determiners, ad-positions, conjunctions, and interjections in comparison to adjectives, verbs and nouns are consistently higher at almost all layers for fine-tuned BERT and HateBERT models in both bullying and non-bullying samples.

- **Negative Words & Attention**
  As discussed in an earlier section , we assume that negative sentiment words will have greater mean attention weights, so we compare these weights with the mean attention weights of positive sentiment words. Also, as mentioned in Section 4.3, we leveraged Vader to generate sentiment scores for all tokens in the reserved test set. We selected four words with greater negative sentiment (f*ck, a*s, b*tch, stu*id) and four words with greater positive sentiment (like, cute, pretty, truth). The Figures 5 and 6 represent mean-attention weights per layer for each of the words. We find that the positive sentiment word *pretty* has a similar mean attention weight as the negative sentiment words *b*tch and a*s* at all layers for both fine-tuned BERT and HateBERT models. This disproves our second assumption that negative sentiment words will have greater mean attention weights. For brevity, our analysis on two sample sentences at every layer and head are briefly discussed in Appendix A.5.

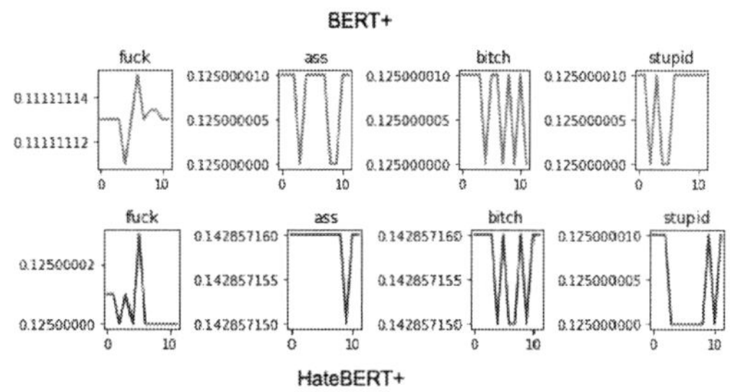

Figure 5: Attention per layer for Negative Sentiment words

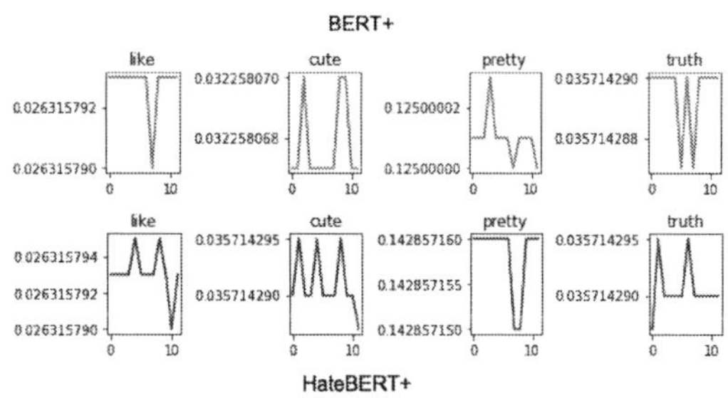

Figure 6: Attention per layer for Positive Sentiment words

6 Conclusion & Future Work

Our comprehensive experiments using two LMs and four grouped real-life cyberbullying datasets from various SNS and MOG platforms revealed that: a) a fine-tuned HateBERT is better at classifying cyberbullying samples as cyberbullying; b) there is almost no correlation between the attention-weights and gradient-based feature importance scores; and c) an attention-based transformer model tuned for cyberbullying classification relies more on syntactical features in text, and d) attention-based transformer model fine-tuned for cyberbullying classification have similar "attention" for both negative and positive sentiment words. While our experiments show that to some level, attention-based transformers fine-tuned on real-life cyberbullying datasets do aid in interpreting and explaining its decision-making based on cyberbullying features, there is still a lot more work to be done in devising transparent and fair LM(s) for cyberbullying detection. While we demonstrate comprehensive methods to interpret and explain fine-tuned LMs on real-life SNS and MOG text cyberbullying classification, we acknowledge that due to the diverse forms and roles of cyberbullying, our work is limited by binary cyberbullying categories. Due to the current paucity of fine-grained cyberbullying datasets, in the future, we will attempt to use the learned representation of these fine-tuned LM(s) on fine-grained pre-adolescent datasets by (Sprugnoli et al., 2018).

7 Acknowledgements

We thank the authors (Van Hee et al., 2018; Reynolds et al., 2011; Xu et al., 2012; Salawu et al., 2020; Hosseinmardi et al., 2015; Rafiq et al., 2015; Bretschneider and Peters, 2016) for sharing the dataset. The research conducted in this publication was funded by the Irish Research Council and Google, Ireland, under grant number EPSPG/2021/161.

References

Amina Adadi and Mohammed Berrada. 2018. Peeking inside the black-box: a survey on explainable artificial intelligence (xai). *IEEE access*, 6:52138–52160.

Mike Ananny and Kate Crawford. 2018. Seeing without knowing: Limitations of the transparency ideal and its application to algorithmic accountability. *new media & society*, 20(3):973–989.

Lobe B, Velicu A, Staksrud E, Chaudron S, and Di Gioia R. 2021. How children (10-18) experienced online risks during the covid-19 lockdown - spring 2020. (KJ-NA-30584-EN-N (online),KJ-NA-30584-EN-C (print)).

Mitra Behzadi, Ian G Harris, and Ali Derakhshan. 2021. Rapid cyber-bullying detection method using compact bert models. In *2021 IEEE 15th International Conference on Semantic Computing (ICSC)*, pages 199–202. IEEE.

Lukas Biewald. 2020. Experiment tracking with weights and biases. Software available from wandb.com.

Uwe Bretschneider and Ralf Peters. 2016. Detecting cyberbullying in online communities.

Chumphol Bunkhumpornpat, Krung Sinapiromsaran, and Chidchanok Lursinsap. 2009. Safe-level-smote: Safe-level-synthetic minority over-sampling technique for handling the class imbalanced problem. In *Advances in Knowledge Discovery and Data Mining*, pages 475–482, Berlin, Heidelberg. Springer Berlin Heidelberg.

Tommaso Caselli, Valerio Basile, Jelena Mitrovic, and Michael Granitzer. 2020. Hatebert: Retraining BERT for abusive language detection in english. *CoRR*, abs/2010.12472.

Eshwar Chandrasekharan, Umashanthi Pavalanathan, Anirudh Srinivasan, Adam Glynn, Jacob Eisenstein, and Eric Gilbert. 2017. You can't stay here: The efficacy of reddit's 2015 ban examined through hate speech. *Proceedings of the ACM on Human-Computer Interaction*, 1(CSCW):1–22.

Edward Choi, Mohammad Taha Bahadori, Jimeng Sun, Joshua Kulas, Andy Schuetz, and Walter Stewart. 2016. Retain: An interpretable predictive model for healthcare using reverse time attention mechanism. *Advances in neural information processing systems*, 29.

Kevin Clark, Urvashi Khandelwal, Omer Levy, and Christopher D. Manning. 2019. What does BERT look at? an analysis of bert's attention. *CoRR*, abs/1906.04341.

Council of European Union. 2016. Regulation (eu) 2016/679 of the european parliament and of the council (general data protection regulation). `https://eur-lex.europa.eu/eli/reg/2016/679/oj`.

Jacob Devlin, Ming-Wei Chang, Kenton Lee, and Kristina Toutanova. 2018. BERT: pre-training of deep bidirectional transformers for language understanding. *CoRR*, abs/1810.04805.

Jesse Dodge, Gabriel Ilharco, Roy Schwartz, Ali Farhadi, Hannaneh Hajishirzi, and Noah A. Smith. 2020. Fine-tuning pretrained language models: Weight initializations, data orders, and early stopping. *CoRR*, abs/2002.06305.

April Edwards, David Demoll, and Lynne Edwards. 2020. Detecting cyberbullying activity across platforms. In *17th International Conference on Information Technology–New Generations (ITNG 2020)*, pages 45–50. Springer.

Fatma Elsafoury, Stamos Katsigiannis, Steven R Wilson, and Naeem Ramzan. 2021. Does bert pay attention to cyberbullying? In *Proceedings of the 44th International ACM SIGIR Conference on Research and Development in Information Retrieval*, pages 1900–1904.

Yong Fang, Shaoshuai Yang, Bin Zhao, and Cheng Huang. 2021. Cyberbullying detection in social networks using bi-gru with self-attention mechanism. *Information*, 12(4):171.

Antigoni Maria Founta, Constantinos Djouvas, Despoina Chatzakou, Ilias Leontiadis, Jeremy Blackburn, Gianluca Stringhini, Athena Vakali, Michael Sirivianos, and Nicolas Kourtellis. 2018. Large scale crowdsourcing and characterization of twitter abusive behavior. In *Twelfth International AAAI Conference on Web and Social Media*.

Tarleton Gillespie. 2018. *Custodians of the Internet*. Yale University Press.

Tarleton Gillespie, Patricia Aufderheide, Elinor Carmi, Ysabel Gerrard, Robert Gorwa, Ariadna Matamoros-Fernández, Sarah T Roberts, Aram Sinnreich, and Sarah Myers West. 2020. Expanding the debate about content moderation: Scholarly research agendas for the coming policy debates. *Internet Policy Review*, 9(4):Article–number.

Yoav Goldberg and Omer Levy. 2014. word2vec explained: deriving mikolov et al.'s negative-sampling word-embedding method. *CoRR*, abs/1402.3722.

Matthew Honnibal and Ines Montani. 2017. spacy 2: Natural language understanding with bloom embeddings, convolutional neural networks and incremental parsing. *To appear*.

Homa Hosseinmardi, Sabrina Arredondo Mattson, Rahat Ibn Rafiq, Richard Han, Qin Lv, and Shivakant Mishra. 2015. Analyzing labeled cyberbullying incidents on the instagram social network. In *International conference on social informatics*, pages 49–66. Springer.

Jeremy Howard and Sebastian Ruder. 2018. Universal language model fine-tuning for text classification. In *Proceedings of the 56th Annual Meeting of the Association for Computational Linguistics (Volume 1: Long Papers)*, pages 328–339, Melbourne, Australia. Association for Computational Linguistics.

Clayton Hutto and Eric Gilbert. 2014. Vader: A parsimonious rule-based model for sentiment analysis of social media text. In *Proceedings of the international AAAI conference on web and social media*, volume 8, pages 216–225.

Sarthak Jain and Byron C Wallace. 2019. Attention is not explanation. *arXiv preprint arXiv:1902.10186*.

A. Funk M.A. Greenwood D. Maynard N. Aswani K. Bontcheva, L. Derczynski. 2013. witie: An open-source information extraction pipeline for microblog text. *Proceedings of the International Conference on Recent Advances in Natural Language Processing*.

Christian Katzenbach and Lena Ulbricht. 2019. Algorithmic governance. *Internet Policy Review*, 8(4):1–18.

Rob Kitchin. 2017. Thinking critically about and researching algorithms. *Information, communication & society*, 20(1):14–29.

Narine Kokhlikyan, Vivek Miglani, Miguel Martin, Edward Wang, Bilal Alsallakh, Jonathan Reynolds, Alexander Melnikov, Natalia Kliushkina, Carlos Araya, Siqi Yan, and Orion Reblitz-Richardson. 2020. Captum: A unified and generic model interpretability library for pytorch.

Tao Lei et al. 2017. *Interpretable neural models for natural language processing*. Ph.D. thesis, Massachusetts Institute of Technology.

André F. T. Martins and Ramón Fernandez Astudillo. 2016. From softmax to sparsemax: A sparse model of attention and multi-label classification. *CoRR*, abs/1602.02068.

Laffan D. O'Higgins Norman J Milosevic, T. 2021. Kidicoti: Kids' digital lives in covid-19 times: A study on digital practices, safety and wellbeing; key findings from ireland. `https://antibullyingcentre.b-cdn.net/wp-content/uploads/2021/12/Short-report_Covid_for-media_TM_with-Author-names-1-2.pdf`.

Tijana Milosevic. 2018. *Protecting children online?: Cyberbullying policies of social media companies*. The MIT Press.

Alejandro Moreo, Andrea Esuli, and Fabrizio Sebastiani. 2016. Distributional random oversampling for imbalanced text classification. In *Proceedings of the 39th International ACM SIGIR Conference on Research and Development in Information Retrieval*, SIGIR '16, page 805–808, New York, NY, USA. Association for Computing Machinery.

James Mullenbach, Sarah Wiegreffe, Jon Duke, Jimeng Sun, and Jacob Eisenstein. 2018. Explainable prediction of medical codes from clinical text. *arXiv preprint arXiv:1802.05695*.

Munipalle Sai Nikhila, Aman Bhalla, and Pradeep Singh. 2020. Text imbalance handling and classification for cross-platform cyber-crime detection using deep learning. In *2020 11th International Conference on Computing, Communication and Networking Technologies (ICCCNT)*, pages 1–7. IEEE.

Justin W Patchin and Sameer Hinduja. 2006. Bullies move beyond the schoolyard: A preliminary look at cyberbullying. *Youth violence and juvenile justice*, 4(2):148–169.

Sayanta Paul and Sriparna Saha. 2020. Cyberbert: Bert for cyberbullying identification. *Multimedia Systems*, pages 1–8.

Ankit Pradhan, Venu Madhav Yatam, and Padmalochan Bera. 2020. Self-attention for cyberbullying detection. In *2020 International Conference on Cyber Situational Awareness, Data Analytics and Assessment (CyberSA)*, pages 1–6. IEEE.

Rahat Ibn Rafiq, Homa Hosseinmardi, Richard Han, Qin Lv, Shivakant Mishra, and Sabrina Arredondo Mattson. 2015. Careful what you share in six seconds: Detecting cyberbullying instances in vine. In *2015 IEEE/ACM International Conference on Advances in Social Networks Analysis and Mining (ASONAM)*, pages 617–622. IEEE.

Kelly Reynolds, April Kontostathis, and Lynne Edwards. 2011. Using machine learning to detect cyberbullying. In *2011 10th International Conference on Machine learning and applications and workshops*, volume 2, pages 241–244. IEEE.

Sebastian Ruder, Matthew E. Peters, Swabha Swayamdipta, and Thomas Wolf. 2019. Transfer learning in natural language processing. In *Proceedings of the 2019 Conference of the North American Chapter of the Association for Computational Linguistics: Tutorials*, pages 15–18, Minneapolis, Minnesota. Association for Computational Linguistics.

Semiu Salawu, Yulan He, and Jo Lumsden. 2020. Bullstop: A mobile app for cyberbullying prevention. In *Proceedings of the 28th International Conference on Computational Linguistics: System Demonstrations*, pages 70–74.

Sofia Serrano and Noah A. Smith. 2019. Is attention interpretable? In *Proceedings of the 57th Annual Meeting of the Association for Computational Linguistics*, pages 2931–2951, Florence, Italy. Association for Computational Linguistics.

Rachele Sprugnoli, Stefano Menini, Sara Tonelli, Filippo Oncini, and Enrico Piras. 2018. Creating a WhatsApp dataset to study pre-teen cyberbullying. In *Proceedings of the 2nd Workshop on Abusive Language Online (ALW2)*, pages 51–59, Brussels, Belgium. Association for Computational Linguistics.

Xiaobing Sun and Wei Lu. 2020. Understanding attention for text classification. In *Proceedings of the 58th Annual Meeting of the Association for Computational Linguistics*, pages 3418–3428, Online. Association for Computational Linguistics.

Mukund Sundararajan, Ankur Taly, and Qiqi Yan. 2017. Axiomatic attribution for deep networks. In *International conference on machine learning*, pages 3319–3328. PMLR.

Valentin Tablan, Ian Roberts, Hamish Cunningham, and Kalina Bontcheva. 2013. Gatecloud.net: a platform for large-scale, open-source text processing on the cloud. *Philosophical Transactions of the Royal Society A: Mathematical, Physical and Engineering Sciences*, 371(1983):20120071.

Jatin Karthik Tripathy, S Sibi Chakkaravarthy, Suresh Chandra Satapathy, Madhulika Sahoo, and V Vaidehi. 2020. Albert-based fine-tuning model for cyberbullying analysis. *Multimedia Systems*, pages 1–9.

David Van Bruwaene, Qianjia Huang, and Diana Inkpen. 2020. A multi-platform dataset for detecting cyberbullying in social media. *Language Resources and Evaluation*, 54(4):851–874.

Cynthia Van Hee, Gilles Jacobs, Chris Emmery, Bart Desmet, Els Lefever, Ben Verhoeven, Guy De Pauw, Walter Daelemans, and Véronique Hoste. 2018. Automatic detection of cyberbullying in social media text. *PloS one*, 13(10):e0203794.

Shikhar Vashishth, Shyam Upadhyay, Gaurav Singh Tomar, and Manaal Faruqui. 2019. Attention interpretability across nlp tasks. *arXiv preprint arXiv:1909.11218*.

Ashish Vaswani, Noam Shazeer, Niki Parmar, Jakob Uszkoreit, Llion Jones, Aidan N. Gomez, Lukasz Kaiser, and Illia Polosukhin. 2017. Attention is all you need. *CoRR*, abs/1706.03762.

Kanishk Verma, Tijana Milosevic, Keith Cortis, and Brian Davis. 2022. Benchmarking language models for cyberbullying identification and classification from social-media texts. In *Proceedings of The First Workshop on Language Technology and Resources for a Fair, Inclusive, and Safe Society within the 13th Language Resources and Evaluation Conference*, pages 26–31, Marseille, France. European Language Resources Association.

Jesse Vig. 2019a. A multiscale visualization of attention in the transformer model. *arXiv preprint arXiv:1906.05714*.

Jesse Vig. 2019b. A multiscale visualization of attention in the transformer model. In *Proceedings of the 57th Annual Meeting of the Association for Computational Linguistics: System Demonstrations*, pages 37–42, Florence, Italy. Association for Computational Linguistics.

Jesse Vig and Yonatan Belinkov. 2019. Analyzing the structure of attention in a transformer language model. In *Proceedings of the 2019 ACL Workshop BlackboxNLP: Analyzing and Interpreting Neural Networks for NLP*, pages 63–76, Florence, Italy. Association for Computational Linguistics.

Zeerak Waseem and Dirk Hovy. 2016. Hateful symbols or hateful people? predictive features for hate speech detection on Twitter. In *Proceedings of the NAACL Student Research Workshop*, pages 88–93, San Diego, California. Association for Computational Linguistics.

Thomas Wolf, Lysandre Debut, Victor Sanh, Julien Chaumond, Clement Delangue, Anthony Moi, Pierric Cistac, Tim Rault, Rémi Louf, Morgan Funtowicz, and Jamie Brew. 2019. Huggingface's transformers: State-of-the-art natural language processing. *CoRR*, abs/1910.03771.

Ellery Wulczyn, Nithum Thain, and Lucas Dixon. 2017. Ex machina: Personal attacks seen at scale. In *Proceedings of the 26th international conference on world wide web*, pages 1391–1399.

Qizhe Xie, Xuezhe Ma, Zihang Dai, and Eduard Hovy. 2017. An interpretable knowledge transfer model for knowledge base completion. *arXiv preprint arXiv:1704.05908*.

Jun-Ming Xu, Kwang-Sung Jun, Xiaojin Zhu, and Amy Bellmore. 2012. Learning from bullying traces in social media. In *Proceedings of the 2012 conference of the North American chapter of the association for computational linguistics: Human language technologies*, pages 656–666.

Kelvin Xu, Jimmy Ba, Ryan Kiros, Kyunghyun Cho, Aaron Courville, Ruslan Salakhudinov, Rich Zemel, and Yoshua Bengio. 2015. Show, attend and tell: Neural image caption generation with visual attention. In *International conference on machine learning*, pages 2048–2057. PMLR.

Jaideep Yadav, Devesh Kumar, and Dheeraj Chauhan. 2020. Cyberbullying detection using pre-trained bert model. In *2020 International Conference on Electronics and Sustainable Communication Systems (ICESC)*, pages 1096–1100. IEEE.

Zhilin Yang, Zihang Dai, Yiming Yang, Jaime G. Carbonell, Ruslan Salakhutdinov, and Quoc V. Le. 2019. Xlnet: Generalized autoregressive pretraining for language understanding. *CoRR*, abs/1906.08237.

Peiling Yi and Arkaitz Zubiaga. 2022. Cyberbullying detection across social media platforms via platform-aware adversarial encoding.

Yujia Zhang, Kuangyan Song, Yiming Sun, Sarah Tan, and Madeleine Udell. 2019. " why should you trust my explanation?" understanding uncertainty in lime explanations. *arXiv preprint arXiv:1904.12991*.

A Appendix

A.1 Data Normalisation Algorithm

As SNS and MOG text is short, an incorrect replacement of misspelt words can make the sentence lose its context. For example, if in the sentence *"i got a tkn to play" "tkn"* is replaced as *"taken"* instead of *"token"*, the sentence will lose its meaning. So, to avoid such an incorrect spell correction, it is important to understand the context of the sentence. To that effect we developed an algorithm 1 to fix spelling spelling errors with the most accurate semantic corrections by leveraging the existing python library py-spell-checker[15] and (Goldberg and Levy, 2014)'s word2vec word embedding technique. The python spell-check library py-spell-checker[16] checks every word for a misspelling and suggests two or more possible correct words. The original sentence is then parsed through the word2vec (Goldberg and Levy, 2014) model to get obtain its word embedding. The candidate words suggested by the spell check library are then replaced in the original sentence, and the new sentence is parsed through the word2vec model again. We then calculate the cosine distances between the original and possible replacement sentences, and the sentence with the highest cosine score or cosine score above 0.9 i.e., most similar to the original sentence, replaces the original sentence in the dataset.

[15] https://pypi.org/project/pyspellchecker/

[16] https://pypi.org/project/pyspellchecker/

Algorithm 1 Algorithm for contextual misspelled word correction using Word2Vec

import spellcheck() ▷ Python Package
import slang word dictionary ▷ Python dictionary of slang words
import word2Vec ▷ Word2Vec Model
for $sentence$ in $list\ sentences$ **do**
    $spellcheck \leftarrow sentence$
    $word2vec \leftarrow sentence$
    $wordoptions \leftarrow spellcheck(sentence)$
    $new_{sentence}$ ←word options+$sentence$
    $new_{word2vec}$ ←new sentence
    similarity = word2vec.cosine - new$_{word2vec}$.$cosine$
    if similarity > threshold (0.90) then sentence = new$_{sentence}$ −
  return $sentences$

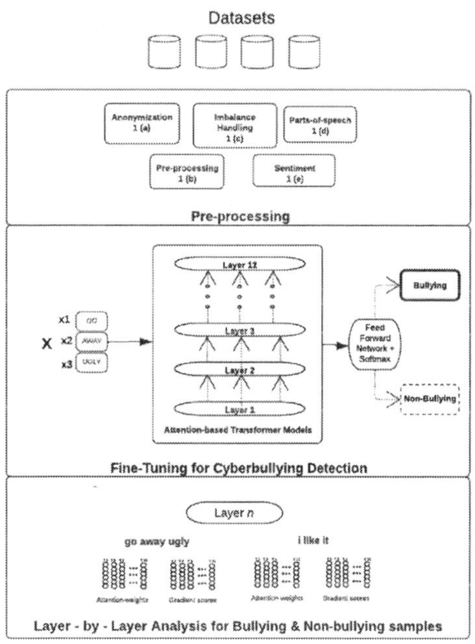

Figure 7: Experiment Schema

A.2 Dataset Split

The table 4 represents each grouped dataset's training, validation, and test-set size.

A.3 Experiment Schema

A.4 Imbalance Handling Results

Table 5 presents the results of no-sampling and over-sampling techniques leveraged in this study

Dataset-Type	Total Size	Training-set	Validation-set	Test-set	
				90% for Performance	10% for Attention
Question-Answering	139,500	111,600	13,950	12,555	1,395
User-Comment	110,323	88,259	11,032	9,929	1,103
Twitter	13,974	11,179	1,397	1,258	140
Gaming	34,229	27,383	3,423	3,081	342

Table 4: Dataset split-size

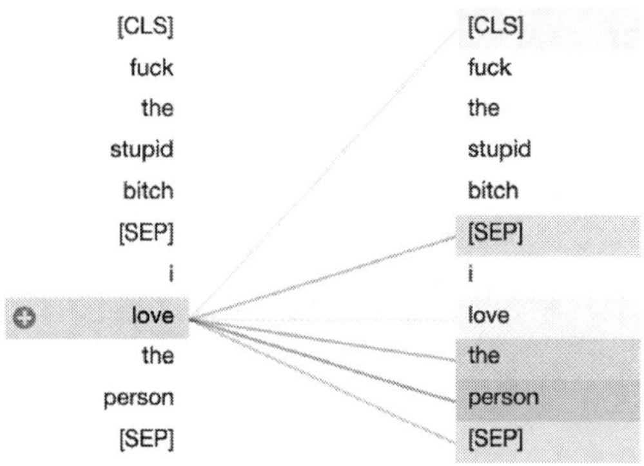

Figure 8: Attention analysis for Positive Sentiment Word

for fine-tuning pre-trained LMs.

A.5 Sentiment Attention Analysis

To analyse if negative and positive sentiment words have more attention in a text sequence. We selected the following two sentences, *"f*ck the st*pid b*tch"* (negative sentiment), and *"i love this person"* (positive sentiment), and visualized the sequence to sequence attention by leveraging BertViz (Vig, 2019b). Our findings for both positive and negative words in sample sentences for almost all layers and attention-heads on both fine-tuned BERT and HateBERT are depicted in Figure 8 and 9. As seen in Figure8, the word *"love"* in positive sentence *"i love the person"*, has higher attention distribution with neutral words like *"the"* and *"person"*. As seen in Figure9, the word *"b*tch"* in negative sentence has higher attention distribution with neutral words like *"i, the"* and *"person"*. This too disproves our hypothesis, and shows attention is not fully at negative sentiment words, instead its similar for positive sentiment words and at times higher for neutral sentiment words.

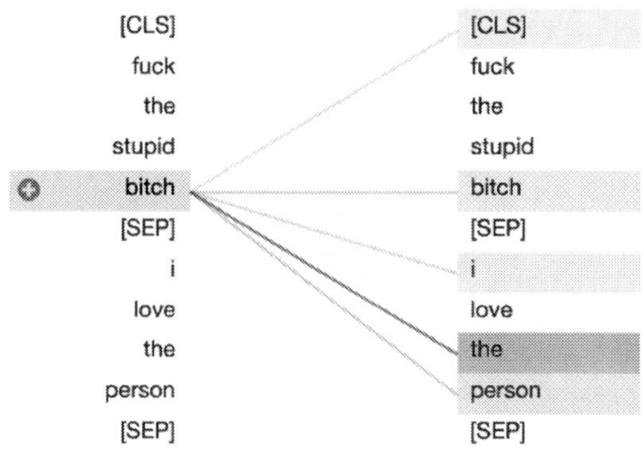

Figure 9: Attention analysis for Negative Sentiment Word

Model	Dataset	No-sampling	Oversampling
BERT+	Gaming	0.7478	**0.7746**
	UC	**0.8476**	0.8224
	QA	**0.9496**	0.939
	Twitter	**0.94**	0.365
HateBERT+	Gaming	0.6857	**0.7468**
	UC	**0.8497**	0.8261
	QA	**0.9498**	0.9076
	Twitter	**0.939**	0.938

Table 5: Model's performance on balanced and imbalanced training datasets
Note: UC $\rightarrow$ user-comment; QA $\rightarrow$ question-answering

Bias, Threat and Aggression Identification using Machine Learning Techniques on Multilingual Comments

Kirti Kumari, Shaury Srivastav, Rajiv Ranjan Suman

Abstract

In this paper, we presented our team "$IIITRanchi$" for the Trolling, Aggression and Cyberbullying (TRAC-3) 2022 shared tasks. Aggression and its different forms on social media and other platforms had tremendous growth on the Internet. In this work we have tried upon different aspects of aggression, aggression intensity, bias of different forms and their usage online and its identification using different Machine Learning techniques. We have classified each sample at seven different tasks namely aggression level, aggression intensity, discursive role, gender bias, religious bias, caste/class bias and ethnicity/racial bias as specified in the shared tasks. Both of our teams tried machine learning classifiers and achieved the good results. Overall, our team "$IIITRanchi$" ranked first position in this shared tasks competition.

Keywords— Aggression, Multilingual comments, Tokenization, TF-IDF, BoG, Logistic Regression.

1 Introduction

Social media is an open platform where users can interact, share, learn and behave openly with other online users. Due to the high demand and popularity of these media, aggression and its manifestations in different forms have taken unprecedented proportions. Users of these media are generally writing their posts in multilingual forms (Kumar et al., 2022; Kumari and Singh, 2020b,a). So, identification of such kinds of aggression, threats and biases are not an easy task due to various reasons like these comments are unstructured, multilingual, short forms and highly contextual in nature. Due to these challenges, the research communities are very much interested in such kinds of automated identification. We have tried to develop systems that could automatically identify and separate these posts from the normal posts on the aggression shared dataset (Kumar et al., 2022).

For the given tasks, we have attempted all seven different categories of the text and classified them into their classes using different machine learning classifiers. The main motive of the work is to develop an efficient Machine Learning system to detect the aggression, biased and threatening contents on the social media platform which can be removed and altered afterwards. This will prevent the negative impact on many users and hate that may spread in society. The proposed models have different machine learning algorithms and we have fine tuned the models with different hyper-parameters which we have found for testing and cross validation phases. We found better results for all the shared tasks and ranked first. Our team (IIITRanchi) ranked first on all the Task1, Task1 surprise tests, and also in Task2.

In the preceding section, we have discussed a detailed description of the some related works, dataset, the preprocessing steps involved, the initial challenges and the models which we used for our use case.

2 Related Work

The variety of aggression related works have been proposed by researchers in the last few years. Aggression related shared tasks were proposed by the organising team of Shared Tasks on Aggression Identification in every second year 2018 (Kumar et al., 2018), 2020 (Bhattacharya et al., 2020) and 2022 (Kumar et al., 2022). Some of the recent works are discussed as:

At first, we are discussing some of the important works on 2018 aggression dataset (Kumar et al., 2018). The work (Risch and Krestel, 2018) used ensemble learning and data augmentation techniques. They augmented English training dataset with the help of machine translation using three languages (French, German and Spanish) by preserving the meaning of comments with different wording. Their system was not stable for Hindi dataset across the platforms (Facebook and Twitter). Their system is not stable, especially for Hindi dataset for the same domain it was performed well, but for other domain, it fails to classify the tweets with good accuracy. Aroyehun and Gelbukh (Aroyehun and Gelbukh, 2018) used various deep learning models such as Long Short Term Memory (LSTM), CNN, and FastText as word representation and data augmentation techniques by machine-translating the original post into different languages and then translated back to the original language. Their system was not clearly classified covertly aggressive comments from overtly aggressive comments with significant accuracy. Julian and Krestel

Proceedings of the 29th International Conference on Computational Linguistic, pages 30–36
October 12–17, 2022.

(Risch and Krestel, 2018) and Aroyehun and Gelbukh (Aroyehun and Gelbukh, 2018) found that augmentation of training data gives a better result. Raiyani et al. (Raiyani et al., 2018) used dense system architecture and compared several models such as dense neural network, FastText and voting-based ensemble model. They found that simple three-layer dense neural network was performing better than the other two (FastText and voting-based ensemble classification) models. Their system has continued to suffer from false-positive cases and has also overlooked words that are not available in their vocabulary.

Some important works on 2020 aggression dataset (Bhattacharya et al., 2020; Kumar et al., 2020). Julian and Krestel (Risch and Krestel, 2020) uses transformer based multiple fine-tuned BERT models based on bagging technique and found very good results. THe work (Mishra et al., 2020) also used the transformer based BERT models and achieved good performance.

3 Dataset

In this section, we discuss brief descriptions about datasets (Kumar et al., 2022) and given shared tasks.

3.1 Tasks

The following tasks defined by the organizing teams as: (a) Aggression, Gender Bias, Racial Bias, Religious Intolerance and Bias and Casteist Bias on social media and (b) the "discursive role" of a given comment in the context of the previous comment(s). Further these task are subdivided into some subclasses as: Gender Bias: It has three subclasses problem: Gender (GEN), Gender Threat (GENT) and Non-Gender (NGEN). Ethnicity/Racial Bias: It has three subclasses Ethnic/Racial comments (ETH), Ethnic/Racial Threat(ETHT), Non Ethnic/Racial comments(NCOM). Communal bias: It has three subclasses Communal (COM), Communal Threat (COMT), Non-Communal (NCOM). Caste/class bias: It has three subclasses Casteist/Classist comments (CAS), Casteist/classist Threat (CAST), Non-Casteist/Classist comments (NCAS). Aggression Level: It has three subclasses 'Overtly Aggressive'(OAG), 'Covertly Aggressive'(CAG) and 'Non-aggressive'(NAG) text data. Aggression Intensity: This level gives a 4-way classification in between 'Physical Threat'(PTH), 'Sexual Threat'(STH), 'Non-threatening Aggression'(NtAG) and 'Curse/Abuse'(CuAG). Religious Bias: At the level E, the task is to develop a 3-way classifier for classifying the text as 'communal' (COM), 'Communal Threat'(COMT) and 'non-communal'(NCOM).

The dataset (Kumar et al., 2022) is multilingual with a total of over 140,000 samples (over 60,000 unique samples) for training and development and over 15,000 unique samples for testing in four Indian languages Meitei, Bangla (Indian variety), Hindi and English. The dataset consists of comments from a total of 158 videos i.e., it has a comment thread in total. All the data is collected from YouTube. This dataset is manually annotated by multiple annotators. The phenomena of aggression/bias is a function of certain parameters. These parameters have been discussed properly in the article (Agha, 2006). The three contextual factors included in the tasks are aggression, gender bias and communal bias. The training data contains a mixed corpus of multilingual code-mixed comments in four Indian languages:

- Meitei
- Bangla
- Hindi
- English

Language-wise distribution is approximately 26.3% Meitei, 27.8% Bangla, 45.9% Hinglish(Hindi and English). The detailed description of the dataset can be found in the article (Kumar et al., 2022).

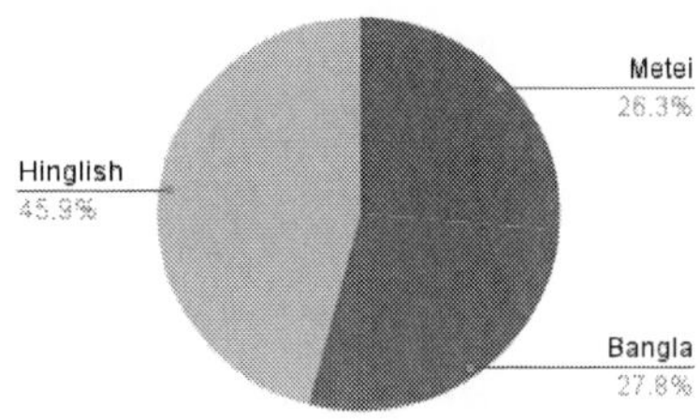

Figure 1: Pie chart for language-wise distribution of the given training dataset.

3.2 Initial challenges

The major challenges in the dataset were the unwanted words and the code-mixed nature of the dataset. We started out by cleaning the dataset with the help of certain techniques. We went for transliteration first but due to the change in meaning of many words we didn't go forward with that method. We then used some of the text data preprocessing techniques and discussed in the following section.

4 Preprocessing

In this section we are going to describe the preprocessing steps we did for cleaning the dataset.

4.1 Removing noise:

The dataset has data from youtube hence mention of users, other hyperlinks are noise for us. Simple regex(regular expression) based rules were used to remove discrepancy : The general method was

- Anything which was followed by @ such as @user was removed as it didn't add much of a context to our tasks.
- Anything starting with https//: was removed.

- Unidentified characters such as emojis with no general meanings were also removed.

4.2 Removing Punctuation and special symbols:

Since, we were going for Bag of Words(BoG) model and Term-Frequency Inverse Document Frequency (TF-IDF) vectorizer concept usage of punctuation didn't have any impact on the dataset, hence we removed the punctuations and other special characters as well.

4.3 Lowering of dataset:

We have lowered the case of the sentences of the dataset to form uniformity in the dataset and we don't have to care about the case of the dataset then for code-mixed data. Words such as 'ACHA' were converted to 'acha' for uniformity and space complexity constraints.

4.4 One Hot Encoding:

Categorical values corresponding to each class were label encoded as 0,1,2,3 to respective tasks having different classes.

4.5 Vectorization:

For vectorization, we used TF-IDF vectorizer as we used classical Machine Learning (ML) models for classification. Since the tasks were binary in nature (mostly as we had to predict whether a certain comment was aggressive or not and then its extent) so just the presence of certain words made it offensive and non-offensive and aggressive and non-aggressive . Therefore a simpler approach such as TF-IDF was used instead of the word2vec technique . Example : @user Agiye cholo aamra aachhi #goodfeels After cleaning we get - Agiye cholo aamra aachhi, goodfeels The final sparse matrix after vectorization was then feeded to the models for predictions.

5 Models

We have considered Naïve Bayes, Decision Tree based Random Forest, Logistic Regression and Support Vector Machines (SVM) for text classifications. We have used training data on each model by performing GridSearchCV for all the combinations of feature parameters. We have analyzed performance on the basis of a weighted average micro f1-score of the cross validation.

5.1 Support Vector Machine

The first model with which we started out was SVM as its state of the art for classification tasks. The parameters we used were C = 1 and the kernel was linear but it didn't perform well mostly due to the non linearly separable nature of the dataset .Then we moved on to the polynomial kernel . With degrees as high as 8-9 also the model didn't perform well as it failed to generalize. The next change we made was : kernel = 'rbf' C = 1 , this performed well on train data. This model generalized well and gave better classification results as compared to above methods.

5.2 Multinomial Bayes (MNB)

The next model we used was Multinomial Bayes which is commonly used for text classification. The initial model didn't perform well with value of = 0 , as the minimum count of many words was zero in many of the cases so the joint probability was returning zero and hence the classes were being misclassified. We used grid search cross validation for finding the best and found best results on train data with = 1e-03 But due to a sparse dataset from TfidfVectorizer it had some limitations and even with hyper parameter tuning the performance didn't improve much.

5.3 Decision Trees and Random Forest

We started the tree methods with a decision trees classifier but even with higher values of max depth and other parameters it didn't perform well. Then we moved to ensemble techniques such as random forest. Random Forest overfitted on the training dataset, and hence it was not able to capture a general trend in the dataset and failed to provide good results on validation set. We choose the criterion for split to be entropy and the max depth of each tree to be 4 in Random Forest.

5.4 Logistic Regression (LR)

The last model, we used was Logistic Regression. A simple classifier model with different C values. Due to its (almost) binary nature and multi-class solver newton-cg logistic regression performed really well on the training dataset. We got a very generalized model for all tasks. We modified the value of penalty parameter C to higher values also and got the best result at C = 5. With the generalized models ready, we used these models to assess the results on the unseen testing data which contained three types - dataset with surprise text, COVID comments dataset and data with no surprise text.

5.5 Ensemble techniques

We then moved on with ensemble based boosting methods. We used XGB Classifier and Adaboost techniques in view of better variance and better results.

5.5.1 XGB classifier

Due to the sparse nature of the data, single decision trees couldn't perform well. We chose many hyperparameters for this model but it failed to provide better results . Hence we didn't move forward with this model in the training phase. We choose the criterion for split to be entropy and the max depth of each tree to be 4 in XGB classifier and the final criteria to be Softmax.

5.5.2 AdaBoost

The last model we used was Ada Boost. Being a boosting method we expected the variance to be better in this case. For base learners we chose a decision tree with max-depth =3 and the criterion of split to be entropy. Since the model was unable to make proper decisions on the basis of sparse data the performance was not par with the models we used before.

Task	SVM	LR	RF	MNB	ADB	XGB
Aggression	0.76	0.78	0.54	0.74	0.52	0.54
Aggression Intensity	0.79	0.76	0.66	0.72	0.63	0.66
Discursive Role	0.91	0.86	0.71	0.85	0.68	0.71
Gender Bias	0.92	0.91	0.82	0.89	0.81	0.82
Communal Bias	0.96	0.95	0.85	0.94	0.82	0.85
Ethnicity-Racial Bias	0.99	0.99	0.867	0.99	0.82	0.867
Caste bias	0.99	0.99	0.87	0.98	0.74	0.87
Overall	**0.90**	0.89	0.75	0.87	0.717	0.75

Table 1: Micro averages of training dataset tasks with different models

Task	SVM	LR	MNB
Aggression	0.66	0.70	0.70
Aggression Intensity	0.66	0.67	0.69
Discursive Role	0.71	0.87	0.82
Gender Bias	0.87	0.89	0.90
Communal Bias	0.93	0.95	0.95
Ethnicity-Racial Bias	0.98	0.99	0.99
Caste bias	0.96	0.98	0.98
Overall	**0.76**	**0.86**	0.84

Table 2: Micro averages of testing dataset on task-1 with different models.

With the generalized models ready, we used these models to assess the results on the unseen testing data which contained three types - dataset with surprise text , covid comments dataset and data with no surprise text.

6 Results and Discussion

In this section, we present our findings and observations of this work.

6.1 Training data

The results, we present here are based on a weighted average micro F1-Score and some abbreviation used as: *LR - logistic regression *MNB - Multinomial bayes *SVM - support vector machines *RF- random forest *ADB - Adaboost * XGB - XG boost

The SVM model tends to fit perfectly to training data with a weighted average micro f1-score over 0.90 for many of the tasks due to its soft margin nature and flexibility in C value . The kernel used is Gaussian hence the model tends to mimic the training data really well.

6.2 Testing data

The testing data consisted of three tasks which had different datasets for evaluation in the competition.

- Task-1 Data without surprise language
- Task -2 Covid comments data
- Task-3 Data with surprise language

6.2.1 Task-1 Data without surprise data

In the above task we have seen, Logistic Regression performs better in all tasks even though SVM performed better on train dataset.

Task	SVM	LR	MNB
2018 Aggression	0.38	0.47	0.48
2020 Aggression	0.45	0.65	0.66
2022 Aggression	0.40	0.70	0.70
covid Aggression	0.30	0.63	0.60
Overall	0.30	**0.63**	0.60

Table 3: Micro averages of testing dataset on Task-2 with different models.

Task	SVM	LR	MNB
Aggression	0.60	0.62	0.63
Aggression Intensity	0.46	0.46	0.47
Discursive Role	0.69	0.88	0.84
Gender Bias	0.91	0.92	0.92
Communal Bias	0.95	**0.96**	0.96
Ethnicity-Racial Bias	0.99	0.99	0.99
Caste bias	0.98	0.98	1.00
Overall	**0.81**	**0.87**	**0.87**

Table 4: Micro averages of testing dataset on task-3 with different models.

6.3 Task-2 Data with Covid-19 comments

This data contains comments in codemixed languages where the context is based on Covid-19. So many of the texts are offensive and many have negative aspects to it as well. Logistic regression again outperforms all other models.

6.3.1 Task-3 Data with surprise data

In this case Logistic Regression and MNB both perform equally but MNB performs well on each of the subtasks individually.

6.4 Reasons for not moving towards deep learning techniques

When we talk about Natural Language Processing task, we directly take into account the popular models such as various forms of BERT models. But since in our case the simpler model (Logistic Regression) was performing well, hence we didn't move on to the deep learning model. While analysing our dataset, we found that the BERT based existing models had tokenizers which use sentence piece methods and hence while our dataset was code-mixed it would break the useful words into irrelevant tokens can be seen in the following example. For example: BERT's tokenizer doesn't have the word 'ANNA' (brother). So, it breaks down the word into 'AN' ,'NA' , which isn't even close to brother. One of the other major reasons was the size of the dataset, since it was small, we couldn't make our own embeddings for better performance as many of the things were required such as sentence piece tokenization and that requires a lot of data. The other reason was, these were simple classification tasks: i.e: whether a sentence is aggressive or not. So the presence of certain words were the only parameters we had to take care of. Hence, in our case Logistic Regression performed really well. We used Sklearn package (Pedregosa et al., 2011) to develop the models.

7 Error Analysis

In this section, we presented error analysis of our models. The size of training data was sufficient for ML models as we came across a large number of vocabulary. Since the metric used was micro F1-Score and most of the tasks had only 2-3 classes we got good results as the micro F1-Score came out to be above 0.70 on an average therefore class wise classification scores were also better. Model performs well on most of the tasks. By good performance, we mean good class wise F1-Score on all the respective classes. Few of the tasks where there was a surplus of one class had a lesser macro average due to absence of context aware classification but mostly the model has outperformed all other techniques. The confusion matrix and classification reports of Logistic Regression model's performance on training data are given below: All the respective classes are encoded to one categorical numeral below is the dictionary for that.

'Aggression': 'CAG': 0, 'OAG': 1, 'NAG': 2,

	precision	recall	f1-score	support
0	0.50	0.73	0.59	14111
1	0.90	0.79	0.84	50217
2	0.80	0.78	0.79	27757
accuracy			0.78	92085
macro avg	0.73	0.77	0.74	92085
weighted avg	0.81	0.78	0.79	92085

Figure 2: Classification report for Aggression task on training data.

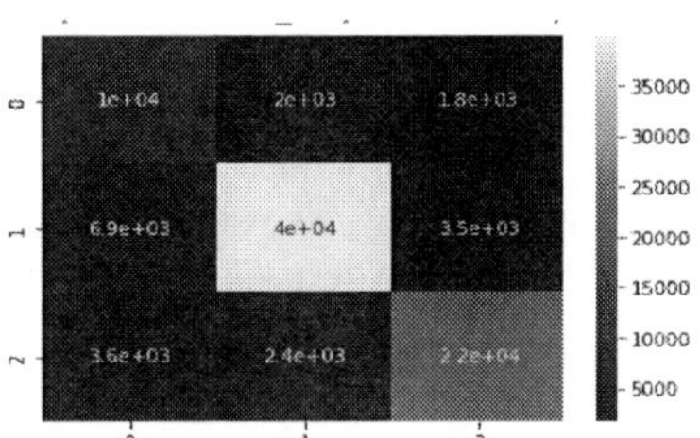

Figure 3: Confusion matrix for Aggression task on training data.

'Aggression Intensity': 'NtAG': 0, 'NA': 1, 'CuAG': 2, 'STH': 3, 'PTH': 4,

'Discursive Role': 'NA': 0,'CNS': 1,'ATK': 2,'AIN': 3,'DFN': 4,'GSL': 5,

'Gender Bias': 'NGEN': 0, 'GEN': 1, 'GENT': 2,

'Communal Bias': 'NCOM': 0, 'COM': 1, 'COMT': 2,

	precision	recall	f1-score	support
0	0.81	0.72	0.76	41573
1	0.78	0.80	0.79	26516
2	0.72	0.81	0.76	21981
3	0.42	0.80	0.55	698
4	0.52	0.86	0.65	1317
accuracy			0.76	92085
macro avg	0.65	0.80	0.70	92085
weighted avg	0.77	0.76	0.77	92085

Figure 4: Classification report for Aggression Intensity task on training data.

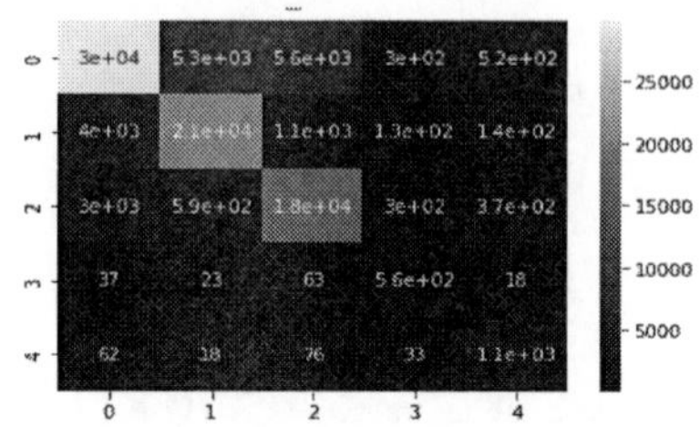

Figure 5: Confusion matrix for Aggression Intensity task on training data.

	precision	recall	f1-score	support
0	0.96	0.87	0.91	70561
1	0.08	0.75	0.15	53
2	0.72	0.84	0.77	20665
3	0.24	0.81	0.37	678
4	0.12	0.78	0.20	128
5	0.00	0.00	0.00	0
accuracy			0.86	92085
macro avg	0.35	0.68	0.40	92085
weighted avg	0.90	0.86	0.88	92085

Figure 6: Classification Report for Discursive Role task on training data.

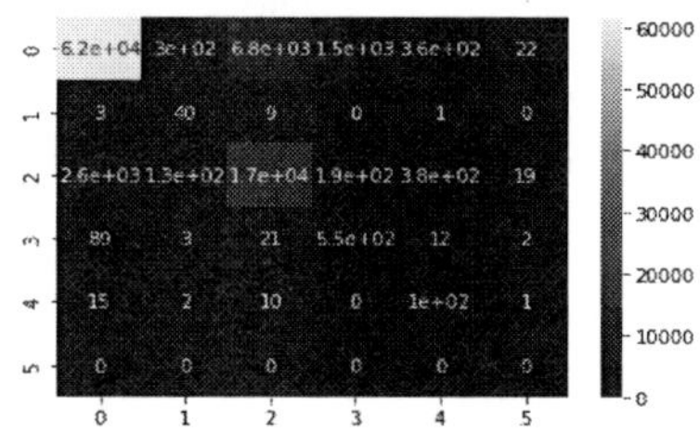

Figure 7: Confusion Matrix for Discursive Role task on training data.

'Caste/Class Bias': 'NCAS': 0, 'CAS': 1, 'CAST': 2,

'Ethnicity/Racial Bias': 'NETH': 0, 'ETH': 1, 'ETHT': 2

8 Conclusion

Our team secured the first position in the competition of the given shared tasks on bias, threat and aggression detection for given datasets. We found that the Logistic

	precision	recall	f1-score	support
0	0.98	0.92	0.95	81216
1	0.58	0.82	0.68	10597
2	0.22	0.85	0.35	272
accuracy			0.91	92085
macro avg	0.60	0.86	0.66	92085
weighted avg	0.93	0.91	0.92	92085

Figure 8: Classification Report for Gender Bias task on training data.

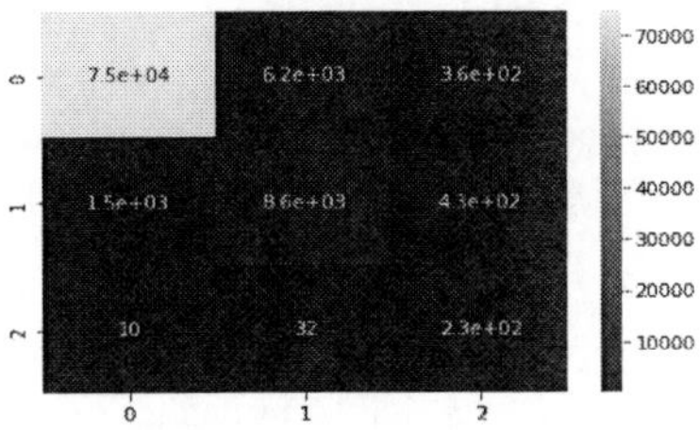

Figure 9: Confusion Matrix for Gender Bias task on training data.

	precision	recall	f1-score	support
0	0.99	0.96	0.98	85176
1	0.65	0.85	0.74	6843
2	0.13	0.80	0.23	66
accuracy			0.95	92085
macro avg	0.59	0.87	0.65	92085
weighted avg	0.96	0.95	0.96	92085

Figure 10: Classification Report for Communal Bias task on training data.

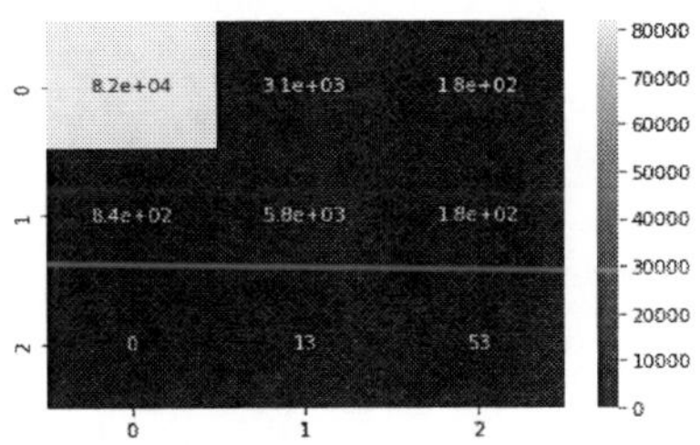

Figure 11: Confusion Matrix for Communal Bias task on training data.

	precision	recall	f1-score	support
0	1.00	0.99	0.99	91577
1	0.35	0.86	0.49	508
2	0.00	0.00	0.00	0
accuracy			0.99	92085
macro avg	0.45	0.62	0.50	92085
weighted avg	1.00	0.99	0.99	92085

Figure 12: Classification Report for Caste/Class Bias task on training data.

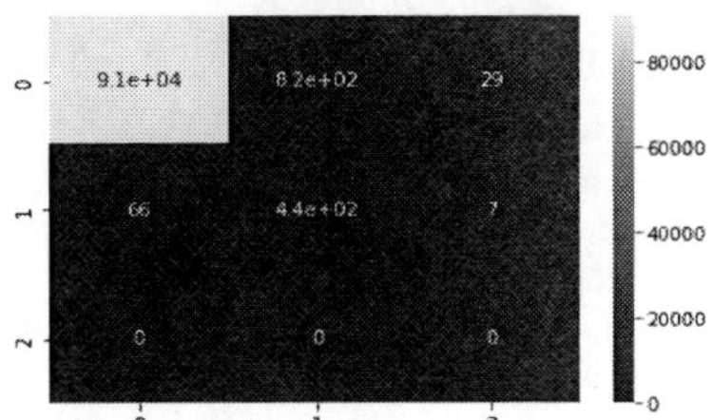

Figure 13: Confusion Matrix for Caste/Class Bias task on training data.

	precision	recall	f1-score	support
0	1.00	0.99	0.99	90554
1	0.50	0.86	0.63	1531
2	0.00	0.00	0.00	0
accuracy			0.98	92085
macro avg	0.50	0.61	0.54	92085
weighted avg	0.99	0.98	0.99	92085

Figure 14: Classification Report for Ethnicity/Racial Bias task on training data.

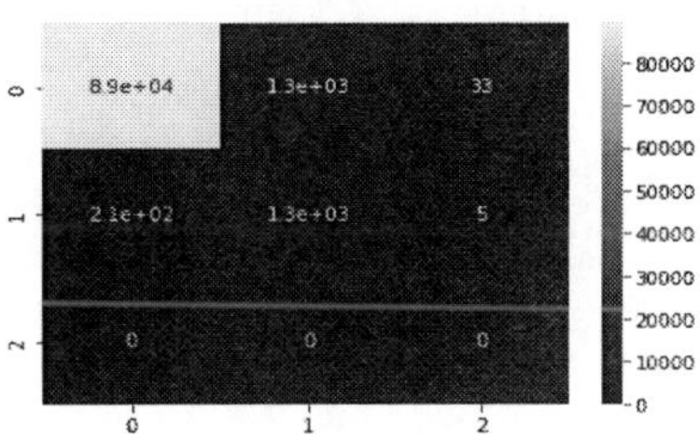

Figure 15: Confusion Matrix for Ethnicity/Racial Bias task on training data.

Regression classifier outperforms all the models on test data due to more generalization and better prediction nature in sparse data. The possible reason was that the dataset in sparse form was linearly separable, but the SVM model being soft margin was not a generalized model for our case. SVM model was overfitting on train data but Logistic Regression generalized the metrics and hence performed really well in our case. At the end, we would like to conclude with the possibility that there exists many of the techniques other than what we have presented in this paper. In order to improve the model's performance, we can go for ensemble techniques of the models which have performed well in order to increase the variance and make the model more generalized.

9 Acknowledgement

We would like to thank Mrinmoy Mahato, Amitesh Patel , Aman Kapoor and Ankit Kumar of Department of Computer Science and Engineering, Indian Institute of Information Technology RANCHI - 834004 for their help in preprocessing steps.

References

Asif Agha. 2006. *Language and social relations*, volume 24. Cambridge University Press.

Segun Taofeek Aroyehun and Alexander Gelbukh. 2018. Aggression detection in social media: Using deep neural networks, data augmentation, and pseudo labeling. In *Proceedings of the First Workshop on Trolling, Aggression and Cyberbullying (TRAC-2018)*, pages 90–97.

Shiladitya Bhattacharya, Siddharth Singh, Ritesh Kumar, Akanksha Bansal, Akash Bhagat, Yogesh Dawer, Bornini Lahiri, and Atul Kr. Ojha. 2020. Developing a multilingual annotated corpus of misogyny and aggression. In *Proceedings of the Second Workshop on Trolling, Aggression and Cyberbullying*, pages 158–168, Marseille, France. European Language Resources Association (ELRA).

Ritesh Kumar, Enakshi Nandi, Laishram Niranjana Devi, Shyam Ratan, Siddharth Singh, Akash Bhagat, and Yogesh Dawer. 2022. The comma dataset v0. 2: Annotating aggression and bias in multilingual social media discourse. In *Proceedings of the Third Workshop on Trolling, Aggression and Cyberbullying*, pages 4149–4161, Marseille, France. European Language Resources Association (ELRA).

Ritesh Kumar, Atul Kr Ojha, Shervin Malmasi, and Marcos Zampieri. 2020. Evaluating aggression identification in social media. In *Proceedings of the second workshop on trolling, aggression and cyberbullying*, pages 1–5.

Ritesh Kumar, Aishwarya N. Reganti, Akshit Bhatia, and Tushar Maheshwari. 2018. Aggression-annotated Corpus of Hindi-English Code-mixed Data. In *Proceedings of the Eleventh International Conference on Language Resources and Evaluation (LREC 2018)*, Miyazaki, Japan. European Language Resources Association (ELRA).

Kirti Kumari and Jyoti Prakash Singh. 2020a. Ai_ml_nit_patna@ hasoc 2020: Bert models for hate speech identification in indo-european languages. In *FIRE (Working Notes)*, pages 319–324.

Kirti Kumari and Jyoti Prakash Singh. 2020b. Ai_ml_nit_patna@ trac-2: deep learning approach for multi-lingual aggression identification. In *Proceedings of the second workshop on trolling, aggression and cyberbullying*, pages 113–119.

Sudhanshu Mishra, Shivangi Prasad, and Shubhanshu Mishra. 2020. Multilingual joint fine-tuning of transformer models for identifying trolling, aggression and cyberbullying at TRAC 2020. In *Proceedings of the Second Workshop on Trolling, Aggression and Cyberbullying*, pages 120–125, Marseille, France. European Language Resources Association (ELRA).

F. Pedregosa, G. Varoquaux, A. Gramfort, V. Michel, B. Thirion, O. Grisel, M. Blondel, P. Prettenhofer, R. Weiss, V. Dubourg, J. Vanderplas, A. Passos, D. Cournapeau, M. Brucher, M. Perrot, and E. Duchesnay. 2011. Scikit-learn: Machine learning in Python. *Journal of Machine Learning Research*, 12:2825–2830.

Kashyap Raiyani, Teresa Gonçalves, Paulo Quaresma, and Vitor Beires Nogueira. 2018. Fully connected neural network with advance preprocessor to identify aggression over facebook and twitter. In *Proceedings of the First Workshop on Trolling, Aggression and Cyberbullying (TRAC-2018)*, pages 28–41.

Julian Risch and Ralf Krestel. 2018. Aggression identification using deep learning and data augmentation. In *Proceedings of the First Workshop on Trolling, Aggression and Cyberbullying (TRAC-2018)*, pages 150–158.

Julian Risch and Ralf Krestel. 2020. Bagging BERT models for robust aggression identification. In *Proceedings of the Second Workshop on Trolling, Aggression and Cyberbullying*, pages 55–61, Marseille, France. European Language Resources Association (ELRA).

The Role of Context in Detecting the Target of Hate Speech

Ilia Markov
CLTL, Vrije Universiteit Amsterdam
Amsterdam, The Netherlands
i.markov@vu.nl

Walter Daelemans
CLiPS, University of Antwerp
Antwerp, Belgium
walter.daelemans@uantwerpen.be

Abstract

Online hate speech detection is an inherently challenging task that has recently received much attention from the natural language processing community. Despite a substantial increase in performance, considerable challenges remain and include encoding contextual information into automated hate speech detection systems. In this paper, we focus on detecting the target of hate speech in Dutch social media: whether a hateful Facebook comment is directed against migrants or not (i.e., against someone else). We manually annotate the relevant conversational context and investigate the effect of different aspects of context on performance when adding it to a Dutch transformer-based pre-trained language model, BERTje. We show that performance of the model can be significantly improved by integrating relevant contextual information.

1 Introduction

Hate speech detection models play an important role in online content moderation and promotion of healthy online debates (Halevy et al., 2020). This has motivated a considerable interest in the task within a variety of disciplines, including social sciences and the natural language processing (NLP) community.

Recent advances in the field of NLP, which include the use of deep learning and ensemble architectures, have led to the development of automated hate speech detection approaches with an increased performance (Kumar et al., 2020; Zampieri et al., 2020; Markov and Daelemans, 2021). However, the task remains challenging from multiple perspectives, e.g., the use of figurative language and cross-domain scalability, amongst others (van Aken et al., 2018; Vidgen and Derczynski, 2020; Pamungkas et al., 2021; Lemmens et al., 2021). These challenges constrain the performance and generalizability of hate speech detection models, and include the problem of integrating contextual information, that is, improving hate speech detection models by making them context aware (Pavlopoulos et al., 2020; Menini et al., 2021; Vidgen et al., 2021).

Modeling contextual information is indisputably important for developing robust hate speech detection systems (de Gibert et al., 2018; Pavlopoulos et al., 2020; Vidgen et al., 2021). For instance, the comment 'go back home' is clearly hate speech if it is posted under a news article about refugees and asylum seekers. However, previous work on detecting both the type and target of online hate speech has mostly focused on message content alone, without accounting for the context of the target comments (Risch and Krestel, 2020; Zampieri et al., 2020). This is partially related to the lack of contextual information in the vast majority of datasets annotated for hate speech, which implies that hate speech detection models cannot exploit the conversational context when they are trained on existing datasets (Vidgen and Derczynski, 2020).

More recent studies have specifically looked into the effect of context on hate speech detection. For instance, Pavlopoulos et al. (2020) experimented with various strategies for integrating contextual information into BiLSTM and BERT models, where context is limited to the preceding ('parent') comment in the Wikipedia conversations dataset. The authors report that though context significantly affects annotation process by both amplifying or mitigating the perceived toxicity of posts, they found no evidence that adding context leads to a large or consistent improvement in performance of the examined models. Menini et al. (2021) highlighted similar challenges: while showing that context affects annotation process (fewer tweets were annotated as abusive when context was provided to annotators), they report that when experimenting with different models (BERT, BiLSTM, SVM) and a context window ranging from one to all preceding tweets, contextual information did not lead to a better classifier performance. Vidgen et al. (2021) introduced

Proceedings of the 29th International Conference on Computational Linguistic, pages 37–42
October 12–17, 2022.

the Contextual Abuse Dataset composed of Reddit messages, where previous or several previous messages were considered as the context and "every annotation has a label for whether contextual information was needed to make the annotation". The authors report that 25-32% of content was labelled as context-dependent, and these messages are more challenging for detection, leaving integrating context for future work.

In this paper, we address hate speech target detection in hateful Dutch Facebook comments: whether the target of hateful content is the social group of interest, that is, migrants or someone else (see Section 2). While in previous work the preceding comment(s) in the discussion thread or the text of the post was used as context (Gao and Huang, 2017; Karan and Šnajder, 2019; Pavlopoulos et al., 2020; Menini et al., 2021; Lemmens et al., 2022), we manually annotate the relevant context, that is, we look specifically at the part of the prior conversation that provides the context, and use that annotation to demonstrate its utility in hate speech target prediction by adding relevant contextual information to a Dutch transformer-based pre-trained language model, BERTje (de Vries et al., 2019).

Hate speech is deeply contextual, and while most previous work ignores the conversational context, and more recent work, which looked into it based on previous comments or post, comes away concluding that such surface-level information is not helpful in prediction, this study shows and quantifies the impact that can be brought by relevant context on classifier performance when detecting the target of online hate speech.

2 Data

We used the LiLaH dataset, as in (Markov et al., 2021). The dataset is composed of Facebook posts by mainstream media outlets in Dutch (i.e., news articles that were published by the media outlets and are (re-)published or shared as Facebook posts) and readers' comments on these posts in a comment section, which were manually annotated by three trained annotators for fine-grained types and targets of hate speech (see below in this section) with a 'moderate' agreement. The annotations were performed in-context, that is, annotators first read entire comment threads and then labeled each comment.

We randomly selected a subset of the dataset composed of 35 posts and around 6,000 comments discussing the migrants topic and annotated this data for context dependency: if context influences the annotators' decision to assign a label to a comment, that is, if assigning hatefulness to a comment depends on understanding its context, or if the target of hate speech is not sufficiently clear without the context, the annotator marked the target comment as context-sensitive and indicated the ID of the post or the ID of the previous comment (not necessarily directly preceding) in the discussion thread that serves as the corresponding context. For example, the comment 'I would have served pork steaks' (*Ik zou varkenslapjes geserveerd hebben*) is hate speech directed against migrants if we take into account that the article is about a Muslim woman who was served alcohol at a show and was upset since this was against her religion. In this case, the annotator would mark the comment as context-dependent and indicate the ID of the post under which the comment was made.

We merged the fine-grained types of hate speech present in the data (e.g., violence, offensiveness, threat) into a single hate speech category, removing comments that belong to the non-hate speech class, which is the commonly used set-up for the hate speech target detection task (Zampieri et al., 2019a,b; Caselli et al., 2021), and used the binary target classes within the hateful messages. That is, we distinguish between migrants as the target of hate speech and merge all other fine-grained target classes into the 'other' category in order to have a sufficient amount of training and test examples per class. In more detail, the 'other' category consists of hate speech directed against (1) the article's author or the media spreading the article; (2) the author of another preceding comment under the same post; (3) other entities related to the migrants group, as they represent a positive attitude towards this group; and (4) people or institutions that do not belong to any of the above categories. For the binary target classes used in this study, the inter-annotator agreement was 'moderate' (Cohen's Kappa = 0.46).

We used training and test partitions splitting the dataset by post boundaries in order to avoid within-post bias, that is, all comments belonging to the same thread are in the same split. The splitting was done so that the distribution of 'migrants' and 'other' classes is as balanced as possible (roughly 40%–60%, respectively), while the proportion of 80% training and 20% test messages is preserved.

	Train (28 posts)		**Test** (7 posts)		**Total** (35 posts)	
	# messages	% context	# messages	% context	# messages	% context
Migrants	1,017	60.2	238	57.6	1,255	59.8
Other	1,660	28.9	431	38.3	2,091	30.8
Total	2,677	40.8	669	45.1	3,346	41.7

Table 1: Statistics of the dataset used in terms of the number of posts, number of comments per class and the percentage of messages annotated as context-dependent within each class.

The statistics of the dataset used in terms of the number of posts and comments in the training and test sets, as well as the percentage of context-dependent messages per class is provided in Table 1. We note that context-sensitive comments are frequent within both categories. Context-dependent messages within the 'migrants' category (59.8%; 750 messages) are more frequent than within the 'other' category (30.8%; 644 messages), which could be explained by the characteristics of the dataset used: it consists of discussion threads on the migrants topic, while in order to direct hate speech against someone else (e.g., previous commenter, article's author) hateful content creators would have to deviate from the original discussion topic by explicitly specifying the target of their hate speech. Out of 1,394 messages labeled as context-dependent, the vast majority (88%) refer to original post as the source of relevant context, 7% to previous comment and 5% to a comment located higher up in the discussion thread.

3 Experiments and Results

We use the monolingual Dutch transformer-based pre-trained language model, BERTje (de Vries et al., 2019), from the Hugging Face transformers library[1], which showed near state-of-the-art results in previous work on Dutch hate speech detection, e.g., (Caselli et al., 2021; Markov et al., 2022). The model was pre-trained using the same architecture and parameters as the original 768-dimensional BERT model (Devlin et al., 2019) on a dataset of 2.4 billion tokens.

We set the maximum sequence length parameter to 512 in order to account for the context, the other parameters have default values, and fine-tune the model for a single epoch. Following the approach proposed in (Pavlopoulos et al., 2020), we concatenate the context and the text of the target comment separated by BERTje's [SEP] token, as in the next sentence prediction task in BERTje's pre-training stage, and fine-tune the model on this data.

We use only the content of the target comment as the baseline and examine the following ways for adding contextual information: (1) adding the text of the post on which the comment was made (comment & post); (2) adding the preceding comment (if any) in the discussion thread (comment & preceding comment); (3) adding the preceding comment and the post (comment & preceding comment & post); and (4) adding the relevant annotated context (comment & context). Since BERTje is sensitive to random seeds, we report the results in terms of precision, recall and F1-score (macro) averaged over five runs, and standard deviations in Table 2.

The obtained results are in line with previous findings in the sense that adding the content of a preceding comment does not facilitate classifier performance (Karan and Šnajder, 2019; Pavlopoulos et al., 2020; Menini et al., 2021). However, we observe a moderate improvement by adding the content of the post (2 F1 points) and a significant improvement (according to McNemar's significance test (McNemar, 1947) with $\alpha < 0.05$) caused by pointing at the actual context in the discussion thread (6 F1 points). The results partially reflect the annotation process, described in Section 2, where most of the hateful messages contain the relevant context in the post text.

To further examine the importance of contextual information, we conducted an additional experiment using only the relevant context (while discarding the content of the target message), obtaining the following results: precision = 0.60 (±0.009), recall = 0.60 (±0.007), F1 = 0.60 (±0.009) (average over 5 runs). Considering that the majority baseline precision = 0.32, recall = 0.50, and F1 = 0.39, this experiment confirms that context contains useful information and can be used in isolation to predict the label of the target message.

The detailed results per class for one of the experiments reported in Table 2 for the baseline (comment only) and 'comment & context' strategies are presented in Table 3. We note that with the

[1] https://huggingface.co/GroNLP/bert-base-dutch-cased

	Precision	Recall	F1-score
Comment (baseline)	0.65 (±0.008)	0.66 (±0.008)	0.63 (±0.011)
Comment & post	0.66 (±0.008)	0.67 (±0.004)	0.65 (±0.008)
Comment & preceding comment	0.64 (±0.007)	0.65 (±0.004)	0.63 (±0.015)
Comment & preceding comment & post	0.64 (±0.004)	0.65 (±0.008)	0.63 (±0.000)
Comment & context	**0.69** (±0.005)	**0.71** (±0.008)	**0.69** (±0.008)

Table 2: Results for the baseline and examined strategies for adding contextual information averaged over five runs. The standard deviations are also reported. The best results are highlighted in bold typeface.

	Comment (baseline)			Comment & context		
	Precision	Recall	F1-score	Precision	Recall	F1-score
Migrants	0.51	0.69	0.58	0.56	0.74	0.64
Other	0.79	0.63	0.70	0.83	0.68	0.74
macro avg	0.65	0.66	0.64	0.69	0.71	0.69

Table 3: Results per class for the baseline and 'comment & context' approaches.

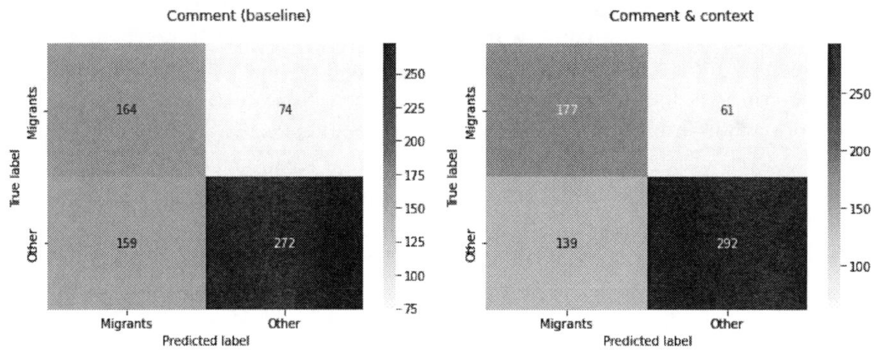

Figure 1: Confusion matrices for the baseline and 'comment & context' approaches.

additional contextual information, there is an improvement in performance for both 'migrants' and 'other' categories in terms of both precision and recall. In line with de Gibert et al. (2018) and Vidgen et al. (2021), we observed that context-sensitive messages are more challenging for classification: out of 302 context-dependent messages within the both categories 57% were identified correctly by the baseline approach, while out of 367 messages not dependent on the context, 71% were assigned the correct label. Integrating the relevant context lead to an improvement for both context-dependent and independent messages, resulting in 60% and 87% correctly-identified messages, respectively.

While for the 'migrants' class integrating the context lead to an improvement for the context-dependent messages (81% instead of 67% were identified correctly after adding the context), and no improvement was observed for the context-independent messages (65% vs. 71% without the context), for the 'other' class, the main source of improvement is the context-independent messages (84% instead of 72% were identified correctly), while the number of correctly-identified context-dependent messages within this category dropped from 48% to 42%. Zooming in on the fine-grained classes within the 'other' category, we note that the results are improved for all the classes, except for the hate speech directed towards article's author or media spreading the news, where only two more messages were misclassified after adding the contextual information.

The confusion matrices for this experiment, presented in Figure 1, demonstrate that integrating the context improves the results both in terms of false positives and false negatives, providing additional evidence that context plays an important role in detecting the target of online hateful comments.

4 Conclusions

Despite recent advances, there are multiple challenges that remain and limit the development of robust real-world hate speech detection systems. One of such challenges, addressed in this work, is to explicitly account for relevant conversational context when developing context-aware hate speech detection approaches.

While prior work has shown that the easy-to-obtain contextual information such as previous comment or post does not provide a large or consistent improvement, we demonstrated that if the model can zoom in on the relevant context, the performance increases significantly.

A limitation of this work is that we use hand-labeled contextual information, and thus report an upper bound of improvement in performance. Nonetheless, we believe that this study is an important step towards developing more robust and context-aware automated hate speech detection approaches.

Given the great potential for encoding contextual information and its significant effect on detecting the target of hate speech presented in this work, the directions for future work include detecting relevant context for a target comment automatically and exploring its effect on performance, as well as investigating the impact of context on detecting fine-grained types and targets of online hate speech.

Acknowledgements

This research has been supported by the Flemish Research Foundation through the bilateral research project FWO G070619N "The linguistic landscape of hate speech on social media". The research also received funding from the Flemish Government (AI Research Program). This research has also been supported by Huawei Finland through the DreamsLab project. All content represented the opinions of the authors, which were not necessarily shared or endorsed by their respective employers and/or sponsors.

References

Tommaso Caselli, Arjan Schelhaas, Marieke Weultjes, Folkert Leistra, Hylke van der Veen, Gerben Timmerman, and Malvina Nissim. 2021. DALC: The Dutch abusive language corpus. In *Proceedings of the 5th Workshop on Online Abuse and Harms*, pages 54–66, Online. ACL.

Ona de Gibert, Naiara Perez, Aitor García-Pablos, and Montse Cuadros. 2018. Hate speech dataset from a white supremacy forum. In *Proceedings of the 2nd Workshop on Abusive Language Online*, pages 11–20, Brussels, Belgium. ACL.

Wietse de Vries, Andreas van Cranenburgh, Arianna Bisazza, Tommaso Caselli, Gertjan van Noord, and Malvina Nissim. 2019. BERTje: A Dutch BERT model. *arXiv/1912.09582*.

Jacob Devlin, Ming-Wei Chang, Kenton Lee, and Kristina Toutanova. 2019. BERT: Pre-training of deep bidirectional transformers for language understanding. In *Proceedings of the 2019 Conference of the North American Chapter of the Association for Computational Linguistics: Human Language Technologies)*, pages 4171–4186, Minneapolis, MN, USA. ACL.

Lei Gao and Ruihong Huang. 2017. Detecting online hate speech using context aware models. In *Proceedings of the International Conference Recent Advances in Natural Language Processing*, pages 260–266, Varna, Bulgaria. INCOMA Ltd.

Alon Halevy, Cristian Canton Ferrer, Hao Ma, Umut Ozertem, Patrick Pantel, Marzieh Saeidi, Fabrizio Silvestri, and Ves Stoyanov. 2020. Preserving integrity in online social networks. *arXiv/2009.10311*.

Mladen Karan and Jan Šnajder. 2019. Preemptive toxic language detection in Wikipedia comments using thread-level context. In *Proceedings of the Third Workshop on Abusive Language Online*, pages 129–134, Florence, Italy. ACL.

Ritesh Kumar, Atul Kr. Ojha, Shervin Malmasi, and Marcos Zampieri. 2020. Evaluating aggression identification in social media. In *Proceedings of the Second Workshop on Trolling, Aggression and Cyberbullying*, pages 1–5, Marseille, France. ELRA.

Jens Lemmens, Tess Dejaeghere, Tim Kreutz, Jens Van Nooten, Ilia Markov, and Walter Daelemans. 2022. Vaccinpraat: Monitoring vaccine skepticism in Dutch Twitter and Facebook comments. *Computational Linguistics in the Netherlands Journal*, 11:173–188.

Jens Lemmens, Ilia Markov, and Walter Daelemans. 2021. Improving hate speech type and target detection with hateful metaphor features. In *Proceedings of the Fourth Workshop on NLP for Internet Freedom: Censorship, Disinformation, and Propaganda*, pages 7–16, Online. ACL.

Ilia Markov and Walter Daelemans. 2021. Improving cross-domain hate speech detection by reducing the false positive rate. In *Proceedings of the Fourth Workshop on NLP for Internet Freedom: Censorship, Disinformation, and Propaganda*, pages 17–22, Online. ACL.

Ilia Markov, Ine Gevers, and Walter Daelemans. 2022. An ensemble approach for Dutch cross-domain hate speech detection. In *Proceedings of the 27th International Conference on Natural Language and Information Systems*, pages 3–15, Valencia, Spain. Springer.

Ilia Markov, Nikola Ljubešić, Darja Fišer, and Walter Daelemans. 2021. Exploring stylometric and emotion-based features for multilingual cross-domain hate speech detection. In *Proceedings of the Eleventh Workshop on Computational Approaches to Subjectivity, Sentiment and Social Media Analysis*, pages 149–159, Kyiv, Ukraine (Online). ACL.

Quinn McNemar. 1947. Note on the sampling error of the difference between correlated proportions or percentages. *Psychometrika*, 12(2):153–157.

Stefano Menini, Alessio Palmero Aprosio, and Sara Tonelli. 2021. Abuse is contextual, what about NLP? The role of context in abusive language annotation and detection. *ArXiv*, abs/2103.14916.

Endang Wahyu Pamungkas, Valerio Basile, and Viviana Patti. 2021. Towards multidomain and multilingual abusive language detection: a survey. *Personal and Ubiquitous Computing*.

John Pavlopoulos, Jeffrey Sorensen, Lucas Dixon, Nithum Thain, and Ion Androutsopoulos. 2020. Toxicity detection: Does context really matter? In *Proceedings of the 58th Annual Meeting of the Association for Computational Linguistics*, pages 4296–4305, online. ACL.

Julian Risch and Ralf Krestel. 2020. Toxic comment detection in online discussions. *Deep Learning-Based Approaches for Sentiment Analysis*, pages 85–109.

Betty van Aken, Julian Risch, Ralf Krestel, and Alexander Löser. 2018. Challenges for toxic comment classification: An in-depth error analysis. *arXiv/1809.07572*.

Bertie Vidgen and Leon Derczynski. 2020. Directions in abusive language training data: Garbage in, garbage out. *arXiv/2004.01670*.

Bertie Vidgen, Dong Nguyen, Helen Margetts, Patricia Rossini, and Rebekah Tromble. 2021. Introducing CAD: the contextual abuse dataset. In *Proceedings of the 2021 Conference of the North American Chapter of the Association for Computational Linguistics: Human Language Technologies*, pages 2289–2303, Online. ACL.

Marcos Zampieri, Shervin Malmasi, Preslav Nakov, Sara Rosenthal, Noura Farra, and Ritesh Kumar. 2019a. Predicting the type and target of offensive posts in social media. In *Proceedings of the 2019 Conference of the North American Chapter of the Association for Computational Linguistics: Human Language Technologies*, pages 1415–1420. ACL.

Marcos Zampieri, Shervin Malmasi, Preslav Nakov, Sara Rosenthal, Noura Farra, and Ritesh Kumar. 2019b. SemEval-2019 task 6: Identifying and categorizing offensive language in social media (OffensEval). In *Proceedings of the 13th International Workshop on Semantic Evaluation*, pages 75–86, Minneapolis, Minnesota, USA. ACL.

Marcos Zampieri, Preslav Nakov, Sara Rosenthal, Pepa Atanasova, Georgi Karadzhov, Hamdy Mubarak, Leon Derczynski, Zeses Pitenis, and Çağrı Çöltekin. 2020. SemEval-2020 task 12: Multilingual offensive language identification in social media. In *Proceedings of the Fourteenth Workshop on Semantic Evaluation*, pages 1425–1447, Barcelona (online). ICCL.

Annotating Targets of Toxic Language at the Span Level

Baran Barbarestani and **Isa Maks** and **Piek Vossen**
CLTL Lab, Vrije Universiteit Amsterdam
De Boelelaan 1105, 1081 HV Amsterdam, The Netherlands
{b.barbarestani, isa.maks, piek.vossen}@vu.nl

Abstract

In this paper, we discuss an interpretable framework to integrate toxic language annotations. Most data sets address only one aspect of the complex relationship in toxic communication and are inconsistent with each other. Enriching annotations with more details and information is, however, of great importance in order to develop high-performing and comprehensive explainable language models. Such systems should recognize and interpret both expressions that are toxic as well as expressions that make reference to specific targets to combat toxic language. We, therefore, create a crowd-annotation task to mark the spans of words that refer to target communities as an extension of the HateXplain data set. We present a quantitative and qualitative analysis of the annotations. We also fine-tune RoBERTa-base on our data and experiment with different data thresholds to measure their effect on the classification. The F1-score of our best model on the test set is 79%. The annotations are freely available and can be combined with the existing HateXplain annotations to build richer and more complete models.

1 Introduction

Communication through social media has exploded in the last decades. The ease of posting opinions and the relative anonymity of posters has also unleashed problematic communication that can take many different forms: offensive language, hate speech, discriminatory language, abusive language, cyberbullying, etc., which can be all captured under the umbrella term *toxic*. Such communication is often very complex and involves different values and perspectives. A comprehensive interpretation of such communication requires different aspects to be detected and combined, among which expressions that make a judgement or suggest negative implications and expressions that refer to targets such as a specific group of people or an individual belonging to such a group. An explainable system that can act as an automated moderator should be capable of "understanding" such phrases, reason over their content and bring specific aspects to posters' attention to explain what is wrong with a post and why it has to be, for example, removed by moderators (Kiritchenko and Nejadgholi, 2020). An explainable model not only produces the desired outputs, but also explains why such output are produced.

The Natural Language Processing community has started many initiatives to automatically detect and classify toxic language and created a plethora of datasets (Vidgen and Derczynski, 2020; Poletto et al., 2021). However, these data sets often address only one of the above-mentioned aspects. Furthermore, they use slightly different terminologies and definitions for annotation and their annotation guidelines lack compatibility, which makes it difficult to combine their annotations. Another problem is that annotation is often done at a global level, such as the whole sentence instead of specific phrases and tokens. Some recent initiatives have started to annotate specific spans within the text itself (Mathew et al., 2020; Pavlopoulos et al., 2021) but this is limited to toxic spans only.

Although previous studies did annotate the target community (e.g., women, Muslims, immigrants, etc.) at the post level, none of these studies marked the words that describe or refer to such a group. Being able to detect these phrases is, however, crucial to reason over who is targeted and how they are referenced. Furthermore, annotating references to targets separately from toxic spans makes it possible to also process larger contexts of communication, among which conversations where references to targets and toxic expressions may be dispersed over multiple posts. By building a framework where target spans are annotated, it is possible to train explainable models that not only tell which community groups are targeted in a piece of text, but

Proceedings of the 29th International Conference on Computational Linguistic, pages 43–51
October 12–17, 2022.

also indicate which words and phrases this decision is based on. This will make the model and its decision more understandable for end users.

In this study, we describe a crowd-annotation task to annotate such target spans. We used this framework to add target spans to the HateXplain data set (Mathew et al., 2020) and tested classification models by fine-tuning with different quality selections of data.

Our contributions are as follows:

- An explainable framework to combine different toxic data annotations has been discussed.
- A crowd-annotation task, which aims at the identification of target spans, i.e., sequences of targeting tokens that together refer to a target community, has been created.
- An existing data set has been extended (Mathew et al., 2020) with annotations of target spans.
- A preliminary quantitative and qualitative analysis of the annotations has been provided.
- Three RoBERTa-base models have been fine-tuned on our data and the results have been reported.

The paper is organized as follows. In Section 2, we summarize the related work on target annotations and position our work. In Section 3, we describe the resources that we use to sample data in order to obtain sufficiently diverse annotations from each source. Section 4 explains our annotation framework and the crowd-annotation task that we designed, while in Section 5 we describe the results of the annotation. In section 6, we report on the language models we fine-tuned with our data and explain the results. We conclude and discuss future work in Section 7.

Please beware that this paper may contain some examples of hateful content. This is strictly for the purpose of enabling this research and we seek to minimize the number of examples wherever possible. Please be aware that this content may be offensive and cause you distress, which is certainly not the intention of the authors of this article.

2 Related work

The number of studies on the automatic identification of hate speech and other forms of toxic language has rapidly increased in recent years. Several definitions for toxic language have been proposed and many different annotation schemes have been designed and applied.

Part of these annotation studies focuses on the target community that has been victimized by such language and acknowledges that the description of these targets is relevant in different ways for the automatic detection of toxic language. Early studies (De Gibert et al., 2018), (Davidson et al., 2017) presented this task as a binary task labeling data as hateful or not. In these studies, only toxic expressions targeting people were considered hateful. For example, according to the annotation guidelines of (De Gibert et al., 2018), an expression should be labeled as hate speech only if all of the three following conditions are met: (1) There is a deliberate attack. (2) The attack is on a specific group of people. (3) The motive for this attack regards aspects of the group's identity. Although the identity of the target group is decisive in determining whether an expression is considered hate speech or not, no details on this were annotated.

Another widely used annotation scheme (see e.g. (Basile et al., 2019), (Zampieri et al., 2020)) was developed by (Zampieri et al., 2019) who addressed the need for identifying more specific information about the target communities and therefore introduced several annotation layers as follows: (1) Determine whether the message is offensive. (2) If the message is offensive, determine whether it is targeting people or not. (3) If the message is targeting people, determine (a) whether the message is targeting an individual, or (b) whether the message is targeting a group or member of a group considered a unity due to the same ethnicity, gender or sexual orientation or any other common characteristic, or (c) whether the message is targeting other entities like an organization, a situation or an event.

Finally and most recently, several studies ((Mollas et al., 2022),(Kennedy et al., 2020), (Vidgen et al., 2021), (Ousidhoum et al., 2019)) have taken the target annotations one step further by providing the group aspect on which basis it was targeted (e.g. gender, race, national origin, disability, religion, sexual orientation, etc.) and by mentioning the specific target communities (e.g. Africans, immigrants, Muslims, homosexuals, politicians, etc.) This information would allow further research into differences in the framing of specific target communities and the building of classifiers that avoid bias in hate speech detection ((Shah et al., 2021)) or permit researchers to delve into issues related to such bias. Although all of these studies considered target detection in hate speech as challenging and important, none of them annotated target spans at the token level.

Our work builds on the already existing annotations of the HateXplain data set (Mathew et al., 2020) by adding such span annotations that refer to a target/ target community. In combination with the annotations already present in HateXplain, this allows us to train systems to detect both the phrases making reference to the targets as well as inferring the group aspect of these targets together with pointing at the phrases that represent the insulting content or judgement expressed about them.

3 Source data overview and sampling

HateXplain is the first hate speech data set that covers many aspects of toxic language (Mathew et al., 2020). Each post in this data set has been annotated from three different perspectives: 1) the three main classes: hate speech, offensive or normal 2) the target community (i.e., the community that has been the victim of hate speech/ offensive language in the post) 3) rationales that are the parts of a post based on which annotators have decided to label it as such. The annotations were carried out at the word and phrase levels except for the target information which was done at the utterance level. According to (Mathew et al., 2020), the data was collected from Twitter and Gab with a total of 9,055 and 11,093 samples, respectively.[1]

For this study, we added target spans to the already existing annotations in this data set. This means that, for each sample targeting a target community, we wanted to determine which tokens in that sentence referred to that target community. For this reason, we selected only those samples that a) were instances of offensive language or hate speech b) targeted only one target community c) at least 2 out of 3 annotators agreed on its target label and d) had more than two and fewer than 61 tokens. We had extracted the distribution graphs of sentences per number of words and noticed that there are very few sentences that had more than 60 words in our data set. Also, the more words a sentence has, the more complex it becomes. In addition sentences with fewer than 3 words seem to have not enough and useful information for analysis. That is why we selected only sentences whose number of words was within the range described. The reason why we chose sentences with only one target group was mainly to be make the task as easy and simple as possible for the crowd. Nonetheless, we later found that there were still a number of sentences that targeted more than one target group even though they were annotated in HateXplain as having only one target group. This is also referred to and explained in 5.4. As a result, a total of 6,445 samples were selected. From these, we selected 3,480 samples that were representative of different target communities and data sources, which constituted about 54% of the full sample set. The number of selected samples per target community are shown in Table 1. Only those target communities that appeared at least 10 times are shown in the table. The rest of them together with the "Other" target community are referred to as "Other target communities".

Target community	Gab	Twitter	Other	Total
Hispanic	160	2	0	162
Men	5	7	0	12
Homosexual	457	331	2	790
Islam	145	111	0	256
Arab	64	39	0	103
Refugee	105	83	1	189
Asian	82	68	0	150
Disability	3	29	0	32
African	355	278	0	633
Jewish	75	47	0	122
Caucasian	47	94	0	141
Women	225	385	0	610
Other target communities	150	130	0	280
Total	1873	1604	3	3480

Table 1: Data selected for annotation across target communities and sources (Gab, Twitter, Other)

To prepare the data set for the crowd-annotation task described in the next section, we sorted the data per target community and created separate batches of 30 samples. Each batch contained 29 samples from HateXplain and 1 attention check sentence randomly selected from a list of 60 sentences. These attention check sentences were manually generated and annotated, and were both targeting and toxic. Attention check sentences were included to inspect the crowd-annotators' annotation and make sure that they did not simply annotate the data samples haphazardly or even skip them. The total number of batches amounted to 120. The first 25 batches only contained "Hispanic" and Homosexual" target communities. From batch 26 onward, however, each batch contained a mix-

[1]However, we observed that only 9,027 samples were labelled with the source Twitter, resulting in 28 samples that were not identified.

ture from different target communities and sources (Gab and Twitter) to reduce imbalanced data bias.

4 Crowd annotation task

For the crowd-annotation task, annotators were provided with batches of 30 toxic sentences presented one-by-one, where each sentence was followed by a list of tokens with tick-boxes. They were asked to read each sentence carefully before determining who the target was and select the tokens that referred to that target. At the start, they received an instruction page with examples. They were instructed to choose all the words - including the pronouns - that referred to the target no matter how many times they appeared in the sentence. Also, complete noun phrases including any adjectives had to be selected. Below are a few examples that demonstrate how sentences should be annotated:

1. You Bangladeshi guys are f***ing gangsta.
   Target spans: You, Bangladeshi, guys

2. Just because we don't let groups of creepy Moroccan rapists into the club doesn't make us racist.
   Target spans: creepy, Moroccan, rapists

3. They do no shit other than going to the mosque.
   Target spans: They

4. Fuck the ignorant assholes from America, UK, and all other countries who try and soil the wonderful ties between all democratic nations.
   Target spans: the, ignorant, assholes, from, America, UK, and, all, other, countries

5. SHUT UP WHITE BOY!
   Target spans: WHITE, BOY

6. What's up nigger?
   Target spans: nigger

7. You spics are worthless.
   Target spans: You, spics

8. He is a stupid Muslim.
   Target spans: He, a, stupid, Muslim

9. I need a new gay hashtag.
   Target spans: gay

It is worth noting that there are certain words and phrases that are toxic and specifically used for referring to a target community, such as "spic" in 7, which generally refers to Hispanics, or "nigger" in 6, which refers to Black people. These words should be also annotated as target words although they are toxic as well, because they are ultimately used to address specific target communities.

We used LINGOTurk (Pusse et al., 2016) as the platform to design our task, which is a free and available crowdsourcing client/ server experiment management system. Furthermore, we used Prolific (Palan and Schitter, 2018), as the online platform for recruiting crowdworkers. The advantage of Prolific over other crowdsourcing platforms, such as Amazon Mechanical Turk, is that it provides more prescreening options, such as nationality, first language, ethnicity, political affiliation, socio-economic status, etc. Also, Prolific is not only limited to US participants. When recruiting annotators, we clearly described the aim of the study to them and explained what they had to do in detail. No specific sensitive information about annotators was stored. We also informed them beforehand that they should be aware of the inappropriate content of the sentences and they were not supposed to participate in this study if they were not comfortable with being exposed to such a language. Since the study was closely related to one's cultural understanding of the context and there were a lot of slang words and phrases used, we recruited only participants that met the following criteria:

- Both their nationality and country of birth had to be at least one of the following: United Kingdom (England, Wales, Scotland, Northern Ireland), United States, Ireland, Australia, Canada, Guyana, Jamaica, Liberia, New Zealand

- Their first, fluent, and primary language had to be English.

In order to determine the optimal number of annotators to recruit for each batch, we ran a test batch with 15 annotators and then extracted 10 random subsets, once with 5 and once with 10 annotators. mathtools

Following the CrowdTruth framework (Dumitrache et al., 2018), we used the Media Unit Quality Score (UQS) to analyze the collected results from different sets of annotators. UQS expresses the overall worker agreement over a so-called media unit. In our case, each token was considered to be a media unit with the binary classification as either targeting (1) or non-targeting (0). In order to calculate the UQS, one needs to first calculate the average cosine similarity between all worker vectors, weighted by the worker quality *(WQS)* and annotation quality *(AQS)*. For more details on how each of these scores is calculated, please refer to (Dumitrache et al., 2018). The advantage of using UQS in comparison to other metrics for calculating the inter-annotator agreement is that CrowdTruth interprets both the disagreement among the annotators and the ambiguity of the token. The quality of an annotation is considered as the interaction between the quality of the annotator in terms of how often she/ he agrees with others as well as the complexity of the input data and set of annotation categories.

We calculated the UQS for the complete set with 15 annotators and each of its subsets including 10 and 5 annotators, respectively. Next, we took the average of the obtained results over all subsets. By doing so, we could test in which cases and with what number of annotators the results were more consistent. In Table 2, the average overall UQS, average UQS for targeting tokens, and average UQS for non-targeting tokens across the test batch with different numbers of annotators are given. Targeting tokens refer to the tokens the majority of annotators labeled as targeting while non-targeting tokens refer to the tokens labeled as non-targeting by the majority. Also, the standard deviations of the 3 metrics per subset are given. In the case where there were 15 annotators, the average was taken over the media units and not different subsets, since no subset was created in this case. The closer the UQS and standard deviation are to 1 and 0, respectively, the higher the quality is.

Number of annotators	15	10	5
Avg UQS	0.81	0.80	0.80
Avg UQS for targeting tokens	0.78	0.80	0.80
Avg UQS for non-targeting tokens	0.86	0.86	0.87
SD of Avg UQSs	0.17	0.18	0.23
SD of Avg UQSs for targeting tokens	0.16	0.14	0.16
SD of Avg UQSs for non-targeting tokens	0.12	0.12	0.14

Table 2: Comparison of the annotation quality with different numbers of annotators. Avg=average; SD = standard deviation;

As can be seen in Table 2, the differences between the values are quite marginal and, especially for 10 and 15 annotators, most values are the same. Therefore, we decided to recruit 10 annotators per batch to do the annotations.

To select 10 annotators within the Prolific platform, the above pre-screening criteria were applied to the total pool of annotators. After running each batch, we analyzed the data to make sure the annotation quality was good enough and annotators acted according to our instructions. In order to do so, we compared the performance of each annotator to that of other participants, validated the attention check sentences, and considered the time taken on the whole for each annotator to finish the task. We also validated the annotations of some other randomly selected sentences. Finally, we checked whether the data provided by each participant corresponded with their Prolific ID and if they had entered a completion code showing that they had completed the whole task. If annotators failed any of the above-mentioned criteria, their submissions were rejected and another annotator was recruited in their place. We added the IDs of rejected annotators to our blocklist after each batch, which would exclude them from the next batches. In the next section, the results will be described in more detail.

5 Annotated Data

5.1 Statistical analysis of the crowd labels

We ran the batches for several weeks on the Prolific platform to obtain 10 annotations per sentence, eliminating problematic annotators as explained above. Table 3 gives a numerical overview of the result of the crowd annotation. In total, 5,799 target spans were identified, of which 4,747 (82%) were single-token. Interestingly, Gab samples had more references to target communities (the average number of target spans per sample was 1,82) than tweets did (with 1,48 spans on average). Additionally, the target spans found in Gab were a bit longer (with 1,52 tokens per span on average) than those found in tweets (1,44 tokens on average). These numbers can be explained by the fact that the Gab samples were generally longer than tweets, having 24,8 tokens on average, whereas this number was 14,6 for Tweets. However, it also shows that the two data sources had different characteristics with respect to how they referred to target communities.

5.2 Gold data annotated by experts

To get an independent evaluation of the quality of the crowd annotation, we did an expert annotation on two batches (2 and 23) through the same

	Gab	Twitter	Total
nr of samples	1873	1604	3480
avg nr of tokens per sample	24,8	14,6	20,3
nr of target spans	3417	2378	5799
avg nr of spans per sample	1,82	1,48	1,66
avg tokens per span	1,52	1,44	1,5

Table 3: Annotation statistics

platform. The annotators were the authors of this paper (A1, A2, A3). We calculated the Cohen's kappa coefficient per pair of annotators. The results can be seen in Table 4.

		A1-A2	A2-A3	A1-A3
Batch 2	Percent agreement	0.90	0.90	0.91
	Kappa score	0.67	0.65	0.67
Batch 23	Percent agreement	0.87	0.89	0.89
	Kappa score	0.62	0.66	0.69

Table 4: Inter-annotator agreements among expert annotators (A1, A2, and A3) on the batches 2 and 23

The results show a reasonable agreement with kappa scores ranging from 0.62 to 0.69 across different annotators, different batches, and different classes (targeting vs. non-targeting). The percent agreement scores are above 87%. We discussed each case of disagreement and resolved these using predefined guidelines in order to have a fully adjudicated gold data set with expert annotations. The adjudicated annotations were used to determine the optimal settings for selecting the final label assigned to each token (see section 5.3).

5.3 Aggregating the crowd annotations

The expert annotation was used to determine the best threshold for selecting the labels of the tokens annotated by 10 annotators. We used the already explained UQS score per token as a basic measure to assign the final label and compared the results with the expert annotations for batches 2 and 23. We repeated this 3 times with different UQS thresholds: 50, 60, and 70. Tokens below these thresholds were considered as non-targeting since the crowd could not reach sufficient consensus. For the tokens with a UQS above these thresholds, we selected the label with the highest majority score, which could be either targeting or non-targeting. Table 5 shows the Kappa scores by comparing the crowd data with different UQS thresholds to the expert annotations.

We can see that the scores are lower than those for the expert annotations, as could be expected, but still reasonably high. Interestingly, we got the

Batch	UQS 50	UQS 60	UQS 70
2	**0.55**	0.48	0.37
23	**0.58**	0.56	0.45

Table 5: Kappa scores comparing the crowd data to the expert data with different UQS thresholds

highest agreement using the lowest UQS threshold, which was 50. Therefore, we selected this threshold for creating a test set from the crowd annotations done on all batches.

5.4 Patterns of agreement and disagreement in the crowd annotations

We performed an error analysis in order to find which disagreement issues occurred most frequently and whether we could find any patterns. We illustrate the issues by making references to the examples below. The tokens marked with [T] are those that were annotated by a vast majority of annotators as targeting, tokens marked with [T*] were annotated by only a small number of annotators as targeting, which caused disagreement. The underlined tokens are those that were considered to be targeting by the authors of this paper.

1. Go back to France[T*] you[T*] anti-american[T] commie[T] socialist[T] traitor[T]

2. One must wonder how long she[T*] will do in jail[T*] on the taxpayers dime before they decide to toss her[T*] spic[T] ass[T] out; as for the guy[T*] castrate[T*] him[T*] and jail[T*] him[T*] for life

3. I[T*] am black[T*] with all white[T*] friends[T*], taco[T] man[T*]

4. the wall is not the final solution these[T*] beaners[T] will keep having babies[T*] keep balkanizing[T*] our society(T*)

5. i saw a[T*] couple[T*] of[T*] baums[T*] and[T*] steins[T*]

6. as if it only okay when you are a cute gay[T] boy

The main sources of disagreement can be summarised as follow:

Length of target span Not all annotators annotated the complete target span. Typically the beginning (cf. *these* in ex. 4 and *her* in ex. 2) or the end (cf. *man* in ex. 3) are missing.

Additional information about the target community It seems that some annotators annotated properties, descriptions and behaviours of the target communities, whereas these tokens are not references to the community, but describing them (cf. *France* in ex. 1; *jail* in ex. 3; *babies, balkanizing, society* in ex. 4)

Inconsistent identification of referring pronouns Pronouns that refer to the target community were often missed (cf. *you* in ex. 1; *she, her, him, him* in ex. 2). This pattern is further confirmed by the words listed in Table 6: the references with the highest agreement were ethnic slurs (right column), whereas the references with the lowest agreement were pronouns (left column).

Multiple candidate target communities Apparently, there was confusion among annotators when multiple communities were referred to. In ex.3, *black* and *white friends* were both incorrectly annotated as targeting, whereas no target community was targeted in this particular sample.

Different interpretations In many cases, annotators did not agree about whether a reference to a target community was toxic or not. For example, those who considered the expression 'Baums and Steins' (cf. ex. 5) to be ironic rather than offensive, did not label it as a targeting expression. xxxxxcbIn these cases it is not much possible to give the correct answers as these considerably depend both on the context and the annotator's individual perspective (cf. (Basile et al., 2021)).

No explicit target word There were cases where no target community was explicitly targeted, but because of the assumption that all sentences must be targeting (as explained in the instructions), annotators selected the existing community referred to in the sentence despite the absence of any obvious toxic reference to it (cf. ex. 6).

The analysis showed that toxic references to the target communities (such as *beaners, her spic ass*) were more easily identified than neutral ones such as *man* and the pronominal references. Moreover, it showed that annotations with a relatively low agreement required further analysis.

6 Automatic classification

After having obtained the labels for each token and having determined the best UQS threshold, we tested how well a language model could learn to detect the target spans and which UQS threshold for the training data would work best. Setting a high UQS threshold would give fewer data with a higher consensus, whereas a UQS threshold of 50, which had resulted in the highest Kappa score when the crowd annotations were compared with the expert annotations, would give us more targeting samples in the training data.

Low UQS	High UQS
You (206)	Nigger (357)
They (90)	Faggot (265)
The (77)	Bitch (211)

Table 6: Most frequent words targeting tokens: high vs. low agreement

To test this, we fine-tuned a pretrained language model for a token classification task to predict whether each token was targeting or non-targeting. In (Sharma et al., 2021), the performances of a number of language models for detecting toxic spans in a sentence were compared. The best-performing model (RoBERTa-base) had the highest F1-score on the test set with a value of 68.41%. Therefore, we chose RoBERTa-base as our pretrained model. For fine-tuning, we converted the data to the IOB (Inside-Outside-Beginning) format, which is widely used in token classification tasks (Evang et al., 2013).

We created a separate test set consisting of 20% of the whole data, but ensured that it was representative of all target communities and data sources. The test set was generated by setting the UQS threshold to 50, as this threshold had previously resulted in the highest agreement when the crowd annotations were compared with the expert annotations. For the training, on the other hand, we generated three different training sets with UQS thresholds of 50, 60, and 70, to test the effects on the predictions. All other hyperparameters and arguments remained the same in all three cases. Furthermore, we selected 10% of the training data as the validation set. The training set, test set, and validation set included each 2227, 696, and 557 samples (sentences), respectively. Arguments and hyperparameters used for the training are as follows: batch size=16; epochs=3; learning rate=2e-5; weight decay=0.01. To prepare the data for fine-tuning our models, they were tokenized using AutoTokenizer from Hugging Face[2].

[2] https://huggingface.co

During fine-tuning, evaluation was done at the end of each epoch. We batched our data with a data collator while using padding to make them all the same size. Each pad was padded to the length of its longest sample. We padded not only the inputs, but also the labels. We evaluated our model and its predictions on the test set with accuracy, precision, recall, and f1-score. After the predictions had been made, we needed to do some postprocessing. We picked the predicted index (with the maximum logit) for each token, converted it to its string label and ignored wherever we put a -100 label.

We repeated the training procedure with the three training sets, each generated with a different UQS threshold as described earlier. Table 7 shows the results on the test data, both overall and per class.

Overall, our model showed a good performance predicting the target spans. The scores for the dominant class "non-targeting" (0) were higher than the scores for the "targeting" class. The Weighted F1 scores ranged from 74 to 79% , which is significantly higher than the results for the toxic span detection task in (Sharma et al., 2021) although the tasks, data and annotations are different across these tasks. The best results were again obtained when the UQS threshold was set to 50.

UQS	Class	Recall	Precision	F1-score	Support
50	All	81%	78%	79%	
	0	96%	97%	96%	14404
	1	73%	73%	73%	2051
	2	75%	64%	69%	906
60	All	75%	81%	77%	
	0	97%	95%	96%	14404
	1	68%	76%	72%	2051
	2	58%	72%	64%	906
70	All	67%	82%	74%	
	0	99%	93%	96%	14404
	1	61%	76%	68%	2051
	2	42%	76%	54%	906

Table 7: Test results overall and per class when the UQS threshold on the training set is 50, 60 or 70; class 0 = non-targeting; class 1= targeting-beginning; class 2= targeting-inside

7 Conclusion

We presented an extension to the HateXplain data set with annotations for target spans using crowd-annotation. The extended data set will enable the community to train and test models that recognize not only toxic language, but also the referents that are targeted. This is essential for future systems that need to comment on "wrong" behaviour in possibly interactive settings, discussing who has been targeted by what aspect and what toxic comments are used against the targeted person or community.

We provided the guidelines and instructions with clear examples of what we meant by target in a toxic sentence. We collected expert-annotated data for two of the batches with reasonable agreement among annotators. We obtained crowd annotations for target tokens in 3,480 sentences that targeted one target community. We also analyzed frequent patterns observed in the annotations and provided a statistical overview of the collected annotations.

We fine-tuned three RoBERTa-base language models with our data and investigated how changing the UQS threshold would affect the results. Our best model resulted in an F1-score of 79% on the test set, which was higher than other works in the field of toxic span classification. All the required information regarding the data and models is available on our Github repository[3]. In future work, we will extend the data to multiple languages as well as to richer and longer contexts, such as in conversational settings, where toxic expressions and targets can be mentioned sparsely. We want to explore other language models and compare their results by changing the hyperparameters and training arguments. Also, we are keen to compare the predictions of these models to the crowd-annotations and perform some error analysis.

Acknowledgements

This research was supported by Huawei Finland through the DreamsLab project. All content represented the opinions of the authors, which were not necessarily shared or endorsed by their respective employers and/ or sponsors.

References

Valerio Basile, Cristina Bosco, Elisabetta Fersini, Debora Nozza, Viviana Patti, Francisco Manuel Rangel Pardo, Paolo Rosso, and Manuela Sanguinetti. 2019. SemEval-2019 task 5: Multilingual detection of hate speech against immigrants and women in Twitter. In *Proceedings of the 13th International Workshop on Semantic Evaluation*, pages 54–63, Minneapolis, Minnesota, USA. Association for Computational Linguistics.

Valerio Basile, Michael Fell, Tommaso Fornaciari, Dirk Hovy, Silviu Paun, Barbara Plank, Massimo Poesio, and Alexandra Uma. 2021. We need to consider

[3]The link to our Github repository: https://github.com/cltl/Target-Spans-Detection

disagreement in evaluation. In *Proceedings of the 1st Workshop on Benchmarking: Past, Present and Future*, pages 15–21, Online. Association for Computational Linguistics.

Thomas Davidson, Dana Warmsley, Michael Macy, and Ingmar Weber. 2017. Automated hate speech detection and the problem of offensive language. In *Proceedings of the International AAAI Conference on Web and Social Media*, volume 11, pages 512–515.

Ona De Gibert, Naiara Perez, Aitor García-Pablos, and Montse Cuadros. 2018. Hate speech dataset from a white supremacy forum. *arXiv preprint arXiv:1809.04444*.

Anca Dumitrache, Oana Inel, Lora Aroyo, Benjamin Timmermans, and Chris Welty. 2018. Crowdtruth 2.0: Quality metrics for crowdsourcing with disagreement. *arXiv preprint arXiv:1808.06080*.

Kilian Evang, Valerio Basile, Grzegorz Chrupała, and Johan Bos. 2013. Elephant: Sequence labeling for word and sentence segmentation. In *EMNLP 2013*.

Brendan Kennedy, Mohammad Atari, Aida Mostafazadeh Davani, Leigh Yeh, Ali Omrani, Yehsong Kim, Kris Koombs, Shreya Havaldar, G J Portillo-Wightman, Elaine Gonzalez, Joe Hoover, Aida Azatian, Alyzeh Hussain, Austin Lara, Gabriel Olmos, Adam Omary, Christina Park, Clarisa Wang, Xin Wang, and Morteza Dehghani. 2020. The gab hate corpus: A collection of 27k posts annotated for hate speech.

Svetlana Kiritchenko and Isar Nejadgholi. 2020. Towards ethics by design in online abusive content detection. *CoRR*, abs/2010.14952.

Binny Mathew, Punyajoy Saha, Seid Muhie Yimam, Chris Biemann, Pawan Goyal, and Animesh Mukherjee. 2020. Hatexplain: A benchmark dataset for explainable hate speech detection. *arXiv preprint arXiv:2012.10289*.

Ioannis Mollas, Zoe Chrysopoulou, Stamatis Karlos, and Grigorios Tsoumakas. 2022. ETHOS: a multi-label hate speech detection dataset. *Complex &amp Intelligent Systems*.

Nedjma Ousidhoum, Zizheng Lin, Hongming Zhang, Yangqiu Song, and Dit-Yan Yeung. 2019. Multilingual and multi-aspect hate speech analysis. In *Proceedings of the 2019 Conference on Empirical Methods in Natural Language Processing and the 9th International Joint Conference on Natural Language Processing (EMNLP-IJCNLP)*, pages 4675–4684, Hong Kong, China. Association for Computational Linguistics.

Stefan Palan and Christian Schitter. 2018. Prolific. ac—a subject pool for online experiments. *Journal of Behavioral and Experimental Finance*, 17:22–27.

John Pavlopoulos, Jeffrey Sorensen, Léo Laugier, and Ion Androutsopoulos. 2021. SemEval-2021 task 5: Toxic spans detection. In *Proceedings of the 15th International Workshop on Semantic Evaluation (SemEval-2021)*, pages 59–69, Online. Association for Computational Linguistics.

Fabio Poletto, Valerio Basile, Manuela Sanguinetti, Cristina Bosco, and Viviana Patti. 2021. Resources and benchmark corpora for hate speech detection: a systematic review. *Language Resources and Evaluation*, 55(2):477–523.

Florian Pusse, Asad Sayeed, and Vera Demberg. 2016. Lingoturk: managing crowdsourced tasks for psycholinguistics. In *Proceedings of the 2016 Conference of the North American Chapter of the Association for Computational Linguistics: Demonstrations*, pages 57–61.

Darsh J Shah, Sinong Wang, Han Fang, Hao Ma, and Luke Zettlemoyer. 2021. Reducing target group bias in hate speech detectors.

Mayukh Sharma, Ilanthenral Kandasamy, and Wb Vasantha. 2021. Youngsheldon at semeval-2021 task 5: Fine-tuning pre-trained language models for toxic spans detection using token classification objective. In *Proceedings of the 15th International Workshop on Semantic Evaluation (SemEval-2021)*, pages 953–959.

Bertie Vidgen and Leon Derczynski. 2020. Directions in abusive language training data: Garbage in, garbage out. *CoRR*, abs/2004.01670.

Bertie Vidgen, Dong Nguyen, Helen Margetts, Patricia Rossini, and Rebekah Tromble. 2021. Introducing CAD: the contextual abuse dataset. In *Proceedings of the 2021 Conference of the North American Chapter of the Association for Computational Linguistics: Human Language Technologies*, pages 2289–2303, Online. Association for Computational Linguistics.

Marcos Zampieri, Shervin Malmasi, Preslav Nakov, Sara Rosenthal, Noura Farra, and Ritesh Kumar. 2019. Predicting the type and target of offensive posts in social media. In *Proceedings of the 2019 Conference of the North American Chapter of the Association for Computational Linguistics: Human Language Technologies, Volume 1 (Long and Short Papers)*, pages 1415–1420, Minneapolis, Minnesota. Association for Computational Linguistics.

Marcos Zampieri, Preslav Nakov, Sara Rosenthal, Pepa Atanasova, Georgi Karadzhov, Hamdy Mubarak, Leon Derczynski, Zeses Pitenis, and Çağrı Çöltekin. 2020. SemEval-2020 Task 12: Multilingual Offensive Language Identification in Social Media (OffensEval 2020). In *Proceedings of SemEval*.

Is More Data Better? Re-thinking the Importance of Efficiency in Abusive Language Detection with Transformers-Based Active Learning

Hannah Rose Kirk[1,2,3‡], **Bertie Vidgen**[1,3], **Scott A. Hale**[1,2,4]
[1]University of Oxford, [2]The Alan Turing Institute, [3]Rewire, [4]Meedan
‡hannah.kirk@oii.ox.ac.uk

Abstract

Annotating abusive language is expensive, logistically complex and creates a risk of psychological harm. However, most machine learning research has prioritized maximizing *effectiveness* (i.e., F1 or accuracy score) rather than data *efficiency* (i.e., minimizing the amount of data that is annotated). In this paper, we use simulated experiments over two datasets at varying percentages of abuse to demonstrate that transformers-based active learning is a promising approach to substantially raise efficiency whilst still maintaining high effectiveness, especially when abusive content is a smaller percentage of the dataset. This approach requires a fraction of labeled data to reach performance equivalent to training over the full dataset.

1 Introduction

Online abuse, such as hate and harassment, can inflict psychological harm on victims (Gelber and McNamara, 2016), disrupt communities (Mohan et al., 2017) and even lead to physical attacks (Williams et al., 2019). Machine learning solutions can be used to automatically detect abusive content at scale, helping to tackle this growing problem (Gillespie, 2020). An *effective* model is one which makes few misclassifications, minimizing the risk of harm from false positives and negatives: false negatives mean that users are not fully protected from abuse while false positives constrain free expression. Most models to automatically detect abuse are trained to maximize effectiveness via "passive" supervised learning over large labeled datasets. However, although collecting large amounts of social media data is relatively cheap and easy, annotating data is expensive, logistically complicated and creates a risk of inflicting psychological harm on annotators through vicarious trauma (Roberts, 2019; Steiger et al., 2021). Thus, an *efficient* model, which achieves a given level of performance with few labeled examples, is highly desirable for abusive content detection.

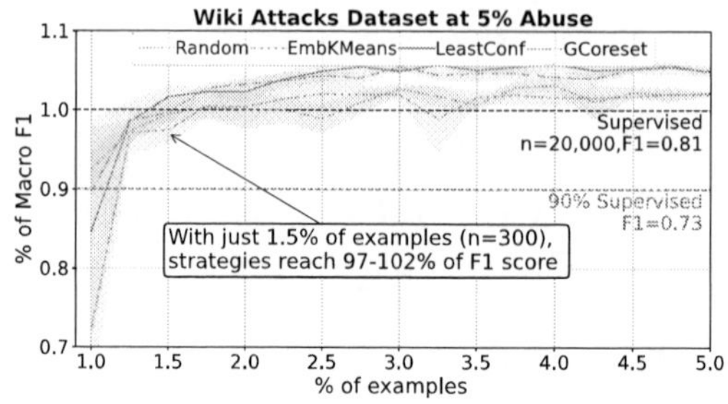

Figure 1: Transformers-based active learning beats fully-supervised baseline with 1.5% of the 20,000 examples.

Our central objective is to demonstrate how to maximize efficiency and effectiveness when training abuse detection systems, and in this paper, we focus on active learning (AL). AL is an iterative human-in-the-loop approach that selects entries for annotation only if they are 'informative' (Lewis and Gale, 1994; Settles, 2009). While AL has shown promise for abusive language dataset creation (Charitidis et al., 2020; Mollas et al., 2020; Rahman et al., 2021; Bashar and Nayak, 2021; Abidin et al., 2021), there are several open questions about the most appropriate configuration and use. In particular, only one paper uses transformers-based AL for abusive language detection (Ein-Dor et al., 2020) to our knowledge, although the benefits of AL for other classification tasks is clear (Schröder et al., 2022; Ein-Dor et al., 2020; Yuan et al., 2020). Pre-trained transformer models have been widely adopted for abuse detection, but while they can be fine-tuned on relatively few examples for specific tasks (Devlin et al., 2018; Qiu et al., 2020), they are still commonly used with large datasets (e.g. Mozafari et al., 2019; Mutanga et al., 2020; Isaksen and Gambäck, 2020; Koufakou et al., 2020). Our first subquestion asks, **RQ1.1:** *What effect do model pre-training and architecture have on efficiency and effectiveness?* To answer RQ1.1, we evaluate transformers- and traditional-based AL

Proceedings of the 29th International Conference on Computational Linguistic, pages 52–61
October 12–17, 2022.

in a simulated setup using two already-labeled abusive language datasets.

One challenge in abusive language detection is class imbalance as, although extremely harmful, abuse comprises a small portion of online content (Vidgen et al., 2019). Prior AL work primarily uses datasets at their given class imbalances and thus has not disentangled how class imbalance versus linguistic features affect the design choices needed for efficient AL. This is a problem given that most abusive language datasets do not reflect the imbalance actually observed in the wild. Our second subquestion addresses this issue, **RQ1.2:** *What effect does class imbalance have on efficiency and effectiveness?* To answer RQ1.2, we artificially-rebalance the datasets at different percentages of abuse.

In addressing these questions, we find that more data is not always better and can actually be worse, showing that effectiveness and efficiency are not always in tension with one another. With extensive pre-training and greater model complexity, a transformers-based AL approach achieves high performance with only a few hundred examples. Crucially, we show that the value of transformers-based AL (relative to random sampling) is larger for more imbalanced data (i.e., data that more closely reflects the real-world). For 5% abuse, the performance of a transformers-based AL strategy over 3% of a 20k dataset can even surpass the F1 of a model passively trained over the full dataset by 5 percentage points (Fig. 1). In §4 we describe caveats of our findings and implications for future research in abusive language detection.[1]

2 Methods

2.1 Active Learning Set-Up

AL typically consists of four components: 1) a classification model, 2) pools of unlabeled data $\mathcal{U}$ and labeled data $\mathcal{L}$, 3) a query strategy for identifying data to be labeled, and 4) an 'oracle' (e.g., human annotators) to label the data. First, seed examples are taken from $\mathcal{U}$ and sent to the oracle(s) for labeling. These examples initialize the classification model. Second, batches of examples are iteratively sampled from the remaining unlabeled pool, using a query strategy to estimate their 'informativeness' to the initialized classification model.[2]

Table 1: Summary of source datasets (in gray) and their artificially-rebalanced versions.

Dataset	Imbalance	Train† abuse	Train† non-abuse	Test* abuse	Test* non-abuse
wiki	12%	10,834	81,852	2,756	20,422
wiki50	50%	10,000	10,000	2,500	2,500
wiki10	10%	2,000	18,000	500	4,500
wiki5	5%	1,000	19,000	250	4,750
tweets	32%	28,955	61,041	3,160	6,840
tweets50	50%	10,000	10,000	2,500	2,500
tweets10	10%	2,000	18,000	500	4,500
tweets5	5%	1,000	19,000	250	4,750

Notes: † Train is used as the unlabeled pool ($n = 20{,}000$)
* Test is used for held-out evaluation ($n = 5{,}000$)

Each queried batch is labeled and added to $\mathcal{L}$. Finally, the classifier is re-trained over $\mathcal{L}$.[3]

2.2 Dataset Selection and Processing

AL is path-dependent—i.e., later decisions are dependent upon earlier ones; so, experimenting in real-world settings is prohibitively costly and risky to annotator well-being. To reproduce the process without labeling new data, we use existing labeled datasets but withhold the labels until the model requests their annotation. We examined a list of publicly available, annotated datasets for abusive language detection[4] and found two that were sufficiently large and contained enough abusive instances to facilitate our experimental approach. The **wiki** dataset (Wulczyn et al., 2017) contains comments from Wikipedia editors, labeled for whether they contain personal attacks. A test set is pre-defined; we take our test instances from this set. The **tweets** dataset (Founta et al., 2018) contains tweets which have been assigned to one of four classes. We binarize by combining the abusive and hate speech classes (=1) and the normal and spam classes (=0) to allow for cross-dataset comparison (Wiegand et al., 2019; Ein-Dor et al., 2020). A test set is not pre-defined; so, we set aside 10% of the data for testing that is never used for training.

To disentangle the merits of AL across class imbalances, we construct three new datasets for both **wiki** and **tweets** that have different class distributions: 50% abuse, 10% abuse and 5% abuse. This creates 6 datasets in total (see Tab. 1). To control

[1]Code at ActiveTransformers-for-AbusiveLanguage.

[2]Note that *batch-mode active learning* is a common application in both research and industry, given its more practical application to annotation workflows and model retraining times (Settles, 2009, p. 35).

[3]We train from scratch to avoid overfitting to previous iterations (Ein-Dor et al., 2020; Hu et al., 2018).

[4]https://hatespeechdata.com

dataset size and ensure we have sufficient positive instances for all imbalances, we assume that each unlabeled pool has 20,000 examples.[5] We experiment with multiple AL strategies to select 2,000 examples for annotation as early experiments showed further iterations did not affect performance.[6]

2.3 Experimental Setup

We use 2 model architectures, 2 query strategies and 6 artificially-rebalanced datasets, giving 24 experiments each of which we repeat with 3 random seeds. Each experiment uses the same sized unlabeled pool, training budget and test set (see Tab. 1). In figures, we present the mean run (line) and standard deviation (shaded). For transformers-based AL, we use distil-roBERTa (**dBERT**), which performs competitively to larger transformer models (Sanh et al., 2019), also in an AL setting (Schröder et al., 2022). For traditional AL without pre-training, we use a linear support vector machine (**SVM**) as a simple, fast and lightweight baseline.[7] For active data acquisition, we try three AL strategies; LeastConfidence, which selects items close to the decision boundary (Lewis and Gale, 1994), is presented in the paper while the other strategies are in the Appendix.[8] For comparison, we randomly sample items from the unlabeled pool at each iteration. Alongside model and query strategy, AL requires an initial seed size, seed acquisition strategy and batch size. We experimentally determined the best values for these parameters: an initial seed of 20 examples selected via a keyword-heuristic (Ein-Dor et al., 2020) and batches of 50 examples.[9]

2.4 Evaluation

As a baseline, we use the passive macro-F1 score over the full dataset of 20,000 entries ($\mathbf{F1_{20k}}$). For each AL strategy, we measure efficiency on the held-out test set as the number of examples needed to surpass 90% of $\mathbf{F1_{20k}}$, which we call $\mathbf{N_{90}}$.[10] For effectiveness, we use the maximum F1 score achieved by each AL strategy, which we call $\mathbf{F1_{AL}}$.

[5]The **wiki** dataset has 10,834 abusive entries; so, at 50% abuse, the upper limit on a rebalanced pool is 21,668.

[6]AL experiments are implemented in the Python `small-text` library (Schröder et al., 2021)

[7]Appendix A presents details of model training.

[8]We also test GreedyCoreSet (Sener and Savarese, 2017) and EmbeddingKMeans (Yuan et al., 2020), but LeastConfidence outperformed them.

[9]We present pilot experiments in Appendix B and C.

[10]To fairly compare models, we calculate $\mathbf{N_{90}}$ relative to *best* $\mathbf{F1_{20k}}$ (achieved by dBERT in all cases).

Table 2: Efficiency and effectiveness of each classifier (transformers vs SVM) with LeastConfidence sampling.

Dataset	Classifier	$\mathbf{F1_{20k}}$†	$\mathbf{F1_{AL}}$	$\mathbf{N_{90}}$
wiki50	dBERT	**0.920**	**0.920**	**170**
	SVM	0.875	0.836	1570
wiki10	dBERT	**0.859**	**0.866**	**170**
	SVM	0.809	0.810	320
wiki5	dBERT	**0.807**	**0.855**	220
	SVM	0.785	0.780	**170**
tweets50	dBERT	**0.939**	**0.938**	**170**
	SVM	0.931	0.926	220
tweets10	dBERT	**0.904**	**0.902**	220
	SVM	0.893	0.901	**170**
tweets5	dBERT	**0.844**	**0.856**	300
	SVM	0.825	0.830	**170**

Notes: † global metric from passive training over full, re-balanced dataset

3 Results

Efficiency & Effectiveness For each dataset, we find active strategies that need just 170 examples (0.8% of the full dataset) to reach 90% of passive supervised learning performance (see Tab. 2). When training over the full dataset, dBERT always outperforms SVM, models have worse performance on more imbalanced datasets, and **wiki** is harder to predict than **tweets** (Tab. 2). In all cases, LeastConfidence outperforms the random baseline, and the gain is larger for lower percentages of abuse: for **wiki10** and **wiki5**, $\mathbf{N_{90}}$ is lower by 150 and 100 examples, respectively. AL can even outperform passive supervised learning over the full dataset, showing there is no efficiency–effectiveness trade-off. For the majority of datasets, dBERT with LeastConfidence over 2,000 examples matches or surpasses the F1 score of a model trained passively over the whole dataset ($\mathbf{F1_{AL}} \geq \mathbf{F1_{20k}}$ in Tab. 2). For **wiki5**, it is 5 percentage points (pp) higher (Fig. 1).

The Effect of Pre-Training We find AL has a bigger impact for SVM than dBERT, shown by the larger gap to the random baselines (Fig. 2). With its extensive pre-training, dBERT achieves high performance with few examples, even if randomly selected. Nonetheless, an AL component still enhances dBERT performance above the random baseline especially with imbalanced data (as found by Schröder et al., 2022; Ein-Dor et al., 2020), requiring 150 and 100 fewer examples for $\mathbf{N_{90}}$, and raising F1 score by 2pp and 4pp, for **wiki5** and **wiki10** respectively.

Train Distribution To assess why AL is more impactful with imbalanced data, we evaluate the

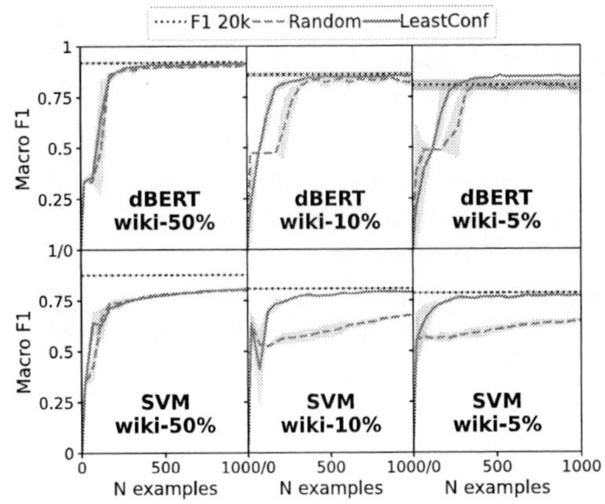

Figure 2: The contribution of pre-training vs active data acquistion.

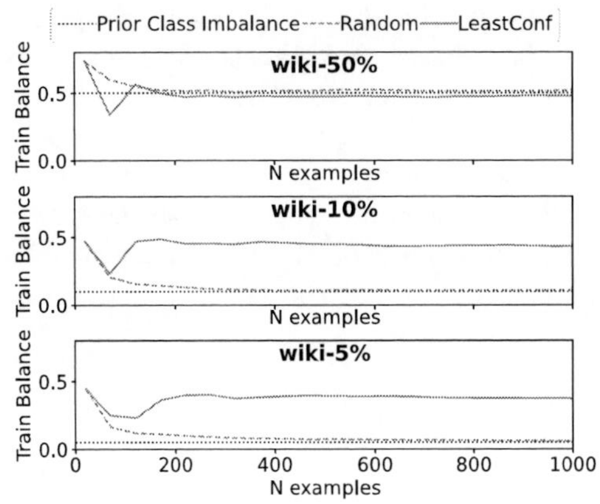

Figure 3: Label imbalance during training (dBERT).

distribution of the labeled pool at each iteration (Fig. 3). The random baseline tends to the original distribution as expected but the LeastConfidence strategy actively selects abusive examples from the pool and tends toward a balanced distribution.

Out-of-domain Testing The high performance of models trained on few examples raises a risk that they are overfitting and may not generalize. We take the models trained on each of the three class imbalances for **wiki** and test them on their equivalent **tweets** dataset, and vice versa. As with in-domain results, models trained on **wiki** and applied to **tweets** reach $\mathbf{F1_{20k}}$ within few iterations. The gap between LeastConfidence and the random baseline is larger for out-of-domain evaluation versus in-domain (Fig. 4). A similar pattern occurs for other imbalances (see Appendix D). This suggests that our results for these two datasets are not overfitting.

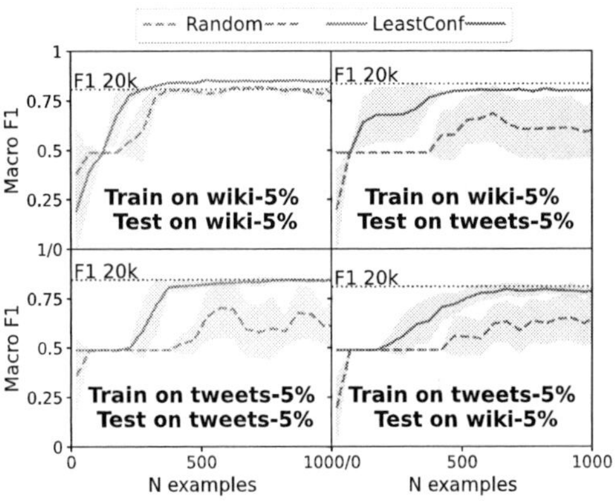

Figure 4: Cross-dataset generalization (dBERT).

4 Discussion

In response to our central research objective, we find strategies which are both effective and efficient, requiring far fewer examples to reach performance equivalent to passive training over the full dataset. These results suggest that passive approaches may be needlessly expensive and place annotators at unnecessary risk of harm. For RQ1.1, we find that coupling pre-trained transformers with AL is a successful approach which leverages the benefits of careful training data selection with the previously demonstrated strong capabilities of pre-trained language models for few-shot learning (Brown et al., 2020; Gao et al., 2021; Schick and Schütze, 2021). However, the compute required to fine-tune a new transformer model in each iteration means AL may have a large environmental footprint (Bender et al., 2021). In some instances, SVMs with AL produce competitive results and have smaller environmental costs. For RQ1.2, we find transformers-based AL is particularly valuable under more extreme class imbalance because it iteratively balances the distribution. Our findings are subject to some limitations, which present avenues for future work.

How does data sampling, class labels and linguistic diversity affect performance? We evaluate against two datasets with pre-existing labels, which we simplify into a binary task. This binarization was required to allow comparison across datasets. The **wiki** dataset samples banned comments and **tweets** samples with keywords and sentiment analysis. While these datasets were the only publicly-available datasets large enough for this work, Wiegand et al. (2019) shows that they lack diversity, contain numerous biases, and cover abuse which is mostly explicit. This may make it easier for models to learn the task and generalize in fewer examples. Future work should evaluate the success and generalizability of AL for fine-grained labels and implicit abuse.

How does the number of model parameters affect performance? For computational feasibility and environmental concerns, we use distil-BERT but future work could assess if larger transformers models set higher baselines from passive training over the full dataset.

Are certain AL strategies well-suited to abusive language detection? We evaluate three commonly-used AL strategies, finding that Least-Confidence performs best, but none are tailored explicitly to abusive language. Constrastive Active Learning (Margatina et al., 2021) may be particularly useful: by finding linguistically similar entries on either side of the decision boundary, it may prevent overfitting to certain slurs, profanities or identities.

Do the experimental findings generalize to real-world settings? Our motivation for maximizing efficiency is to reduce financial costs and risk of harm to annotators, which we operationalize in terms of the number of labeled examples they view. In practice, costs are variable because entries which are more 'uncertain' to the model may also be more time-consuming, challenging or harmful for humans to label (Haertel et al., 2015). In a real-world setting, the work of the human annotators must be scaled up and down in response to labeling demands, which may incur additional costs. Crowd-sourced annotators can provide labels on demand when a new batch of entries is launched. With an expert annotation team, there may be a cost of paying annotators during re-training. Furthermore, it is important to note that the scope and scale of realized harm depends on both the total number of annotators as well as their identity, positionality and working conditions. While our approach simulates the labeling process with one groundtruth label, we make no assumptions on how this groundtruth is obtained—either via a single annotator or with some aggregation function over multiple annotator votes—so, our method is applicable to any number or constitution of annotators. We only make the light assumption that less exposure to harm is a good thing—whether that is many people being exposed a little less or few people being exposed a lot less. Future work is needed beyond our simulated set-up to calculate a more realistic cost-benefit ratio of AL, both in terms of financial and psychological costs.

We are exploring these questions in future work but simultaneously encourage the community to consider the need for efficiency in abusive language detection because of the costs, complexities and risk of harm to annotator well-being from inefficient data labeling.

Acknowledgments

This work was supported in part by JADE: Joint Academic Data science Endeavour - 2 under the EPSRC Grant EP/T022205/1, and by the The Alan Turing Institute under EPSRC grant EP/N510129/1. Hannah Rose Kirk was supported by the Economic and Social Research Council grant ES/P000649/1. We thank Paul Röttger and our anonymous reviewers for their comments.

References

Muhammad Ilham Abidin, Khairil Anwar Notodiputro, and Bagus Sartono. 2021. Improving Classification Model Performances using an Active Learning Method to Detect Hate Speech in Twitter. *Indonesian Journal of Statistics and Its Applications*, 5(1):26–38.

Md Abul Bashar and Richi Nayak. 2021. Active Learning for Effectively Fine-Tuning Transfer Learning to Downstream Task. *ACM Transactions on Intelligent Systems and Technology (TIST)*, 12(2).

Emily M. Bender, Timnit Gebru, Angelina McMillan-Major, and Shmargaret Shmitchell. 2021. On the dangers of stochastic parrots: Can language models be too big? 🦜. In *Conference on Fairness, Accountability, and Transparency (FAccT '21)*. ACM, New York, NY, USA.

Tom Brown, Benjamin Mann, Nick Ryder, Melanie Subbiah, Jared D Kaplan, Prafulla Dhariwal, Arvind Neelakantan, Pranav Shyam, Girish Sastry, Amanda Askell, Sandhini Agarwal, Ariel Herbert-Voss, Gretchen Krueger, Tom Henighan, Rewon Child, Aditya Ramesh, Daniel Ziegler, Jeffrey Wu, Clemens Winter, Chris Hesse, Mark Chen, Eric Sigler, Mateusz Litwin, Scott Gray, Benjamin Chess, Jack Clark, Christopher Berner, Sam McCandlish, Alec Radford, Ilya Sutskever, and Dario Amodei. 2020. Language Models are Few-Shot Learners. In *Advances in Neural Information Processing Systems*, volume 33, pages 1877–1901. Curran Associates, Inc.

Polychronis Charitidis, Stavros Doropoulos, Stavros Vologiannidis, Ioannis Papastergiou, and Sophia Karakeva. 2020. Towards countering hate speech against journalists on social media. *Online Social Networks and Media*, 17:100071.

Thomas Davidson, Dana Warmsley, Michael Macy, and Ingmar Weber. 2017. Automated Hate Speech Detection and the Problem of Offensive Language. In *Proceedings of the 11th International AAAI Conference on Web and Social Media*, ICWSM '17, pages 512–515.

Jacob Devlin, Ming-Wei Chang, Kenton Lee, and Kristina Toutanova. 2018. BERT: Pre-training of Deep Bidirectional Transformers for Language Understanding. *NAACL HLT 2019 - 2019 Conference of the North American Chapter of the Association for Computational Linguistics: Human Language Technologies - Proceedings of the Conference*, 1:4171–4186.

Liat Ein-Dor, Alon Halfon, Ariel Gera, Eyal Shnarch, Lena Dankin, Leshem Choshen, Marina Danilevsky, Ranit Aharonov, Yoav Katz, and Noam Slonim. 2020. Active Learning for BERT: An Empirical Study. In *Proceedings ofthe 2020 Conference on Empirical Methods in Natural Language Processing*, pages 7949–7962.

Mai ElSherief, Vivek Kulkarni, Dana Nguyen, Wang William Y., and Elizabeth Belding. 2018a. Hate Lingo: A Target-based Linguistic Analysis of Hate Speech in Social Media. In *Proceedings of the 12th International AAAI Conference on Web and Social Media*, ICWSM '18.

Mai ElSherief, Shirin Nilizadeh, Dana Nguyen, Vigna Giovanni, and Elizabeth Belding. 2018b. Peer to Peer Hate: Hate Instigators and Their Targets. In *Proceedings of the 12th International AAAI Conference on Web and Social Media*, ICWSM '18.

Antigoni-Maria Founta, Constantinos Djouvas, Despoina Chatzakou, Ilias Leontiadis, Jeremy Blackburn, Gianluca Stringhini, Athena Vakali, Michael Sirivianos, and Nicolas Kourtellis. 2018. Large Scale Crowdsourcing and Characterization of Twitter Abusive Behavior. *12th International AAAI Conference on Web and Social Media, ICWSM 2018*, pages 491–500.

Robert J Gabriel. 2018. Full List of Bad Words and Top Swear Words Banned by Google.

Tianyu Gao, Adam Fisch, and Danqi Chen. 2021. Making Pre-trained Language Models Better Few-shot Learners. In *Proceedings of the 59th Annual Meeting of the Association for Computational Linguistics and the 11th International Joint Conference on Natural Language Processing (Volume 1: Long Papers)*, pages 3816–3830, Online. Association for Computational Linguistics.

Katharine Gelber and Luke McNamara. 2016. Evidencing the harms of hate speech. *Social Identities*, 22(3):324–341.

Tarleton Gillespie. 2020. Content moderation, AI, and the question of scale. *Big Data & Society*, 7(2):205395172094323.

Robbie Haertel, Eric Ringger, Kevin Seppi, and Paul Felt. 2015. An Analytic and Empirical Evaluation of Return-on-Investment-Based Active Learning. In *Proceedings of The 9th Linguistic Annotation Workshop*, pages 11–20. Association for Computational Linguistics.

Peiyun Hu, Zachary C. Lipton, Anima Anandkumar, and Deva Ramanan. 2018. Active Learning with Partial Feedback. *7th International Conference on Learning Representations, ICLR 2019*.

Vebjørn Isaksen and Björn Gambäck. 2020. Using transfer-based language models to detect hateful and offensive language online. In *Proceedings of the Fourth Workshop on Online Abuse and Harms*, pages 16–27, Online. Association for Computational Linguistics.

Anna Koufakou, Endang Wahyu Pamungkas, Valerio Basile, and Viviana Patti. 2020. HurtBERT: Incorporating lexical features with BERT for the detection of abusive language. In *Proceedings of the Fourth Workshop on Online Abuse and Harms*, pages 34–43, Online. Association for Computational Linguistics.

David D Lewis and William A Gale. 1994. A Sequential Algorithm for Training Text Classifiers. In *SIGIR '94*, pages 3–12. Springer London, London.

Katerina Margatina, Giorgos Vernikos, Loïc Barrault, and Nikolaos Aletras. 2021. Active learning by acquiring contrastive examples. In *Proceedings of the 2021 Conference on Empirical Methods in Natural Language Processing*, pages 650–663.

Shruthi Mohan, Apala Guha, Michael Harris, Fred Popowich, Ashley Schuster, and Chris Priebe. 2017. The Impact of Toxic Language on the Health of Reddit Communities. In *Lecture Notes in Computer Science (including subseries Lecture Notes in Artificial Intelligence and Lecture Notes in Bioinformatics)*, volume 10233 LNAI, pages 51–56. Springer, Cham.

Ioannis Mollas, Zoe Chrysopoulou, Stamatis Karlos, and Grigorios Tsoumakas. 2020. ETHOS: an Online Hate Speech Detection Dataset.

Marzieh Mozafari, Reza Farahbakhsh, and Noel Crespi. 2019. A bert-based transfer learning approach for hate speech detection in online social media. In *International Conference on Complex Networks and Their Applications*, pages 928–940. Springer.

R Mutanga, Nalindren Naicker, and Oludayo O Olugbara. 2020. Hate speech detection in twitter using transformer methods. *International Journal of Advanced Computer Science and Applications*, 11(01).

Xi Peng Qiu, Tian Xiang Sun, Yi Ge Xu, Yun Fan Shao, Ning Dai, and Xuan Jing Huang. 2020. Pre-trained models for natural language processing: A survey. *Science China Technological Sciences 2020 63:10*, 63(10):1872–1897.

Md Mustafizur Rahman, Dinesh Balakrishnan, Dhiraj Murthy, Mucahid Kutlu, and Matthew Lease. 2021. An Information Retrieval Approach to Building Datasets for Hate Speech Detection. *35th Conference on Neural Information Processing Systems (NeurIPS 2021) Track on Datasets and Benchmarks.*

Sarah T. Roberts. 2019. *Behind the Screen: Content Moderation in the Shadows of Social Media.* Yale University Press, New Haven, CT.

Victor Sanh, Lysandre Debut, Julien Chaumond, and Thomas Wolf. 2019. Distilbert, a distilled version of bert: smaller, faster, cheaper and lighter. *arXiv preprint arXiv:1910.01108.*

Timo Schick and Hinrich Schütze. 2021. It's Not Just Size That Matters: Small Language Models Are Also Few-Shot Learners. In *Proceedings of the 2021 Conference of the North American Chapter of the Association for Computational Linguistics: Human Language Technologies*, pages 2339–2352, Online. Association for Computational Linguistics.

Christopher Schröder, Lydia Müller, Andreas Niekler, and Martin Potthast. 2021. Small-text: Active Learning for Text Classification in Python.

Christopher Schröder, Andreas Niekler, and Martin Potthast. 2022. Revisiting Uncertainty-based Query Strategies for Active Learning with Transformers. In *Findings of the Association for Computational Linguistics: ACL 2022*, pages 2194–2203, Dublin, Ireland. Association for Computational Linguistics.

Ozan Sener and Silvio Savarese. 2017. Active Learning for Convolutional Neural Networks: A Core-Set Approach. *6th International Conference on Learning Representations, ICLR 2018 - Conference Track Proceedings.*

Burr Settles. 2009. Active Learning Literature Survey. Technical Report, University of Wisconsin-Madison Department of Computer Sciences.

Miriah Steiger, Timir J Bharucha, Sukrit Venkatagiri, Martin J. Riedl, and Matthew Lease. 2021. The Psychological Well-Being of Content Moderators. *CHI '21: Proceedings of the 2021 CHI Conference on Human Factors in Computing Systems*, pages 1–14.

Bertie Vidgen, Helen Margetts, and Alex Harris. 2019. How much online abuse is there? A systematic review of evidence for the UK. Technical report, The Alan Turing Institute.

Michael Wiegand, Josef Ruppenhofer, and Thomas Kleinbauer. 2019. Detection of Abusive Language: The Problem of Biased Datasets. In *Proceedings of the 2019 Conference of the North American Chapter of the Association for Computational Linguistics: Human Language Technologies, Volume 1 (Long and Short Papers)*, pages 602–608. Association for Computational Linguistics.

Matthew L. Williams, Pete Burnap, Amir Javed, Han Liu, and Sefa Ozalp. 2019. Hate in the Machine: Anti-Black and Anti-Muslim Social Media Posts as Predictors of Offline Racially and Religiously Aggravated Crime. *The British Journal of Criminology*, 60(1):93–117.

Thomas Wolf, Lysandre Debut, Victor Sanh, Julien Chaumond, Clement Delangue, Anthony Moi, Pierric Cistac, Tim Rault, Rémi Louf, Morgan Funtowicz, Joe Davison, Sam Shleifer, Patrick von Platen, Clara Ma, Yacine Jernite, Julien Plu, Canwen Xu, Teven Le Scao, Sylvain Gugger, Mariama Drame, Quentin Lhoest, and Alexander M. Rush. 2019. HuggingFace's Transformers: State-of-the-art Natural Language Processing.

Ellery Wulczyn, Nithum Thain, and Lucas Dixon. 2017. Ex Machina: Personal Attacks Seen at Scale. In *Proceedings of the 26th International Conference on World Wide Web*, pages 1391–1399, Republic and Canton of Geneva, Switzerland. International World Wide Web Conferences Steering Committee.

Michelle Yuan, Hsuan-Tien Lin, and Jordan Boyd-Graber. 2020. Cold-start active learning through self-supervised language modeling. In *Proceedings of the 2020 Conference on Empirical Methods in Natural Language Processing (EMNLP)*, pages 7935–7948.

A Details of Dataset Processing and Model Training

We use two English-language datasets which were curated for the task of automated abuse detection (Wulczyn et al., 2017; Founta et al., 2018). The **wiki** dataset can be downloaded from `https://github.com/ewulczyn/wiki-detox` and is licensed under Apache License, Version 2.0. The **tweets** dataset can be downloaded with tweet ids from `https://github.com/ENCASEH2020/hatespeech-twitter`. These datasets cover two different domains: Wikipedia and Twitter. Each dataset is cleaned by removing extra white space, dropping duplicates and converting usernames, URLs and emoji to special tokens.

We fine-tune distil-roBERTa using the `transformers` integration with the `small-text` python package (Wolf et al., 2019; Schröder et al., 2021). distil-roBERTa has six layers, 768 hidden units, and 82M parameters. We encode input texts using the distil-roBERTa tokenizer, with added special tokens for usernames, URLs and emoji. All models were trained for 3 epochs with early stopping based on the cross-validation loss, a learning rate of $2e-5$ and a weighted Adam optimizer. All other hyperparameters are set to their `small-text` defaults. In each active learning iteration, we use 10% of each labeled batch for validation. As a baseline to transformers-based AL, we use a support vector machine with no pre-training which we implement with `sklearn`. To encode a vector representation of input texts, we use a TF-IDF transformation fitted to the training dataset.

All experiments were run on the JADE-2 cluster using one NVIDIA Tesla V100 GPU per experiment. For transformer-models, it took on average 1.5 hours to run each experiment. For SVM, it took less than a minute to run each experiment and these can be easily be run on a CPU. We repeat each experiment three times using three seeds to initialize a pseudo-random number generator.

B Sampling with Keywords

We use a heuristic to weakly label examples from the unlabeled pool to be selected for the initial seed. Keywords are a commonly-used approach (e.g. see Ein-Dor et al., 2020) and searching for text matches is computationally efficient over a large pool of unlabeled examples. However, the keyword heuristic only approximates the true label and can introduce biases due to non-abusive use of offense and profanities. In our data, we rely on a keyword density measure (K) which equals the number of keyword matches over the total tokens in a text instance. We then experiment with varied thresholds of $K \in [1\%, 5\%, 10\%, 25\%]$ for a weak label of abusive text. A higher threshold reduces false positives but also decreases true positives. We find a threshold of 5% best balances these directional effects. Making predictions using a keyword heuristic with a 5% cut-off achieves an F1-score relative to the true labels of 69% for wiki and 80% for tweets. Using this threshold, examples are expected to be abusive if the percentage of keywords in total tokens exceeds 5%. We then sample equal numbers of expected abusive and non-abusive examples from the pool, reveal their true labels and initialize the classifier by training over this seed.

Table 3: The effect of varied keyword density thresholds on F1, false positive rate (FPR) and false negative rate (FNR).

K	F1	FPR	FNR
		wiki	
1.0%	76.0%	2.7%	52.8%
5.0%	69.0%	0.5%	71.8%
10.0%	91.0%	0.1%	87.4%
25.0%	49.0%	0.0%	98.4%
		Tweets	
1.0%	85.0%	4.5%	29.6%
5.0%	80.0%	2.9%	42.7%
10.0%	83.0%	0.9%	76.4%
25.0%	75.0%	0.2%	98.5%

C Additional Experimental Analysis

Table 4: The best AL parameters and performance for each classifier (transformers vs SVM).

		Best AL Combinations*				Metrics		
Dataset	**Classifier**	**Seed**	**Cold**	**Batch**	**Query**	$\mathbf{F1_{20k}}$†	$\mathbf{F1_{AL}}$	N_{90}
wiki50	dBERT	20	Random	50	LC	**0.920**	**0.922**	**170**
	SVM	20	Random	50	LC	0.875	0.838	1520
wiki10	dBERT	20	Heuristic	50	LC	**0.859**	**0.866**	**170**
	SVM	20	Heuristic	50	LC	0.809	0.810	320
wiki5	dBERT	20	Heuristic	50	LC	**0.807**	**0.855**	220
	SVM	20	Heuristic	50	LC	0.785	0.780	**170**
tweets50	dBERT	20	Random	50	LC	**0.939**	**0.938**	**170**
	SVM	20	Random	50	LC	0.931	0.926	220
tweets10	dBERT	20	Heuristic	50	LC	**0.904**	**0.902**	220
	SVM	20	Random	50	LC	0.893	0.901	**170**
tweets5	dBERT	200	Heuristic	50	LC	**0.844**	**0.856**	300
	SVM	20	Heuristic	50	LC	0.825	0.830	**170**

Notes: † global metric from passive training over the full dataset
* calculated by averaging the rank performance on $\mathbf{F1_{AL}}$, N_{90}

Tab. 4 shows the best parameters for each dataset and each classifier. In Fig. 6, we present the learning curve and comparisons of each experimental variable for both datasets and classifiers. In each panel of Fig. 6, we vary one parameter whilst holding all others fixed. This allows us to evaluate the impact of one variable, *ceteris paribus*. Namely, the reference values are those reported in the main paper: seed size of 20 selected by heuristics-based sampling and a batch size of 50 queried by LeastConfidence strategy.

Seed and Batch Size We test two choices for seed size (20, 200), and three choices for batch size (50, 100, 500). We find AL is more efficient with smaller seeds and batch sizes. The F1 score achieved with a seed of 20 and four AL iterations of 50 ($|\mathcal{L}| = 220$) exceeds that reached with a seed of 200 and 0 iterations ($|\mathcal{L}| = 200$) by 55pp for **wiki50**, 4pp for **wiki10**, and 10pp for **wiki5**. Batch sizes of 100 and 500 are less efficient than 50, with 700–1,100 and 150–200 more examples needed for $\mathbf{N_{90}}$, respectively.

Seed Acquisition Strategy (Cold) We evaluate two choices to select the examples for the seed. (1) **Random:** Seed examples are randomly selected. Depending on the class distribution of the unlabeled pool (which, in real world settings, is unknown) only non-abusive content might be identified. For datasets expected to be approximately balanced, a randomly-selected seed has a high probability of including both class labels. (2) **Heuristics:** Seed examples are selected using keywords ($n = 652$), taken from the abusive language literature (Davidson et al., 2017; ElSherief et al., 2018a,b; Gabriel, 2018). For **wiki50**, random- and heuristics-based initialization achieve equivalent $\mathbf{N_{90}}$. However, with a seed of 20, a third of randomly-initialized experiments fail on **wiki10** and all experiments fail for **wiki5**. This shows that when the data is imbalanced, a random seed is suboptimal because both class labels are not observed.

Query Strategy In addition to LeastConfidence (LC), we evaluate two further strategies coupled with dBERT: 1) **GreedyCoreSet** is a data-based diversity strategy which selects items representative of the full set (Sener and Savarese, 2017) and 2) **EmbeddingKMeans** is a data-based diversity strategy which uses a dense embedding representation (such as BERT embeddings) to cluster and sample from the nearest neighbors of the k centroids (Yuan et al., 2020). On our datasets, these two strategies are high performing in terms of the maximum F1 score they achieve over 2,000 examples, but take longer to learn and are less efficient than LeastConfidence.

D Generalizability of Performance

In the main paper, we present the results of cross-dataset generalization with 5% abuse. In Fig. 5, we demonstrate the equivalent results for all class imbalances and both datasets. In general, tweets is harder to predict than wiki, so we see a larger change in performance when training on tweets and evaluating on wiki. For 50% and 10% abuse, performance is similar across test sets. For 5% abuse, there is a larger difference especially for the random baseline. However, in all cases, the performance of the LeastConfidence strategy generalizes well to out-of-domain testing, at least for these two datasets which are similar in their proportion of explicit abuse (Wiegand et al., 2019).

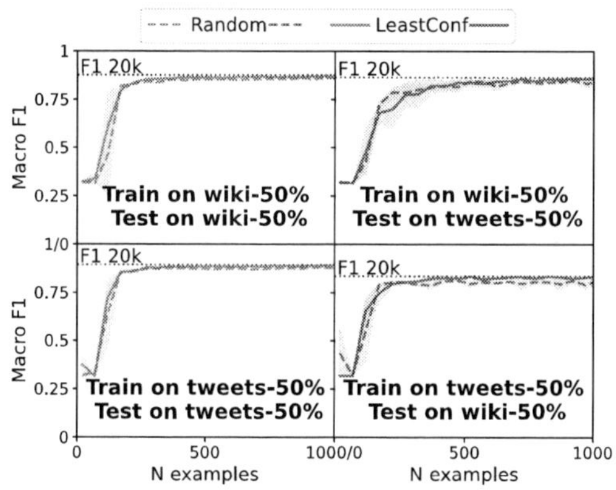

(a) Models trained on 50% abuse

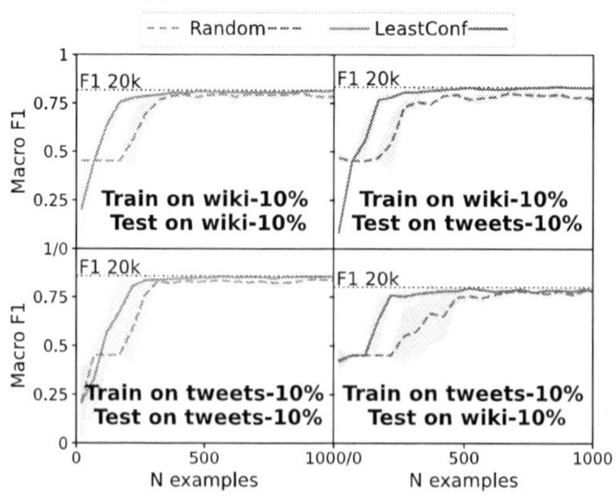

(b) Models trained on 10% abuse

Figure 5: Cross-dataset generalization (dBERT) for 50% and 10% abuse.

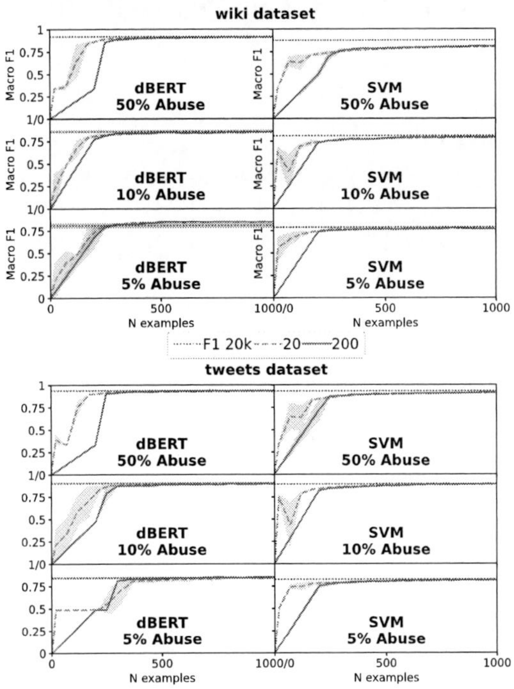

(a) Seed Size

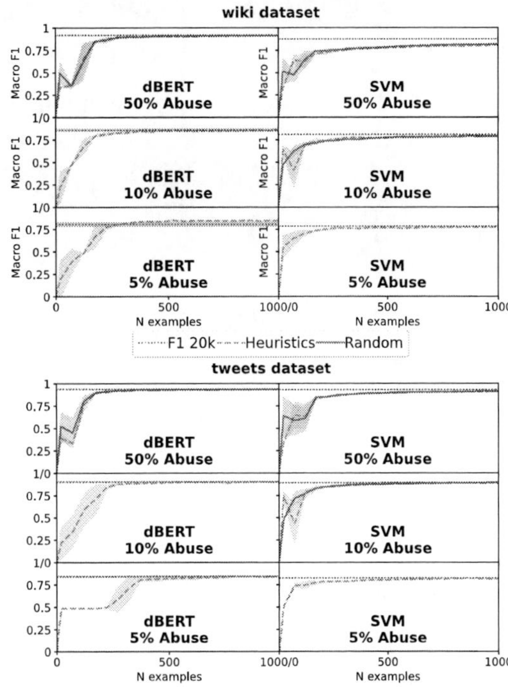

(b) Cold Strategy

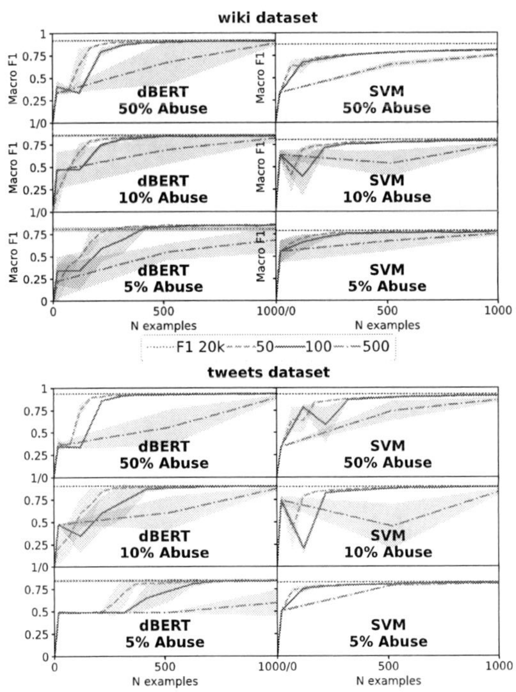

(c) Batch Size

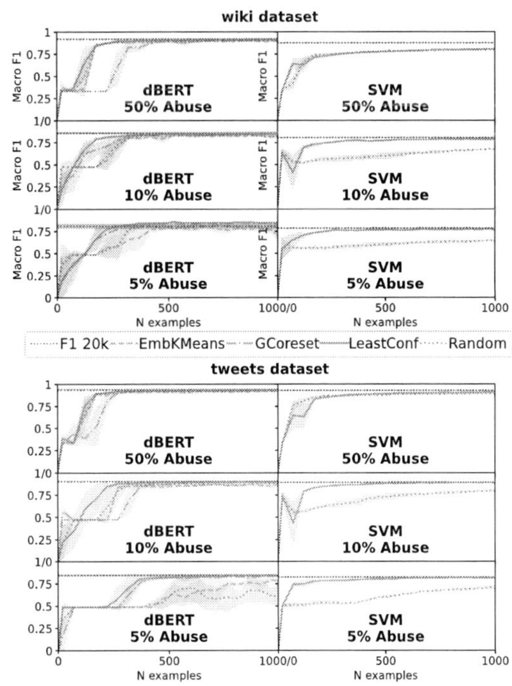

(d) Query Strategy

Figure 6: Learning curves per dataset-class imbalance pair showing the effect of isolated experimental variables on traditional (SVM) and transformers-based (dBERT) active learning.

A Lightweight yet Robust Approach to Textual Anomaly Detection

Leslie Barrett, Robert Kingan, Alexandra Ortan and **Madhavan Seshadri**
Bloomberg LP
{lbarrett4, rkingan, aortan, mseshadri}@bloomberg.net

Abstract

Highly imbalanced textual datasets continue to pose a challenge for supervised learning models. However, viewing such imbalanced text data as an anomaly detection (AD) problem has advantages for certain tasks such as detecting hate speech, or inappropriate and/or offensive language in large social media feeds. There the unwanted content tends to be both rare and non-uniform with respect to its thematic character, and better fits the definition of an anomaly than a class. Several recent approaches to textual AD use transformer models, achieving good results but with trade-offs in pre-training and inflexibility with respect to new domains. In this paper we compare two linear models within the NMF family, which also have a recent history in textual AD. We introduce a new approach based on an alternative regularization of the NMF objective. Our results surpass other linear AD models and are on par with deep models, performing comparably well even in very small outlier concentrations.

1 Introduction

Anomaly detection (AD), also known as Outlier Detection, is a well-researched area of machine learning. Traditional machine learning approaches to AD include proximity-based models where points that are separated from the rest of the data by a certain distance are considered outliers. These fall into several subclasses. There are cluster-based methods, such as k-means (MacQueen, 1967), where the point is an outlier if there is a large distance between the point and the nearest cluster, density-based methods, such as LOF (Breunig et al., 2000) and DBSCAN (Ester et al., 1996), where an object is an outlier if its density is lower than that of its neighbors and distance-based methods, such as k-NN (Cover and Hart, 1967), where the outlier neighborhood has few other points.

Most recently, Transformer models (Manolache et al., 2021) and word embeddings with multi-head self-attention (Ruff et al., 2019) have been applied in textual AD models, surpassing previously top-performing reconstruction-based approaches using Non-negative Matrix Factorization (NMF) as in (Kannan et al., 2017).

But detecting hate speech and offensive language is a challenging task because these may take various forms, change dynamically and be found in only a small minority of relatively short texts. Recent studies (Yin and Zubiaga, 2021) have pointed to concerns about generalizing results where even the best performing models show large variances in quality from one dataset to another in this domain.

We propose a new NMF-based approach as an alternative to recent transformer models. We improve upon previous NMF outlier detection approaches by replacing the usual squared norm of the error term in the objective function by a correntropy-based metric, which we argue is better tailored for textual outliers. This approach, we argue, is not only well-suited to the task of textual AD in general due to its lightweight architecture and flexibility but is also the better choice versus recent supervised models for hate-speech detection.

This paper is organized as follows: Previous approaches are discussed in Section 2, Data and Methods are discussed in Section 3, our results are in Section 4 and the Conclusion and plans for future work in section 5. Code to reproduce our results can be found here: (github repo provided upon acceptance)

2 Previous Work

While Anomaly Detection in text does not have a particularly deep history in the literature, there is some notable research. For example, Guthrie (2008) and Guthrie et al. (2007) consider texts that are unusual because of author, genre, style or emotional tone.

Peng et al. (2014), analyzed idiom recognition as a type of outlier detection. Idioms have certain key properties that make detection more likely using methods for finding outliers. Examples in English include "kick the bucket" or "have a cow" where the non-compositionality yields highly unusual lexical properties that can be recognized as anomalies.

Other studies (Manevitz and Yousef (2002), Kannan et al. (2017), Barrett et al. (2019), Ruff et al. (2019), Manolache et al. (2021)), treat textual anomalies as topical intrusions, where the texts from one topic constitute the "inliers" and a smaller set of intrusion texts constitute the "outliers". We use this data definition for our anomaly detection task.

Among topic-intrusion type models, the cur-

Proceedings of the 29th International Conference on Computational Linguistic, pages 62–67
October 12–17, 2022.

rently best-performing is the transformer approach in Manolache et al. (2021), a discriminator-generator model that outperformed the previously top performing OCSVM approach in Ruff et al. (2019). A non-negative matrix factorization model was used in Kannan et al. (2017). All three approaches have outperformed traditional AD models like Isolation Forests (Désir et al., 2013) on text.

3 Proposed Methods

We propose a lightweight alternative Non-negative Matrix Factorization (NMF) model that improves upon the results of Kannan and also provides comparable results to deep models without pre-training, or attention layers. We use simple frequency-based document representations and do not rely on trained embeddings. We show results on benchmark datasets and also on a dataset of hate speech in order to show the power and adaptability of our approach to an important NLP problem. Overall, our model is tested on four datasets in multiple combinations with different outlier-inlier concentrations.

Matrix factorization models like TONMF find outliers through a reconstruction process that isolates outlier documents as residual noise. In this approach, $\mathbf{A}$ is the term-document matrix where terms correspond to rows and documents correspond to columns, $\mathbf{W}$ is the term-topic matrix and $\mathbf{H}$ is the topic-document matrix. The residual matrix $\mathbf{Z}$ is intended to capture outliers depending on the configuration of its norm. The idea is that if a document is not representable as a linear combination of topics, the corresponding column in $\mathbf{Z}$ will have more entries. The quality of the result depends on manipulating norms on both the residual matrix and the low-rank approximation of the input matrix. Kannan et al. (2017) for example use the following optimization:

$$\underset{\mathbf{W}\geq 0, \mathbf{H}\geq 0; \mathbf{Z}}{\arg\min} \ \frac{1}{2}\|\mathbf{A}-\mathbf{WH}-\mathbf{Z}\|_F^2 + \alpha\|\mathbf{Z}\|_{1,2} + \beta\|\mathbf{H}\|_1 \tag{1}$$

Here, the standard Frobenius norm is applied to the main error term. The $\ell_{1,2}$ penalty norm is applied to the outlier matrix $\mathbf{Z}$ in order to minimize the sum of ℓ_2 column norms, which can be seen as the outlier scores of each document. The last term is added for regularization, to produce a more interpretable low rank matrix $\mathbf{WH}$ with sparse coefficients. The α and β parameters control the weight of the residual and regularization terms over the recovery of a low-rank approximation to $\mathbf{A}$.

3.1 Matrix Factorization with Additional Constraints

We used the basic model architecture in Kannan et al. (2017) to gauge the effect of changing the main objective function. This design includes a residual matrix representing the outlying points not reproducible by the main factorization process.

We set up two competing NMF-based models. Our baseline model is a hierarchical least-squares (HALS) approach (Cichocki et al., 2008), which is the base model architecture of Kannan et al. (2017). HALS solves the non-negative least squares sub-problem by updating each column of $\mathbf{W}$ separately, and generally can converge to a stationary point. Each column of $\mathbf{W}$ is successively updated, using gradient descent to solve each column-wise sub-problem. This has been shown to converge faster than a matrix-wise iterative updating procedure (Cichocki et al., 2008). We refer to this approach as H-NMF, henceforth in this paper.

3.2 Alternative Updating

Our experimental model uses a different updating approach entirely, replacing the squared error function with an alternative. We use an NMF approach leveraging the Correntropy-induced metric (Liu et al., 2006) in which the similarity between two variables (or sub-matrices in the NMF case) is determined through applying the Gaussian kernel to the error term:

$$V_\sigma(x,y) = \frac{1}{n}\sum_{i=1}^{n} k_\sigma(x_i - y_i) \tag{2}$$

where k_σ is the kernel function. CIM-based NMF substitutes the squared error on each entry with the kernel function. We take this a step farther following Du et al. (2012), wherein the CIM-based NMF optimizes on the row level, substituting the squared residuals on each row rather than each entry. We combine this optimization with the constrained residual matrix in the objective function as follows:

$$\frac{1}{2}\sum_{i=1}^{n}\left[w_i\|(\mathbf{A}-\mathbf{Z})_{i*} - \mathbf{W}_{i*}\mathbf{H}^T\|^2 + \phi(w_i)\right] + \alpha\|\mathbf{Z}\|_{1,2} \tag{3}$$

where the weight factor is defined as:

$$w_i = exp\left(-\frac{\|(\mathbf{A}-\mathbf{Z})_{i*} - \mathbf{W}_{i*}\mathbf{H}^T\|^2}{2\sigma^2}\right) \tag{4}$$

The half-quadratic optimization method used here and in Du et al. (2012) has been used in the past to detect and correct errors in facial recognition problems (He et al., 2014). This method sets up a robust strategy for identifying text segments that are topically anomalous not just because of bursty word distributions but because of the topicality of the entire segment. We refer to this approach as R-NMF, henceforth in this paper.

Both our baseline and experimental models leave the residual matrix constraints fixed and focus on the main objective function, in an effort to improve the quality of outliers that are passed as residuals.

4 Experimental Results

Below we describe the datasets and preparation. All models were run on four public datasets representing distinct genres (listserv, news, wiki and hate speech). We used three outlier-inlier concentrations for each.

4.1 Data and Experimental Design

The 20Newsgroups dataset is a publicly available collection of approximately 20,000 newsgroup documents organized into 20 topical subgroups[1]. Some newsgroups are similar (e.g., IBM/Mac hardware), while others are highly unrelated (e.g., for sale/Christian religion).

Reuters-21578 is a publicly available dataset of stories appearing on Reuters' newswire in 1987[2]. It contains 21,578 documents indexed and assigned categories by members of the Reuters Ltd. staff.

WikiPeople is the subset of the English language Wikipedia dump[3] consisting of the 945,662 articles in the category "living people".

Our dataset of Hate Speech is from de Gibert et al. (2018) and contains 9,916 samples in total of forum posts from Stormfront, a white-supremacy based forum where the "hate" class represents 11 percent of the corpus.

For each dataset, we blend the inlier classes listed in Table 1 with a sample from the outlier class to achieve three concentrations: .01, .025 and .05. The size of these concentrations is based on rare event analysis where such events have a chance of occurrence of < 0.05. In this case it would correspond to selecting an anomalous sample from our dataset. When such a sample is too small, we omit the .01 concentration. Our strategy for selecting inlier and outlier samples was to select topics that had reasonably close topical content. That is, avoiding highly diverse samples which might make the classification task easier than it should be to create a robust test of the compared approaches.

When evaluating, we take the number of top results corresponding to our outlier concentration and record the number of actual outlier samples in that concentration.

For both NMF models, we parse the input text into word count vectors using sklearn's CountVectorizer with all default parameters.We call the factorization routine on the sparse word-document matrix to obtain low-rank matrices $\mathbf{W}$ and $\mathbf{H}$ and outlier matrix $\mathbf{Z}$. Following the methodology in Kannan et al. (2017), we then use the ℓ_2 norm of each column in the $\mathbf{Z}$ matrix as the outlier score for every document. For both models, we use 3 CPU cores with 8Gb RAM.

We also train the DATE model (Manolache et al., 2021) on our data as a benchmark, as it represents the current SOTA on textual AD. We use the the code provided by the authors[4] to run experiments. We use a learning rate of $1e^{-5}$ and sequences of maximum length 128. Training is stopped at convergence, which occurs after 5000 steps on average. We use the same evaluation framework as proposed by the authors to report results. For the DATE experiments, we use 2 Tesla V100 GPU nodes each with 32 GB RAM and 6 CPU cores.

4.2 Model Results

We show results from H-NMF, R-NMF and the DATE model of Manolache et al. (2021). Model results are shown in Table 1. We list the AUC results for each dataset for each sample and concentration, along with the inlier and outlier classes we used to create each sample. For background on reporting AD model quality as AUC see Aggarwal (2016). The size of the inlier class is listed in parenthesis below the inlier class name. The outliers are sampled at random from the outlier class so as to achieve the specified outlier/inlier concentration. Winners are shown in bold.

The results are the best from a sweep of eight values of the hyper-parameter k within the range [1,128] and 5 values of alpha within the range [1,16], for both the H-NMF baseline and R-NMF. The beta parameter, commonly used for the degree of sparseness is only used for H-NMF, and there we use a sweep in the range [1,16][5].

4.3 Results Analysis

The results show that the rCIM model (R-NMF) outperforms baseline (H-NMF) overall and in particular on Reuters and WikiPeople but is outperformed by DATE on 20Newsgroups and Reuters in the larger concentrations using the "trade" class as outliers. For the Hate Speech corpus, rCIM does better in the lowest concentration, whereas HALS has a slight edge in larger concentrations. Both NMF-based models outperform DATE on this dataset in all concentrations. DATE generally seems to favor the larger concentrations slightly but the NMF-based approaches do not show that same trend.

All models achieved the best AUC on the Reuters data, with the more challenging datasets being WikiPeople and 20Newsgroups.The greatest difference between the two NMF-based approaches is found on the Reuters data where rCIM has the stronger results. Note that the results are better for all three models when the outlier class is "trade" than when it is "interest", possibly because the "interest" topic is more closely related to and thus harder to distinguish from the inlier topics "earn" and "acq".

In the Hate Speech data, both NMF-based models outperform the transformer-based model. In addition our model required considerably fewer compute resources, running on 3 CPU cores, compared to 2 GPUs and 6 cores for the transformer. Other recent supervised models trained on Hate Speech alone (not developed for AD) (Wullach et al. (2021)), show good performance for corpora including the de Gibert et al. (2018), but

[1] https://archive.ics.uci.edu/ml/datasets/Twenty+Newsgroups

[2] https://archive.ics.uci.edu/ml/datasets/reuters-21578+text+categorization+collection

[3] https://dumps.wikimedia.org/

[4] https://github.com/bit-ml/date

[5] Du et al. (2012) find that using an L1 norm would cause the rCIM objective function to be dominated by the datapoints with near-zero fitting error and actually reduce the quality of row-based outliers.

Dataset	Inliers	Outliers	Concentration	H-NMF	R-NMF	DATE
20Newsgroups	pc/mac.hardware	ms-windows.misc	0.025	0.600	0.592	**0.650**
	(2000)		0.05	0.543	0.559	**0.767**
20Newsgroups	pc/mac.hardware	comp.windows.x	0.025	0.567	0.595	**0.691**
	(2000)		0.05	0.557	0.555	**0.712**
Reuters-21578	earn+acq	interest	0.01	0.741	**0.769**	0.691
	(5795)		0.025	0.725	**0.766**	0.712
			0.05	0.716	**0.777**	0.725
Reuters-21578	earn+acq	trade	0.01	0.871	**0.889**	0.886
	(5795)		0.025	0.826	0.859	**0.905**
			0.05	0.848	0.877	**0.894**
WikiPeople	life	career	0.025	0.675	**0.694**	0.548
	(5000)		0.05	0.690	**0.707**	0.617
Hate Speech	noHate	hate	0.01	0.688	**0.702**	0.508
	(9507)		0.025	**0.697**	0.693	0.499
			0.05	**0.679**	0.675	0.505

Table 1: AUROC Results. Bolded values indicate the best performance for each dataset blend.

train on large numbers of hate speech samples that may not be available in all real-life circumstances. Our rCIM model on the other hand shows the best performance on very small concentrations. Since posts containing hate speech or offensive language tend to be in a small minority in the real world, our model is ideally suited for practical application and does not have to compensate for data imbalance issues.

5 Conclusion and Future Work

Although recent approaches to textual Anomaly Detection using deep models are very robust, our model performs comparably and even outperforms the state of the art on the majority of AD datasets including a hate speech dataset. We improve upon recent NMF-based AD by combining a row-centric approach with a separate residual matrix. Our approach requires no pretraining or fine tuning, making it highly adaptable to different data sets with different concentrations of anomalous texts in a low compute resource setting. The model is well-suited both to the task of identifying hate speech and topical-intrusion-type textual anomalies in general.

We plan to continue further experiments on new AD data sets, including those containing hate speech and offensive language.

6 Ethical Considerations

Anomaly detection is a type of classification model which may have imperfect Precision and Recall. As such it may classify hateful or toxic language incorrectly and should be subject to human review in contexts of high risk. Risks if deployed in the context of a real listserv or subscription media product could include users being banned due to false positive outputs as well as unwanted or offensive posts being allowed due to false negatives.

References

Charu C. Aggarwal. 2016. *Outlier Analysis*, 2nd edition. Springer Publishing Company, Incorporated.

Leslie Barrett, Sidney Fletcher, Robert Kingan, Mrinal Kumar, Anu Pradhan, and Ryon Smey. 2019. Textual outlier detection and anomalies in financial reporting. KDD '19, New York, NY, USA. Association for Computing Machinery.

Markus M. Breunig, Hans-Peter Kriegel, Raymond T. Ng, and Jörg Sander. 2000. Lof: Identifying density-based local outliers. 29(2).

A. Cichocki, R. Zdunek, and S. Amari. 2008. Nonnegative matrix and tensor factorization [lecture notes]. *IEEE Signal Processing Magazine*, 25(1):142–145.

T. Cover and P. Hart. 1967. Nearest neighbor pattern classification. *IEEE Transactions on Information Theory*, 13(1):21–27.

Ona de Gibert, Naiara Perez, Aitor García-Pablos, and Montse Cuadros. 2018. Hate speech dataset from a white supremacy forum. In *Proceedings of the 2nd Workshop on Abusive Language Online (ALW2)*, pages 11–20, Brussels, Belgium. Association for Computational Linguistics.

Chesner Désir, Simon Bernard, Caroline Petitjean, and Laurent Heutte. 2013. One class random forests. *Pattern Recogn.*, 46(12):3490–3506.

L. Du, X. Li, and Y. Shen. 2012. Robust nonnegative matrix factorization via half-quadratic minimization. In *2012 IEEE 12th International Conference on Data Mining*, pages 201–210.

Martin Ester, Hans-Peter Kriegel, Jörg Sander, and Xiaowei Xu. 1996. A density-based algorithm for discovering clusters in large spatial databases with noise. In *Proceedings of the Second International Conference on Knowledge Discovery and Data Mining*, KDD'96, page 226–231. AAAI Press.

David Guthrie. 2008. Unsupervised detection of anomalous text.

David Guthrie, Louise Guthrie, Ben Allison, and Yorick Wilks. 2007. Unsupervised anomaly detection. In *IJCAI 2007, Proceedings of the 20th International Joint Conference on Artificial Intelligence, Hyderabad, India, January 6-12, 2007*, pages 1624–1628.

Ran He, Wei-Shi Zheng, Tieniu Tan, and Zhenan Sun. 2014. Half-quadratic-based iterative minimization for robust sparse representation. *IEEE Trans. Pattern Anal. Mach. Intell.*, 36(2):261–275.

Ramakrishnan Kannan, Hyenkyun Woo, Charu C. Aggarwal, and Haesun Park. 2017. Outlier detection for text data : An extended version.

Weifeng Liu, P. P. Pokharel, and J. Príncipe. 2006. Correntropy: A localized similarity measure. *The 2006 IEEE International Joint Conference on Neural Network Proceedings*, pages 4919–4924.

J. B. MacQueen. 1967. Some methods for classification and analysis of multivariate observations. In *Proc. of the fifth Berkeley Symposium on Mathematical Statistics and Probability*, volume 1, pages 281–297. University of California Press.

Larry M. Manevitz and Malik Yousef. 2002. One-class svms for document classification. *J. Mach. Learn. Res.*, 2:139–154.

Andrei Manolache, Florin Brad, and Elena Burceanu. 2021. DATE: Detecting anomalies in text via self-supervision of transformers. In *Proceedings of the 2021 Conference of the North American Chapter of the Association for Computational Linguistics: Human Language Technologies*, pages 267–277, Online. Association for Computational Linguistics.

Jing Peng, Anna Feldman, and Ekaterina Vylomova. 2014. Classifying idiomatic and literal expressions using topic models and intensity of emotions. In *Proceedings of the 2014 Conference on Empirical Methods in Natural Language Processing (EMNLP)*, pages 2019–2027, Doha, Qatar. Association for Computational Linguistics.

Lukas Ruff, Yury Zemlyanskiy, Robert Vandermeulen, Thomas Schnake, and Marius Kloft. 2019. Self-attentive, multi-context one-class classification for unsupervised anomaly detection on text. In *Proceedings of the 57th Annual Meeting of the Association for Computational Linguistics*, pages 4061–4071, Florence, Italy. Association for Computational Linguistics.

Tomer Wullach, Amir Adler, and Einat Minkov. 2021. Fight fire with fire: Fine-tuning hate detectors using large samples of generated hate speech. In *Findings of the Association for Computational Linguistics: EMNLP 2021*, pages 4699–4705, Punta Cana, Dominican Republic. Association for Computational Linguistics.

Wenjie Yin and Arkaitz Zubiaga. 2021. Towards generalisable hate speech detection: a review on obstacles and solutions. *PeerJ Computer Science*, 7.

A Appendix: Examples

Examples of Hate Speech from the de Gibert et al. (2018) corpus are shown in Table 2.

TEXT	CLASS
As of March 13th , 2014 the booklet had been downloaded over 18,300 times and counting .	no_hate
In order to help increase it would be great if all Stormfronters who had YouTube accounts , could display the following text in the description boxes of their uploaded YouTube videos .	no_hate
Simply copy and paste the following text into your YouTube videos description boxes	no_hate
Click below for a FREE download of a colorfully illustrated 132 page e-book on the Zionist-engineered INTENTIONAL destruction of Western civilization .	hate
She may or may not be a Jew she seems to think the Blacks wo n't kill her alongside every other White they can get their dirty hands on , what a muppet !	hate
Thank you for posting your story .	no_hate
I think you should write a book as well	no_hate
And the sad thing is the white students at those schools will act like that too .	hate

Table 2: Examples of inliers (no_hate) and outliers (hate) from the hate speech dataset.

B Appendix: Hyper-parameters

The hyper-parameter values that yielded the best results for each dataset blend. These were obtained from a sweep of eight values of k within the range [1,128], 5 values of alpha within the range [1,16], and 5 values of beta within the range [1,16]. The beta parameter is only used for H-NMF.

Dataset	Inliers/Outliers	Concentration	Best Model	k	alpha	beta
20Newsgroups	pc/mac.hardware	0.025	H-NMF	100	1	16
	ms-windows.misc	0.05	R-NMF	64	1	
20Newsgroups	pc/mac.hardware	0.025	R-NMF	64	2	
	comp.windows.x	0.05	H-NMF	32	1	1
Reuters-21578	earn+acq	0.01	R-NMF	16	16	
	interest	0.025	R-NMF	16	16	
		0.05	R-NMF	16	16	
Reuters-21578	earn+acq	0.01	R-NMF	16	16	
	trade	0.025	R-NMF	8	16	
		0.05	R-NMF	8	8	
WikiPeople	life	0.025	R-NMF	8	16	
	career	0.05	R-NMF	8	8	
Hate Speech	noHate	0.01	R-NMF	8	8	
	hate	0.025	H-NMF	8	8	1
		0.05	H-NMF	16	8	1

Table 3: Best hyper-parameters for each dataset blend.

Detection of Negative Campaign in Israeli Municipal Elections

Natalia Vanetik **Sagiv Talker** **Or Machlouf** **Marina Litvak**

Department of Software Engineering

Shamoon College of Engineering

{natalyav,Orma5,Sagivta,marinal}@ac.sce.ac.il

Abstract

Political competitions are complex settings where candidates use campaigns to promote their chances to be elected. One choice focuses on conducting a positive campaign that highlights the candidate's achievements, leadership skills, and future programs. The alternative is to focus on a negative campaign that emphasizes the *negative aspects of the competing person* and is aimed at *offending opponents or the opponent's supporters*. In this proposal, we concentrate on negative campaigns in Israeli elections. This work introduces an empirical case study on automatic detection of negative campaigns, using machine learning and natural language processing approaches, applied to the Hebrew-language data from Israeli municipal elections. Our contribution is multi-fold: (1) We provide TONIC—daTaset fOr Negative polItical Campaign in Hebrew—which consists of annotated posts from Facebook related to Israeli municipal elections; (2) We introduce results of a case study, that explored several research questions. **RQ1**: Which classifier and representation perform best for this task? We employed several traditional classifiers which are known for their excellent performance in IR tasks and two pre-trained models based on BERT architecture; several standard representations were employed with traditional ML models. **RQ2**: Does a negative campaign always contain offensive language? Can a model, trained to detect offensive language, also detect negative campaigns? We are trying to answer this question by reporting results for the transfer learning from a dataset annotated with offensive language to our dataset. **RQ3**: Does a negative campaign necessarily express negative sentiment? Can sentiment analysis help to detect negative campaigns? We experiment with sentiment labels to enrich data representation and report our findings.

Our dataset and pre-trained models will be freely available for researchers.

1 Introduction

Political competitions aim at promoting the candidates' chances to be elected. The main decision in such competitions regards the nature of the campaign – that is, whether a candidate should apply a positive campaign that highlights the candidate's achievements, leadership skills, and future programs, or focus on a negative campaign that emphasizes the negative sides of the competitors (Bernhardt and Ghosh, 2020; Invernizzi, 2019; Martin, 2004; Skaperdas and Grofman, 1995).

Our work introduces a new dataset of Facebook posts, published by candidates during municipal elections in Israel. We annotated this dataset with binary labels, where we distinguish between negative campaigns and other campaign-related content. In addition to the dataset, we report the results of extensive experiments, aimed at answering multiple research questions: Which supervised model and representation are more effective at automatically detecting negative campaigns? Can we effectively detect negative campaigns with a model trained to identify offensive language? Can sentiment analysis boost negative campaign detection?

Our contribution is multi-fold: (1) We introduce a new annotated dataset in Hebrew for negative campaign detection; (2) We report results of multiple classifiers and their combination with various representations on our dataset; (3) We explore possible relations between sentiment analysis and negative campaign and (4) between offensive language and negative campaign.

2 Related Work

The scholarly literature has investigated various aspects related to negative campaigns (Asunka et al., 2019; Chaturvedi, 2005; Martin, 2004; Skaperdas and Grofman, 1995). It points out that this phenomenon exists in many areas such as competition over jobs in the workplace, yet in the politi-

Proceedings of the 29th International Conference on Computational Linguistic, pages 68–74
October 12–17, 2022.

cal arena there are several special characteristics. A major characteristic is a fact that participants in electoral competition often hold positions of power as well as public and private resources to finance their efforts (Bernhardt and Ghosh, 2020; Invernizzi, 2019). In many cases, they also set the rules of the competition as opposed to other areas where the contest organizer sets the rules of the game. Indeed, in recent years, we witness more and more political candidates that do not play by the rules, both formally and informally. A specific feature of this trend is the intensive use of negative campaigns which target the weaknesses and failures of the opponents promising to do the opposite (Invernizzi, 2019; Martin, 2004; Skaperdas and Grofman, 1995).

The implementation of language technologies in the political sciences is recently in high demand. While computational political scientists are looking for NLP tools to assist automatic analysis of campaign-related content and predict outcomes, computational linguistics explores real-world use cases in political domains. The recent Workshop on Natural Language Processing for Political sciences (PoliticalNLP) (Afli et al., 2022) is an example of the rising popularity of this interdisciplinary research. However, despite some works dedicated to the analysis of elections-related materials (Baran et al., 2022; Abdine et al., 2022; Sanders and van den Bosch, 2022), in this workshop or anywhere else, we were unable to find any work on automated negative campaign analysis and detection.

As a majority of text classification tasks last years are efficiently performed by pre-trained language models and transformers, we follow this approach in our study. We apply BERT, its multilingual (mBERT) and Hebrew (AlephBERT) versions. mBERT serves us both as an encoder (feature extractor) and end-to-end classifier.[1] In addition to the introduction of a new dataset, we explore possible relations between sentiment analysis and negative campaigns and between offensive language and negative campaigns.

[1]We did not apply AlephBERT as feature extractor because its implementation does not comply with the sentence transformers package and does not allow extraction of sentence vectors.

3 Case Study

3.1 TONIC dataset

The data was collected from Facebook accounts of local politicians from several big Israeli cities running for mayor's offices. There were total of 12 cities and 27 mayor candidates whose number for elections that took place in 2018. Data statistics appear in Table 1. The data is freely available for download from GitHub at `https://github.com/NataliaVanetik1/TONIC`.

Table 3 displays two instances of comments from the TONIC dataset that have been translated into English.

The collected posts were first manually filtered as related or unrelated to political campaigns, and only campaign-related messages were kept. Those texts were annotated as either negative or not by two independent annotators; in case of a disagreement between them, the third annotator decided on a final label. The annotators were instructed to label a post as "negative campaign" only if it contained a negative (but not necessarily offensive) content about the opponent of the post's owner or her supporter. Kappa agreement between the annotators was 0.862, which is considered to be an excellent agreement. The statistics for campaign-related posts for all cities are given in Table 2.

3.2 Method

Our approach to text representation and classification consists of the following steps:

1. Representing texts with one of the following:
    - tf*idf vectors, where every post is treated as a separate document;
    - character n-grams with $n = 1, 2, 3$;
    - pre-trained BERT vectors obtained from a multilingual BERT model (Sanh et al., 2019).
2. Enhancing the above representations with sentiment weights produced by the pre-trained HeBERT model (Chriqui and Yahav, 2021). This model produces weights as a probability distribution for positive, negative, and neutral sentiments.
3. Training and application of supervised ML models (see Section 3.4) on all of the above data representations.

The approach is depicted in Figure 1.

Table 1: Collected data by city

city	candidates	post num	avg words in post	avg characters in post
Ashdod	4	644	64.2	367.9
Netanya	4	571	49.2	292.0
Jerusalem	3	516	65.5	386.8
Ashkelon	3	683	61.4	358.4
Petah Tikva	4	669	61.7	359.0
Haifa	1	104	51.7	304.4
Rishon LeZion	1	239	87.2	523.7
Dimona	1	95	57.2	338.2
Hod Hasharon	2	366	71.0	416.1
Tel Aviv	1	233	70.8	410.2
Beer Sheva	1	34	139.8	866.4
Herzliya	2	272	92.4	549.4
Total	27	4426	65.6	385

Table 2: TONIC statistics

post num	pos	neg	majority	avg words	avg chars
2632	568	2064	0.784	85.2	500.6

Table 3: Two sample comments from the TONIC dataset

Translated comment	Label
Good week to all residents of Ashdod! Let's talk about Ashdod-Yam Park. Who does the park belong to? Does the park belong to the residents of the city at all or only to the ultra-Orthodox residents (and non-residents)? Ashdod-Yam Park has been an attraction for the ultra-orthodox public from all over the country for years. I really don't have a problem with it, or most residents of Ashdod, but as soon as the park and its facilities are closed on Shabbat, the message to the non-Orthodox residents of Ashdod is simple: you are not welcome in your city. Unless you are...that's right - ultra-Orthodox. This week the municipality of Ashdod decided that as part of the closing of the park's facilities on Shabbat, the only cafe in the park will also be closed on Shabbat. Another conquest of the ultra-Orthodox businessmen with the kind help of Yehiel Lesri. We must return the city to all residents. The city was not intended only for the ultra-Orthodox. With your help I will be the mayor and then Ashdod will serve you all!	yes
What has already become a procedure, the week is closed with the dear residents of the city! Today we visited the 11th and 12th districts and were happy to meet the residents, to hear what they like in the city, what they dislike and what problems they suffer from. On 30.10.18 we will be able to start providing better service to the resident and take care of the needs of every district and every community in the city. Many thanks to the dear activists who accompany me all along the way.	no

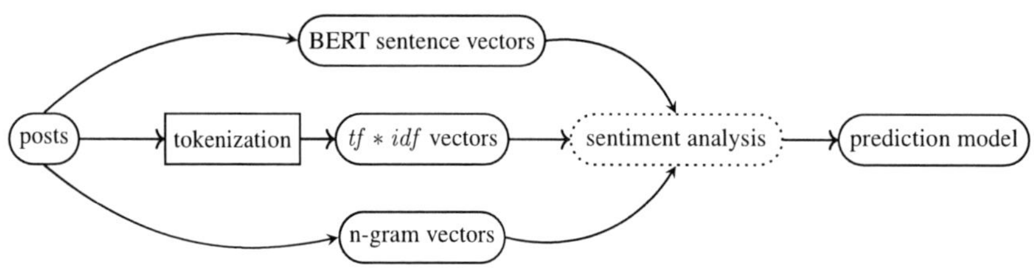

Figure 1: Political posts classification pipeline.

3.3 Data representation

We employed three different representation models for input texts, as follows.

Tf-idf, short for term frequency-inverse document frequency, is a numerical statistic that is intended to reflect how important a word is to a document in a collection or corpus. The tf-idf value increases proportionally to the number of times a word appears in the document and is offset by the number of documents in the corpus that contain the word. In our case, we treated every post as a separate document and the whole dataset as a corpus.

N-grams are the sequences of n consecutive words seen in the text, where n is a parameter. In our evaluation, we used the values $n = 1, 2, 3$.

BERT sentence embeddings of length 512 were obtained using the pre-trained multilingual BERT model trained in 104 languages, including Hebrew.

3.4 Models

We applied three traditional ML algorithms—Random Forest (RF) (Pal, 2005), Logistic Regression (LR) (Wright, 1995), and Extreme Gradient Boosting (XGB) (Chen et al., 2015). All three were applied to texts represented by each of three representations, described in Section 3.3.

Also, we employed the BERT transformer (Devlin et al., 2018) trained for sentence classification. We applied two different pre-trained models for our task. The first one is a multilingual model called *bert-base-multilingual-cased* (denoted as mBERT) introduced in (Devlin et al., 2018). The second is the AlephBERT (Seker et al., 2021), a large pre-trained language model for Modern Hebrew, which is trained on a larger vocabulary and a larger dataset than any Hebrew pre-trained language model before. Both of these models were fine-tuned on the train portion of our data.

3.5 Experiments

Our experiments aim at evaluation of and comparison of various models and text representations for the purpose of detecting negative campaigns in political posts. Additionally, we explore two research questions.

In the first one, we want to understand whether general offensive language data in the same language (Hebrew) can be used for transfer learning with the proposed methodology. For answering that, we perform cross-domain experiments with a dataset with Hebrew messages annotated with offensive language.

In the second question, we explore whether the sentiment analysis can boost the negative campaign detection accuracy. For answering that, we compare between performance scores of our models with and without sentiment labels in the data representation.

3.6 Data Setup

For the experiments on TONIC, RF, LR, and XGB were trained on 80% of the data and evaluated on the remaining 20%. Fine-tuned BERT was trained a 75% of the data with the validation set containing 5% of the data, and it was tested on the remaining 20%. Fine-tuning was run for 10 epochs with batch size 16.

For the cross-domain experiments, we used the Hebrew offensive language dataset (Litvak et al., 2021) called OLaH. It is composed of Facebook comments written in Hebrew and annotated by humans. The dataset contains 2,025 annotated comments, out of which 821 are labeled positive (i.e., they do contain offensive content).

3.7 Software Setup

For the purpose of reproducibility, we present below the setup of our experiments. All non-neural models are implemented in sklearn (Pedregosa et al., 2011) python package. Our neural model is implemented with Keras (Chollet et al., 2015) with the TensorFlow backend (Abadi et al., 2015). Experiments were performed on google colab (Bisong, 2019) with standard settings and GPU runtime type. Runtime for every experiment setting (mono- or cross-domain) was less than 10 minutes.

3.8 Evaluation Results

Table 4: Mono-domain evaluation results on the TONIC dataset

Model	P	R	F1	Acc
AlephBERT	0.7318	0.6616	0.6949	0.7040
mBERT	0.7288	0.6792	0.7031	0.7590
RF_{tfidf}	0.8004	0.5490	0.6513	0.8008
$RF_{tfidf+SA}$	0.8507	0.6550	0.7401	0.8425
RF_{ng1}	0.7774	0.5597	0.6508	0.8027
RF_{ng1+SA}	0.8517	0.6877	0.7610	0.8539
RF_{ng2}	0.8157	0.5414	0.6508	0.7989
RF_{ng2+SA}	0.8372	0.6168	0.7103	0.8273
RF_{ng3}	0.771	0.5239	0.6239	0.7913
RF_{ng3+SA}	0.8482	0.6506	0.7364	0.8406
RF_{bert}	0.8485	0.5383	0.6587	0.7989
$RF_{bert+SA}$	0.8508	0.7355	0.7890	0.8691
LR_{tfidf}	0.7731	0.5358	0.6329	0.7951
$LR_{tfidf+SA}$	**0.8530**	0.7399	0.7924	0.8710
LR_{ng1}	0.7341	0.6571	0.6935	0.8159
LR_{ng1+SA}	0.8474	**0.7928**	**0.8192**	**0.8843**
LR_{ng2}	0.6551	0.6491	0.6521	0.7685
LR_{ng2+SA}	0.7455	0.7501	0.7478	0.8273
LR_{ng3}	0.6551	0.6491	0.6521	0.7685
LR_{ng3+SA}	0.7455	0.7501	0.7478	0.8273
LR_{bert}	0.7864	0.6075	0.6855	0.8178
$LR_{bert+SA}$	0.8096	0.7851	0.7972	0.8672
XGB_{tfidf}	0.8195	0.5948	0.6893	0.8178
$XGB_{tfidf+SA}$	0.8151	0.7724	0.7932	0.8672
XGB_{ng1}	0.8007	0.5892	0.6789	0.8140
XGB_{ng1+SA}	0.8303	0.7879	0.8085	0.8767
XGB_{ng2}	0.7168	0.5978	0.6519	0.8027
XGB_{ng2+SA}	0.8121	0.7787	0.7950	0.8672
XGB_{ng3}	0.7241	0.5991	0.6557	0.8046
XGB_{ng3+SA}	0.8072	0.7699	0.7881	0.8634
XGB_{bert}	0.6733	0.5798	0.6231	0.7894
$XGB_{bert+SA}$	0.8208	0.7887	0.8044	0.8729

Evaluation results for the TONIC dataset as both train and test sets are presented in Table 4. We can make the following conclusions from these results.

First, there is a shred of strong evidence that sentiment labels boost classification performance. Second, the best recall, f-measure, and accuracy were produced by LR with unigrams enriched with sentiment labels, and the best precision was obtained by the same LR but with tf-idf and sentiment labels.

Table 5: Cross-domain evaluation results: OLaH→TONIC

Model	P	R	F1	Acc
AlephBERT	0.4988	0.3916	0.4387	0.7818
mBERT	0.5135	**0.6025**	0.5545	0.7799
RF_{tfidf}	0.4536	0.4959	0.4738	0.7723
$RF_{tfidf+SA}$	0.5356	0.5054	0.5201	0.7723
RF_{ng1}	0.4530	0.4779	0.4651	0.7192
RF_{ng1+SA}	0.5599	0.5079	0.5326	0.7761
RF_{ng2}	0.4779	0.4886	0.4832	0.7211
RF_{ng2+SA}	0.5222	0.5072	0.5146	0.7552
RF_{ng3}	0.4727	0.4867	0.4796	0.7230
RF_{ng3+SA}	0.5031	0.5009	0.5020	0.7552
RF_{bert}	0.3910	0.4952	0.4370	0.7761
$RF_{bert+SA}$	0.4628	0.4971	0.4793	0.7742
LR_{tfidf}	0.3918	0.5000	0.4393	0.7837
$LR_{tfidf+SA}$	0.3914	0.4976	0.4382	0.7799
LR_{ng1}	0.4723	0.4850	0.4786	0.7154
LR_{ng1+SA}	0.5222	0.5072	0.5146	0.7552
LR_{ng2}	0.5417	0.5396	0.5406	0.6964
LR_{ng2+SA}	0.5484	0.5382	0.5433	0.7192
LR_{ng3}	0.5417	0.5396	0.5406	0.6964
LR_{ng3+SA}	0.5484	0.5382	0.5433	0.7192
LR_{bert}	0.4623	0.4942	0.4777	0.7647
$LR_{bert+SA}$	0.5592	0.5039	0.5301	0.7799
XGB_{tfidf}	0.5352	0.5027	0.5184	0.7780
$XGB_{tfidf+SA}$	0.7265	0.5076	0.5976	0.7856
XGB_{ng1}	0.4617	0.4914	0.4761	0.7552
XGB_{ng1+SA}	**0.7946**	0.5163	**0.6259**	**0.7894**
XGB_{ng2}	0.5315	0.5174	0.5244	0.7362
XGB_{ng2+SA}	0.6214	0.5262	0.5699	0.7799
XGB_{ng3}	0.5609	0.5388	0.5496	0.7400
XGB_{ng3+SA}	0.5789	0.5162	0.5458	0.7742
XGB_{bert}	0.4680	0.4892	0.4784	0.7419
$XGB_{bert+SA}$	0.5460	0.5113	0.5281	0.7666

Cross-domain experiments in Table 5 show that using an offensive language dataset as a training set decreases classification accuracy for all the models, indicating that the task of detecting negative campaigns is different from the task of offensive language detection. Despite enhancing data with SA obviously improve results, only a few models trained on offensive language data achieved accuracy that is slightly higher than or equal to the majority rule. XGB with unigrams and sentiment labels achieved the best precision, f-measure, and accuracy, while the best recall was obtained by mBERT.

3.9 Error Analysis

We used the top-performing model $(LRng1 + SA)$ to analyze the misclassification errors in the mono-domain classification instance (Logistic Regression with unigrams and sentiment labels as a text representation). This model's confusion matrix is as follows: $TP = 72$, $TN = 394$, $FP = 19$, and $FN = 42$, with precision of 0.79 and recall of 0.63 respectively. These results show that the model does a good job of identifying and eliminating negative samples (non-negative campaigns), but it misses positive samples (negative campaign). As a result, TN is the most important accuracy compound, while FN represents the biggest amount of errors.

In a 30 misclassified case sample that we manually examined, 22 cases are from the FN group and only 8 cases are from the FP category. The majority of errors (23), including 19 samples incorrectly identified as negative campaigns when we actually found them to be neutral and 4 samples incorrectly labeled as neutral, were the result of incorrect labeling by our annotators. Due to a variety of factors, the model incorrectly classified four neutral posts as negative campaigns, including one sample that was actually negative but was correctly categorized as neutral because it wasn't addressed to a specific person, and two samples that contained words that were likely to have influenced the classification. One sample was incorrectly categorized for an unidentified reason; the cause is likely due to the negative campaign writing style, which is characterized by frequent mentions of individuals. The model missed three unfavorable marketing materials, most likely as a result of the neutral vocabulary (no offensive content in these samples).

4 Future Work and Conclusions

In this paper, we introduce a new dataset that can help researchers to study negative campaigns. The dataset contains only Hebrew-written content posted by Israeli politicians on Facebook. We report the results of extensive experiments which include multiple classifiers and representations and answer two research questions: whether transfer learning from offensive language to negative campaign can be efficiently applied and whether sentiment analysis can boost negative campaign detection. We can conclude that traditional models with unigrams and sentiment labels as text representations performed best in both scenarios. This is probably due to a small training set which is not sufficient for efficient fine-tuning of pre-trained transformers with a large number of parameters, but big enough to train a relatively simple classification function with fewer parameters. Also, unigrams seem to be most efficient in representing Hebrew texts — due to the rich morphology of Hebrew and ambiguous tokenization, simple BOW (and tf-idf) cannot provide enough semantic information. It also might be the case of political rhetoric which is similar across candidates and campaigns of different political parties. Based on our results, we can conclude that sentiment analysis obviously boosts negative campaign detection. However, there is no strong relation between offensive language and negative campaigns. Therefore, transfer learning with models trained to detect offensive content is inefficient for the detection of a negative campaign.

In the future, we plan to apply our analysis to elections to the Israeli government. We also would like to see whether cross-lingual and cross-country learning is efficient for negative campaign detection. We'd like to explore the common characteristics and differences between political campaigns in different countries. We hypothesize that an engagement of a candidate in a negative campaign can be dependent on the candidate's gender, perceived strength, initial support, etc. We intend to study these possible relations in the future.

References

Martín Abadi, Ashish Agarwal, Paul Barham, Eugene Brevdo, Zhifeng Chen, Craig Citro, Greg S. Corrado, Andy Davis, Jeffrey Dean, Matthieu Devin, Sanjay Ghemawat, Ian Goodfellow, Andrew Harp, Geoffrey Irving, Michael Isard, Yangqing Jia, Rafal Jozefowicz, Lukasz Kaiser, Manjunath Kudlur, Josh Levenberg, Dandelion Mané, Rajat Monga, Sherry Moore, Derek Murray, Chris Olah, Mike Schuster, Jonathon Shlens, Benoit Steiner, Ilya Sutskever, Kunal Talwar, Paul Tucker, Vincent Vanhoucke, Vijay Vasudevan, Fernanda Viégas, Oriol Vinyals, Pete Warden, Martin Wattenberg, Martin Wicke, Yuan Yu, and Xiaoqiang Zheng. 2015. TensorFlow: Large-scale machine learning on heterogeneous systems. Software available from tensorflow.org.

Hadi Abdine, Yanzhu Guo, Virgile Rennard, and Michalis Vazirgiannis. 2022. Political communities on twitter: Case study of the 2022 french presidential election. In *Proceedings of The LREC 2022 workshop on Natural Language Processing for Political Sciences*, pages 62–71, Marseille, France. European Language Resources Association.

Haithem Afli, Mehwish Alam, Houda Bouamor, Cristina Blasi Casagran, Colleen Boland, and Sahar Ghannay, editors. 2022. *Proceedings of The LREC 2022 workshop on Natural Language Processing for Political Sciences*. European Language Resources Association, Marseille, France.

Joseph Asunka, Sarah Brierley, Miriam Golden, Eric Kramon, and George Ofosu. 2019. Electoral fraud or violence: The effect of observers on party manipulation strategies. *British Journal of Political Science*, 49(1):129–151.

Mateusz Baran, Mateusz WÃ³jcik, Piotr Kolebski, MichaÅ, Bernaczyk, Krzysztof Rajda, Lukasz Augustyniak, and Tomasz Kajdanowicz. 2022. Electoral agitation dataset: The use case of the polish election. In *Proceedings of The LREC 2022 workshop on Natural Language Processing for Political Sciences*, pages 32–36, Marseille, France. European Language Resources Association.

Dan Bernhardt and Meenakshi Ghosh. 2020. Positive and negative campaigning in primary and general elections. *Games and Economic Behavior*, 119:98–104.

Ekaba Bisong. 2019. *Building machine learning and deep learning models on Google cloud platform: A comprehensive guide for beginners*. Apress.

Ashish Chaturvedi. 2005. Rigging elections with violence. *Public Choice*, 125(1):189–202.

Tianqi Chen, Tong He, Michael Benesty, Vadim Khotilovich, Yuan Tang, Hyunsu Cho, Kailong Chen, et al. 2015. Xgboost: extreme gradient boosting. *R package version 0.4-2*, 1(4):1–4.

François Chollet et al. 2015. Keras. `https://github.com/fchollet/keras`.

Avihay Chriqui and Inbal Yahav. 2021. Hebert & hebemo: a hebrew bert model and a tool for polarity analysis and emotion recognition. *arXiv preprint arXiv:2102.01909*.

Jacob Devlin, Ming-Wei Chang, Kenton Lee, and Kristina Toutanova. 2018. BERT: pre-training of deep bidirectional transformers for language understanding. *CoRR*, abs/1810.04805.

Giovanna Maria Invernizzi. 2019. Electoral competition and factional sabotage. *Available at SSRN 3329622*.

Marina Litvak, Natalia Vanetik, Yaser Nimer, Abdulrhman Skout, and Israel Beer-Sheba. 2021. Offensive language detection in semitic languages. In *Multimodal Hate Speech Workshop 2021*, pages 7–12.

Paul S Martin. 2004. Inside the black box of negative campaign effects: Three reasons why negative campaigns mobilize. *Political psychology*, 25(4):545–562.

Mahesh Pal. 2005. Random forest classifier for remote sensing classification. *International journal of remote sensing*, 26(1):217–222.

F. Pedregosa, G. Varoquaux, A. Gramfort, V. Michel, B. Thirion, O. Grisel, M. Blondel, P. Prettenhofer, R. Weiss, V. Dubourg, J. Vanderplas, A. Passos, D. Cournapeau, M. Brucher, M. Perrot, and E. Duchesnay. 2011. Scikit-learn: Machine learning in Python. *Journal of Machine Learning Research*, 12:2825–2830.

Eric Sanders and Antal van den Bosch. 2022. Correlating political party names in tweets, newspapers and election results. In *Proceedings of The LREC 2022 workshop on Natural Language Processing for Political Sciences*, pages 8–15, Marseille, France. European Language Resources Association.

Victor Sanh, Lysandre Debut, Julien Chaumond, and Thomas Wolf. 2019. Distilbert, a distilled version of bert: smaller, faster, cheaper and lighter. *arXiv preprint arXiv:1910.01108*.

Amit Seker, Elron Bandel, Dan Bareket, Idan Brusilovsky, Refael Shaked Greenfeld, and Reut Tsarfaty. 2021. Alephbert: A hebrew large pre-trained language model to start-off your hebrew nlp application with. *arXiv preprint arXiv:2104.04052*.

Stergios Skaperdas and Bernard Grofman. 1995. Modeling negative campaigning. *American Political Science Review*, 89(1):49–61.

Raymond E Wright. 1995. Logistic regression.

Hypothesis Engineering for Zero-Shot Hate Speech Detection

Janis Goldzycher and **Gerold Schneider**
Department of Computational Linguistics
University of Zurich
{goldzycher,gschneid}@cl.uzh.ch

Abstract

Standard approaches to hate speech detection rely on sufficient available hate speech annotations. Extending previous work that repurposes natural language inference (NLI) models for zero-shot text classification, we propose a simple approach that combines multiple hypotheses to improve English NLI-based zero-shot hate speech detection. We first conduct an error analysis for vanilla NLI-based zero-shot hate speech detection and then develop four strategies based on this analysis. The strategies use multiple hypotheses to predict various aspects of an input text and combine these predictions into a final verdict. We find that the zero-shot baseline used for the initial error analysis already outperforms commercial systems and fine-tuned BERT-based hate speech detection models on HateCheck. The combination of the proposed strategies further increases the zero-shot accuracy of 79.4% on HateCheck by 7.9 percentage points (pp), and the accuracy of 69.6% on ETHOS by 10.0pp.[1]

1 Introduction

With the increasing popularity of social media and online forums, phenomena such as hate speech, offensive and abusive language, and personal attacks have gained a powerful medium through which they can propagate fast. Due to the sheer number of posts and comments on social media, manual content moderation has become unfeasible, thus the automatic detection of harmful content becomes essential. In natural language processing, there now exist established tasks with the goal of detecting offensive language (Pradhan et al., 2020), abusive language (Nakov et al., 2021), hate speech (Fortuna and Nunes, 2018) and other related types of harmful content (Poletto et al., 2021). In this work, we focus on the detection of hate speech, which is typically defined as attacking, abusive or discriminatory language that targets people on the basis of identity defining group characteristics such as gender, sexual orientation, disability, race, religion, national origin etc. (Fortuna and Nunes, 2018; Poletto et al., 2021; Yin and Zubiaga, 2021). Most current hate speech detection approaches rely on either training models from scratch or fine-tuning pre-trained language models (Jahan and Oussalah, 2021). Both types of approaches need large amounts of labeled data which are only available for a few high-resource languages (Poletto et al., 2021) and costly to create. Therefore, exploring data-efficient methods for hate speech detection is an attractive alternative.

In this paper, we build on Yin et al. (2019) who proposed to re-frame text classification tasks as natural language inference, enabling high accuracy zero-shot classification. We exploit the fact that we can create arbitrary hypotheses to predict aspects of an input text that might be relevant for hate speech detection. To identify effective hypotheses, we first find a well-performing hypothesis formulation that claims that the input text contains hate speech. An error analysis based on HateCheck (Röttger et al., 2021) shows that given a well-performing formulation the model still struggles with multiple phenomena, including (1) abusive or profane language that does not target people based on identity-defining group characteristics, (2) counterspeech, (3) reclaimed slurs, and (4) implicit hate speech. To mitigate these misclassifications, we develop four strategies. Each strategy consists of multiple hypotheses and rules that combine these hypotheses in order to address one of the four identified error types.

We show that the combination of all proposed strategies improves the accuracy of vanilla NLI-based zero-shot prediction by 7.9pp on HateCheck (Röttger et al., 2021) and 10.0pp on ETHOS (Mollas et al., 2022). An error analysis shows that

[1]The code and instructions to reproduce the experiments are available at https://github.com/jagol/nli-for-hate-speech-detection.

Proceedings of the 29th International Conference on Computational Linguistic, pages 75–90
October 12–17, 2022.

the overall gains in accuracy largely stem from increased performance on previously identified weaknesses, demonstrating that the strategies work as intended.

Overall, our primary contributions are the following:

C1 An error analysis of vanilla NLI-based zero-shot hate speech detection.

C2 Developing strategies that combine multiple hypotheses to improve zero-shot hate speech detection.

C3 An evaluation and error analysis of the proposed strategies.

2 Background and Related Work

Early approaches to hate speech detection have focused on English social media posts, especially Twitter, and treated the task as binary or ternary text classification (Waseem and Hovy, 2016; Davidson et al., 2017; Founta et al., 2018). In more recent work, additional labels have been introduced that indicate whether the post is group-directed or not, who the targeted group is, if the post calls for violence, is aggressive, contains stereotypes, if the hate is expressed implicitly, or if sarcasm or irony is used (Mandl et al., 2019, 2020; Sap et al., 2020; ElSherief et al., 2021; Röttger et al., 2021; Mollas et al., 2022). Sometimes hate speech is not directly annotated but instead labels, such as *racism*, *sexism*, *homophobia* that already combine hostility with a specific target are annotated and predicted (Waseem and Hovy, 2016; Waseem, 2016; Saha et al., 2018; Lavergne et al., 2020).

While early approaches relied on manual feature engineering (Waseem and Hovy, 2016), most current approaches are based on pre-trained transformer-based language models that are then fine-tuned on hate speech datasets (Florio et al., 2020; Uzan and HaCohen-Kerner, 2021; Banerjee et al., 2021; Lavergne et al., 2020; Das et al., 2021; Nghiem and Morstatter, 2021).

Some work has focused on reducing the need for labeled data by multi-task learning on different sets of hate speech labels (Kapil and Ekbal, 2020; Safi Samghabadi et al., 2020) or adding sentiment analysis as an auxiliary task (Plaza-Del-Arco et al., 2021). Others have worked on reducing the need for non-English annotations by adapting hate speech detection models from high- to low-resource languages in a cross-lingual zero-shot setting (Stappen et al., 2020; Pamungkas et al., 2021). However the approach has been criticized for being unreliable when encountering language-specific taboo interjections (Nozza, 2021).

name	# examples	classes
HateCheck	3,728	hateful (68.8%), non-hate (31.2%)
ETHOS (binary)	997	hate speech (64.1%), not-hate speech (25.9%)

Table 1: The number of examples and the class balance of the datasets.

2.1 Zero-Shot Text Classification

The advent of large language models has enabled zero-shot and few-shot text classification approaches such as prompting (Liu et al., 2021), and task descriptions (Raffel et al., 2020), which convert the target task to the pre-training objective and are usually only used in combination with large language models. Chiu and Alexander (2021) use the prompts *"Is this text racist?"* and *"Is this text sexist?"* to detect hate speech with GPT-3. Schick et al. (2021) show that toxicity in large generative language models can be avoided by using similar prompts to self-diagnose toxicity during the decoding.

In contrast, NLI-based prediction in which a target task is converted to an NLI-task and fed into an NLI model converts the target task to the fine-tuning task. Here, a model is given a premise and a hypothesis and tasked to predict if the premise entails the hypothesis, contradicts it, or is neutral towards it. Yin et al. (2019) proposed to use an NLI model for zero-shot topic classification, by inputting the text to classify as the premise and constructing for each topic a hypothesis of the form "This text is about <topic>". They map the labels *neutral* and *contradiction* to *not-entailment*. We can then interpret a prediction of entailment as predicting that the input text belongs to the topic in the given hypothesis. Conversely, *not-entailment* implies that the text is not about the topic. Wang et al. (2021) show for a range of tasks, including offensive language identification, that this task reformulation also benefits few-shot learning scenarios. Recently, AlKhamissi et al. (2022) obtained large performance improvements in few-shot learning for hate speech detection by (1) decomposing the task into four subtasks and (2) additionally training the few-shot model on a knowledge base.

3 Data

HateCheck Röttger et al. (2021) introduce this English, synthetic, evaluation-only dataset, annotated for a binary decision between hate speech and not-hate speech. It covers 29 functionalities that are either a type of hate speech or challenging types of non-hate speech that could be mistaken for hate speech by a classifier. The examples for each of these functionalities have been constructed on the basis of conversations with NGO workers. Each of these templates contains one blank space to be filled with a protected group. The authors fill these templates with seven protected groups, namely: women, gay people, transgender people, black people, Muslims, immigrants, and disabled people. Overall the dataset contains 3,728 examples.

ETHOS The ETHOS dataset (Mollas et al., 2022) is split into two parts: one part is annotated for the presence of hate speech. The other part contains fine-grained annotations that indicate which characteristics have been targeted (gender, sexual orientation, race, ethnicity, religion, national origin, disability), whether the utterance calls for violence, and whether it is directed at an individual or a general statement about a group. The dataset is based on English comments from Youtube and Reddit. For this work, we will only make use of the binary hate speech annotations. These annotations are continuous values between 0 (indicating no hate speech at all) and 1 indicating clear hate speech. We rounded all annotations to either 0 or 1 using a threshold of 0.5.

Table 1 displays the class balances of the two datasets.

4 Evaluating Standard Zero-Shot Prediction

The evaluation of standard zero-shot NLI-based hate speech detection has two goals: To (1) obtain an error analysis that serves as the starting point for developing zero-shot strategies in Section 5, and (2) establish a baseline for those strategies.

Experiment setup To test if an input text contains hate speech, we need a hypothesis expressing that claim. However, there are many ways how the claim, that a given text contains hate speech, can be expressed. Choosing a sub-optimal way to express this claim will result in lower accuracy. Wang et al. (2021) already tested four different hypotheses for hate speech or offensive language. We conduct an extensive evaluation by constructing and testing all grammatically correct sentences built with the following building blocks: *It/That/This + example/text + contains/is + hate speech/hateful/hateful content.* We conduct all experiments with a BART-large model (Lewis et al., 2020) that was fine-tuned on the **M**ulti-Genre **N**atural **L**anguage **I**nference dataset (MNLI) (Williams et al., 2018) and has been made available via the Huggingface transformers library (Wolf et al., 2020) as `bart-large-mnli`. This model predicts either *contradiction*, *neutral*, or *entailment*. We follow the recommendation of the model creators to ignore the logits for *neutral* and perform a softmax over the logits of *contradiction* and *entailment*. If the probability for entailment is equal or higher than 0.5 we consider this a prediction of *entailment* and thus *hate speech*.[3] We evaluate on HateCheck since the functionalities in this dataset allow for an automatic in-depth error analysis and compare our results to the baselines provided by Röttger et al. (2021).

system	acc. (%)
BART-MNLI 0-shot results	
That example is hate speech. / That is hateful.	66.6
That contains hate speech.	79.4
average	75.1
Systems evaluated by Röttger et al. (2021)	
SiftNinja	33.2
BERT fine-tuned on Davidson et al. (2017)	60.2
BERT fine-tuned on Founta et al. (2018)	63.2
Google Jigsaw Perspective [2]	76.6

Table 2: Evaluation of hypotheses for zero-shot hate speech detection on HateCheck. The top rows contain the two lowest scoring hypotheses, the highest scoring hypothesis and the average score for all tested hypotheses. The bottom rows contain the HateCheck baselines computed by Röttger et al. (2021). The full results for all tested hypotheses are listed in Appendix A.

Results Table 2 shows an abbreviated version of the results. The full results are given in Appendix A. The hypothesis "That contains hate speech." obtains the highest accuracy and beats the Google-Jigsaw API by 2.8pp. This is remarkable, since we can assume that the commercial systems were all trained to detect hateful content or hate speech, while this model has not been trained on a single

[2]Google Jigsaw has since released a new version of the model powering the Perspective API (Lees et al., 2022). We assume that the new model would score higher on HateCheck.

[3]This procedure is equal to taking the argmax over *contradiction* and *entailment*.

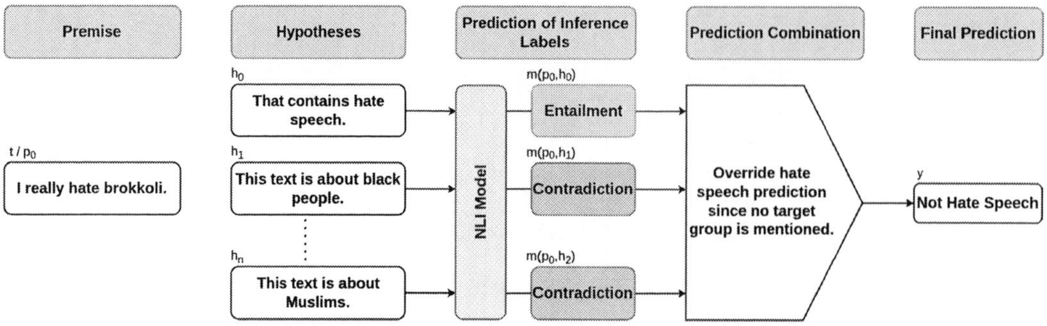

Figure 1: **FBT** Standard zero-shot entailment predictions would wrongly predict the input text as containing hate speech. Using additional hypotheses it is possible to check if a protected group is targeted and if necessary to override the original prediction.

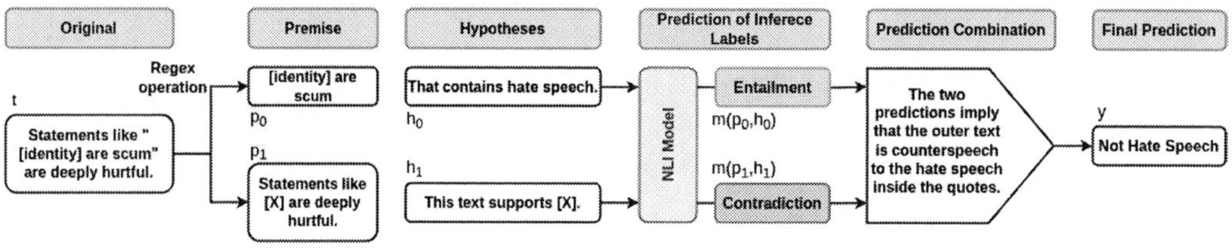

Figure 2: **FCS** If a text contains quotations the quoted text is replaced with a variable X using a regular expression. Then, then two hypotheses are tested: The first hypothesis serves as a test checking if the text inside the quotes is hate speech. If that is predicted to be the case, the second hypothesis is used to predict if the quoted text is supported or denounced by the post.

example of hate speech detection or a similar task. The two lowest scoring hypotheses lead to an accuracy of 66.6% meaning that an unlucky choice of hypothesis can cost more than 12pp accuracy.

Error Analysis Column "No Strat." in Table 4 shows the accuracy per HateCheck functionality for the hypothesis "That contains hate speech.". Most notably, the model wrongly predicted all denouncements of hate (F20 and F21) as hate speech. In four functionalities (F22, F11, F23, F20) the model predicted hate speech even though no one or no relevant group was targeted. Finally, we see that the model often fails at analyzing sentences with negations (F15) and that it fails at recognizing when slurs are reclaimed and used in a positive way (F9). In what follows, we will present and evaluate strategies to avoid these errors.

5 Methods

In this section, we present four methods, which we call strategies, that aim to improve zero-shot hate speech detection. A strategy has the following components and structure: The aim is to assign a label $y = \{0, 1\}$ to input text t, where 1 corresponds to the class *hate speech* and 0 corresponds to the class *not-hate speech*. The input text t can be used in one or multiple a premises p_0 to p_m, that are used in conjunction with the main hypothesis h_0 and one or multiple supporting hypotheses $[h_1, ..., h_n]$ to obtain NLI model predictions $m(p_i, h_j) \in \{0, 1\}$ where 0 corresponds to contradiction and 1 corresponds to entailment. The variables i and j are defined as: $i \in [0, ..., m]$ and $j \in [0, ..., n]$. The rules for how to combine model predictions to obtain the final label y are given by the individual strategies. As the main hypothesis we use "That contains hate speech.", since it lead to the highest accuracy on HateCheck in Section 4. The supporting hypotheses used to implement the strategies are listed in Table 3.

5.1 Filtering By Target (FBT)

The error analysis showed that we can improve zero-shot classification accuracy significantly by avoiding predictions of hate speech where no relevant target group occurs. We thus propose to avoid false positives by constructing a set of supporting hypotheses $[h_1, ..., h_n]$ to predict if text t actually targets or mentions a protected group or characteristic. If no protected group or characteristic is

FBT groups	This text is about women. This text is about trans people. This text is about gay people. This text is about black people. This text is about disabled people. This text is about Muslims. This text is about immigrants.
FBT characteristics	This text is about gender. This text is about sexual orientation. This text is about race. This text is about ethnicity. This text is about disability. This text is about religion. This text is about national origin.
FCS	This text supports [X].
FRS	This text is about myself.
CDC	This text is about insects. This text is about apes. This text is about primates. This text is about rats. This text is about a plague. This text has a negative sentiment.

Table 3: The supporting hypotheses used to implement the proposed strategies. For filtering by target we used the group-hypotheses for the HateCheck dataset and the characteristics-hypotheses for the ETHOS dataset, to account for differing hate speech definitions.

predicted to occur in t, a potential prediction of *hate speech* is overridden to *not-hate speech*. Figure 1 illustrates the method.

5.2 Filtering Counterspeech (FCS)

Our zero-shot model wrongly classifies all examples of counterspeech that quote or reference hate speech as actual hate speech. References to hate speech without quotation marks are hard to identify. Thus, for this work, we limit ourselves to counterspeech that quotes hate speech explicitly. We propose a three-stage strategy to this phenomenon: (1) quotation identification, (2) hate speech classification of the quoted content, (3) detecting the stance of the post towards the quoted content. Formally, the input text t is divided into premise p_0 which contains the quoted text and premise p_1 which contains the text around the quotes. The quoted text is represented as "$[X]$" in p_1. Using the main hypothesis h_0 we predict if p_0 contains hate speech or not. We use the supporting hypothesis "This text supports $[X]$." (h_1) to predict the stance of p_1 towards p_0. If p_0 contains hate speech and p_1 has a supportive stance towards p_0, t is classified as *hate speech*, otherwise it is classified as *not-hate speech*. The strategy is depicted in Figure 2.

5.3 Filtering Reclaimed Slurs (FRS)

As shown in Table 4, slurs that are reclaimed by members of a targeted group are often missclassified as hate speech. Based on the observation that a reclaimed slur is often ascribed to oneself, we propose to use a supporting hypothesis that indicates if text is self-directed.[4] If the model predicts self-directedness a potential prediction of *hate speech* is overridden to *not-hate speech*.

5.4 Catching Dehumanizing Comparisons (CDC)

One way of expressing hate towards a group and dehumanizing said group is to draw unflattering comparisons with animals. Such comparisons tend to be missed by hate speech detection systems, since the use of hateful or aggressive words is not needed to convey the hateful message. In HateCheck, this phenomenon is subsumed under "Implicit derogation". Standard zero-shot prediction obtains a moderately good accuracy of 89.3%. We test if false negatives can be caught with a three-step combination of supporting hypotheses: (1) use the supporting hypotheses of FBT to predict if a protected group is mentioned in text t, (2) predict if t has a negative sentiment, and (3) predict if t has is about animals typically used when making dehumanizing comparisons (such as insects, rats, or monkeys). If all conditions are met, override a prediction of *not-hate speech* to *hate speech*.

6 Experiments

We use the same model and adopt the entailment threshold of 0.5 from Section 4 for the main and all supporting hypotheses. Further, we take the hypothesis leading to the highest accuracy in Section 4 as the main hypothesis.

Since the main hypothesis in our experiments is chosen for maximum accuracy on HateCheck (based on the experiment in Section 4) and the strategies developed are based on an error analysis on HateCheck, the overall system might be overfitting on this specific dataset. An evaluation on this dataset might thus lead to results that overestimate a potential positive effect of the proposed strategies. We therefore also evaluate on ETHOS as an "unseen" dataset.

[4]Of course there are counterexamples to this rule, where reclaimed slurs are directed to others and not oneself. However, as long this approximation, as crude as it may be, helps to reduce false positives, it is a useful approximation.

Functionality	No Strat.	FBT	FCS	FRS	CDC	All
F1: Expression of strong negative emotions (explicit)	100.0	+0.0	+0.0	+0.0	+0.0	+0.0
F2: Description using very negative attributes (explicit)	98.6	+0.0	+0.0	+0.0	+0.0	+0.0
F3: Dehumanisation (explicit)	100.0	+0.0	+0.0	+0.0	+0.0	+0.0
F4: Implicit derogation	89.3	-5.0	+0.0	-10.0	+0.0	-12.9
F5: Direct threat	100.0	+0.0	+0.0	-3.0	+0.0	-3.0
F6: Threat as normative statement	99.3	+0.0	+0.0	+0.0	+0.0	+0.0
F7: Hate expressed using slur	85.4	-14.6	+0.0	+0.0	+2.8	-12.5
F8: Non-hateful homonyms of slurs	76.7	+6.7	+0.0	+0.0	+0.0	+6.7
F9: Reclaimed slurs	33.3	+0.0	+0.0	+32.1	+0.0	+32.1
F10: Hate expressed using profanity	97.9	-0.7	+0.0	+0.0	+0.0	-0.7
F11: Non-hateful use of profanity	43.0	+49.0	+0.0	+23.0	+0.0	+50.0
F12: Hate expressed through reference in subsequent clauses	100.0	+0.0	+0.0	-2.9	+0.0	-2.9
F13: Hate expressed through reference in subsequent sentences	97.7	+0.0	+0.0	+0.0	+0.0	+0.0
F14: Hate expressed using negated positive statement	100.0	-2.9	+0.0	+0.0	+0.0	-2.9
F15: Non-hate expressed using negated hateful statement	33.1	+5.3	+0.0	+0.0	+0.0	+5.3
F16: Hate phrased as a question	99.3	+0.0	+0.0	-5.0	+0.0	-5.0
F17: Hate phrased as an opinion	100.0	+0.0	+0.0	-2.3	+0.0	-2.3
F18: Neutral statements using protected group identifiers	96.0	+0.0	+0.0	+0.0	+0.0	+0.0
F19: Positive statements using protected group identifiers	97.4	+0.0	+0.0	+0.0	+0.0	+0.0
F20: Denouncements of hate that quote it	0.0	+8.7	+100.0	+0.0	+0.0	+100.0
F21: Denouncements of hate that make direct reference to it	0.0	+7.8	+0.0	+1.4	+0.0	+8.5
F22: Abuse targeted at objects	63.1	+36.9	+0.0	+9.2	+0.0	+36.9
F23: Abuse targeted at individuals (not as member of a prot. group)	7.7	+70.8	+0.0	+0.0	+0.0	+70.8
F24: Abuse targeted at nonprotected groups (e.g. professions)	11.3	+83.9	+0.0	+3.2	+0.0	+83.9
F25: Swaps of adjacent characters	97.7	+0.0	+0.0	+0.0	+0.0	+0.0
F26: Missing characters	88.6	-1.4	+0.0	+0.0	+0.7	-0.7
F27: Missing word boundaries	87.9	-4.3	+0.0	+0.0	+1.4	-3.5
F28: Added spaces between chars	97.7	-11.0	+0.0	-0.6	+0.0	-11.6
F29: Leet speak spellings	93.1	-12.7	+0.0	+0.0	+0.6	-12.1
Overall	79.4	+3.3	+4.6	+0.7	+0.2	+7.9

Table 4: Analysis of how individual functionalities are affected by the proposed strategies. The functionality descriptions are taken from Röttger et al. (2021). *No Strat.* refers to using only the hypothesis "That contains hate speech.". Accuracies below 70% are marked in red. *All* refers to combining all four proposed strategies. The columns *FBT*, *FCS*, *FRS*, *CDC* and *All* contain the difference in percentage point (pp) accuracy compared to *No Strat.*.

ETHOS does not refer to protected groups in its definition and annotation of hate speech, but instead to protected characteristics. Thus, in the hypotheses for FBT we replace protected groups with the protected characteristics listed in Table 3.

6.1 Results

HateCheck The bottom row *Overall* in Table 4 shows the results for the proposed strategies and their combination on the HateCheck dataset. Each strategy leads to an improvement in accuracy. But while FBT and FCS lead to large increases, FRS and CDC only lead to minor increases. Combining all proposed strategies leads to an increase in accuracy of 7.9pp.

strategies	accuracy (%)	Δ
(ETHOS) SVM	66.4	-
(ETHOS) BERT	80.0	-
(ETHOS) DistilBERT	80.4	-
"That contains hate speech."	69.6	+0.0
FBT (TG)	75.5	+5.9
FBT (TC)	78.7	+9.1
FCS	69.6	+0.0
FRS	71.3	+1.7
CDC (TC)	69.5	-0.1
FBT (TC) + FCS	78.7	+9.1
FBT (TC) + FRS	79.7	+10.1
FCS + FRS	71.3	+1.7
FBT (TC) + FCS + FRS	79.7	+10.1
CDC (TC) + FBT (TC) + FCS + FRS	79.6	+10.0

Table 5: Accuracy scores on ETHOS. The three top rows show baselines computed by Mollas et al. (2022). TG refers to using *target groups* to implement FBT and TC refers to using *target characteristics* for FBT.

ETHOS The results of evaluating the same strategies on ETHOS (Mollas et al., 2022) are given in Table 5. As additional baselines compared to zero-shot prediction using just one hypothesis, we include the performance of three models trained on ETHOS by Mollas et al. (2022).

The combination of all strategies leads to a increase of 10.0pp, which is an even greater increase than on HateCheck. However, the gains are more unevenly distributed across the proposed strategies. Filtering by target characteristics alone leads to an increase of 9.1pp. Filtering reclaimed slurs still has a positive effects of 1.7pp. However, filtering counterspeech, the best performing strategy on HateCheck, does not have any effect at all. And catching dehumanizing comparisons even reduces performance by 0.1pp.

The comparison to the baselines provided by Mollas et al. (2022) shows that zero-shot prediction using the hypothesis "That contains hate speech." already outperforms a trained SVM by more than 3pp but still underperforms the fine-tuned BERT by more than 10pp. However, applying the proposed strategies almost closes the gap to the fine-tuned models.

6.2 Analysis of Affected Functionalities

We analyse if the observed performance gains actually stem from improvements on the functionalities targeted by the proposed strategies. Table 4 shows for each functionality how it was affected by each strategy.

Filtering by Target The results for filtering by target show dramatic accuracy increases for HateCheck functionalities containing abuse and profanity that is not targeted at a protected group. These are exactly the functionalities this strategy aimed at. The performance for spelling variations and implicit derogation decreases slightly. This can be explained by the model failing to correctly recognize spelling variations of target groups and by the fact that the target group might only be implied in implicit derogation leading to false negatives.

Filtering Counterspeech The counterspeech filter increases the accuracy of the respective functionality from 0% to 100%. Thus, detecting quoted hate speech as well as detecting the stance towards the quote worked exactly as intented on HateCheck.

Filtering Reclaimed Slurs The functionality with the largest gains when filtering reclaimed slurs is "reclaimed slurs", showing that the strategy works as intended. However, the performance increase of this method is not as high as for example filtering by target. The functionality "non-hateful use of profanity" also benefits from this strategy. We assume that such uses of profanity often are also not directed at other people and thus sometimes predicted to be directed at oneself. This is a beneficial side-effect of the strategy.

Catching Dehumanizing Comparisons This strategy only leads to minor a minor overall improvement of 0.2pp. We observe no effect on the targeted functionality, but a small positive effect on F7, "Hate expressed using slur", which could

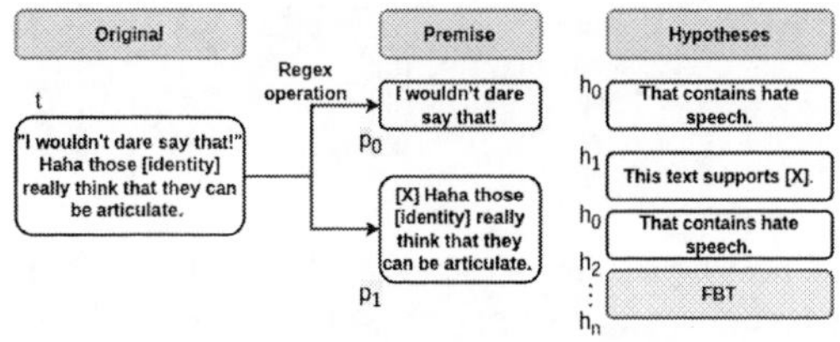

Figure 3: Counterspeech filter adjusted for detecting hate speech where quotes are present but the hate speech is outside of the quote - i.e. in the outer text.

indicate that the model associates slurs with negatively coded animals. Additionally, the strategy has minor positive effects on functionalities that contain spelling variations.

7 Discussion

Supporting Hypotheses The performance of NLI-strategies largely depends on the accuracy of the supporting hypotheses. Testing the accuracy of each supporting hypothesis is not always possible, since annotated data for the predicted aspect of the input text might not be available. Indeed, one of the strengths of our approach is that it can use aspects for which no annotated data exists. Another uncertainty lies in the formulation of supporting hypotheses. A suboptimal formulation of supporting hypotheses negatively affects the overall results. By using annotated targets in HateCheck and inferring stance labels as well as self-directedness from HateCheck functionalities, we compute and compare the accuracy of multiple supporting hypothesis formulations. The results (in Appendix B) show that testing for the presence of a target group mostly leads to accuracies above 90%, independent of the specific formulation. Detecting the outer stance towards the inner text obtained a perfect accuracy of 100% and testing for self-directedness leads to low accuracies, which are probably partly due to faulty label inferences from functionalities. Overall, the results indicate that the supporting hypotheses provide reliable information.

Generality There are two ways in which the proposed strategies might not generalize. First, the strategies might be specific to the model used for the experiments. In order to answer this question, repeating the experiments with other NLI models will be necessary. Second, the strategies might be specific to HateCheck and not generalize to other datasets, since they specifically target HateCheck functionalities. The evaluation on ETHOS shows

strategy	F20	overall
No strategy	0.0	79.4
FCS	+100	+4.6
FCS_{p_1}	+0.0	+0.0
$FCS_{p_1 FBT}$	+6.9	+0.3

Table 6: Evaluation of FCS variants. The two bottom rows display the variants adjusted for detecting Hate Speech in p_1. The functionality F20 contains *Denouncements of hate that quote it.* The scores are given in accuracy (%) and change in accuracy compared to *No strategy.*

that this is generally not case, since the results for the best strategy combination on ETHOS even exceed the results for the best combination on HateCheck.

While our experiments did not show problems in generalization, we can imagine the following weakness for the FCS strategy: Given an input text t that contains a quote and hate speech, where the hate speech does not occur inside of the quotes, the current FCS strategy would fail, since it only detects hate speech in p_0, that is inside the quotes. Such an example is given in Figure 3.

The obvious solution to avoid this problem is to not only apply the main hypothesis h_0 on the premise p_0 but also on premise p_1, which contains the text outside the quotes. In a follow-up experiment we implement this modified strategy (FCS_{p_1}) and evaluated it on HateCheck. Note, that since such a case is not covered by HateCheck or ETHOS there is no increase in accuracy to be expected - we can only test if accounting for this case leads to a decrease in accuracy through unwanted side effects.

The results, displayed in Table 6 show that this modification removes all the gains obtained through FBT. We assume that this is due to the fact that the counterspeech often also conveys strong negative emotions that are mistaken by the model for hate speech.

We further test if this problem can be alleviated by applying the FBT strategy if hate speech is detected in p_1 (i.e. outside of the quotes) as depicted in Figure 3. The results in Table 6 (row $FCS_{p_1 FBT}$) show that additionally applying FBT only recovers a fraction of the positive effect of FCS. We assume that this is due to counterspeech including or being associated with target groups. Thus, further research that investigates how the problem can be alleviated is needed.

Efficiency In the proposed setup each new hypothesis necessitates an additional forward pass, which means that the computational cost linearly increases with adding new hypotheses. This leads to a difficult trade-off between accuracy and efficiency. A possible solution was recently proposed by Müller et al. (2022), who embed premises and hypotheses independently, thereby keeping the computational cost during inference time with respect to the number of hypotheses constant.

Prerequisites of FBT FBT presumes that the target groups or characteristics are known beforehand. This prerequisite is unproblematic when using FBT to detect hate speech against well known targets of hate speech or discrimination. However, it makes this method unsuitable for tasks such as vulnerable group identification (Mossie and Wang, 2020).

Flexibility Single hypotheses or entire strategies can be easily added to or removed from a system. This modularity makes the approach easily adjustable to different scenarios or use cases. For example, if precision is the main concern, the *catching dehumanizing comparisons* can be dropped and if recall is the main concern, filters can be removed. Instead of adding or removing strategies, it is also possible to manipulate the precision-recall trade-off by adjusting confidence thresholds for particular hypotheses.

8 Conclusion

In this work, we combine hypotheses to create more accurate NLI-based zero-shot hate speech detection systems. Specifically, we develop four simple strategies, *filtering by target*, *filtering counter speech*, *filtering reclaimed-slurs*, and *catching dehumanizing comparisons*, that target specific model weaknesses. We evaluate the strategies on HateCheck, which served as the basis for developing these strategies, and on ETHOS, which acts as an "unseen" dataset. The NLI-based zero-shot baseline already outperforms fine-tuned models on HateCheck and beats an SVM baseline on ETHOS. Using all four proposed strategies leads to a further performance increase of 7.9% on HateCheck and 10.0% on ETHOS. However, the contribution of the strategies to the performance increases varies, with *catching dehumanizing comparisons* even having a small negative effect on the accuracy on ETHOS.

The proposed approach is simple and modular making it easy to implement and adjust to different scenarios.

In future work, we plan to evaluate such strategies in a multi-lingual setup and in a few-shot scenario. Further, this works leads to the question how effective supporting hypotheses could be searched and generated automatically.

Acknowledgements

We thank Chantal Amrhein, Jonathan Schaber, Aneta Zuber, and the anonymous reviewers for their helpful feedback. This work was funded by the University of Zurich Research Priority Program (project "URPP Digital Religion(s)"[5]).

Ethical Considerations

The goal of this article is to contribute to the development of sophisticated hate speech detection methods, and thus to contribute to an online environment that is less hateful. However, we can imagine multiple ways how such methods, and our proposed approach in particular, can lead to harm: (1) Deploying the exact system that we propose would lead to not detecting hate speech against protected groups that are not explicitly included in the two datasets we worked with and thus not covered by the FBT-method. Thus, before deploying such a method, careful consideration of which protected groups or group characteristics are covered is needed. (2) Overconfident claims about the accuracy of hate speech detection methods could lead to the false impression that content moderation can be left to automatic methods with no human intervention. (3) Hate speech detection in general is prone to misuse and repurposing in order to prohibit other kinds of speech. Detecting if a text revolves around a protected group could be misused to detect and prohibit important discussion around topics connected to a protected group.

However, we believe that a decomposition of hate speech into more specific aspects is important for more accurate, interpretable and modular hate speech detection methods (Khurana et al., 2022). Thus, detecting such components of hate speech is also strongly beneficial for effective content moderation and a less hateful online environment.

[5] https://www.digitalreligions.uzh.ch/en.html

References

Badr AlKhamissi, Faisal Ladhak, Srini Iyer, Ves Stoyanov, Zornitsa Kozareva, Xian Li, Pascale Fung, Lambert Mathias, Asli Celikyilmaz, and Mona Diab. 2022. ToKen: Task Decomposition and Knowledge Infusion for Few-Shot Hate Speech Detection. arXiv. ArXiv ID: arXiv:2205.12495 [cs].

Somnath Banerjee, Maulindu Sarkar, Nancy Agrawal, Punyajoy Saha, and Mithun Das. 2021. Exploring Transformer Based Models to Identify Hate Speech and Offensive Content in English and Indo-Aryan Languages. *arXiv:2111.13974 [cs]*. ArXiv: 2111.13974.

Ke-Li Chiu and Rohan Alexander. 2021. Detecting Hate Speech with GPT-3. *arXiv:2103.12407 [cs]*. ArXiv: 2103.12407.

Sourav Das, Prasanta Mandal, and Sanjay Chatterji. 2021. Probabilistic Impact Score Generation using Ktrain-BERT to Identify Hate Words from Twitter Discussions. *arXiv:2111.12939 [cs]*. ArXiv: 2111.12939.

Thomas Davidson, Dana Warmsley, Michael Macy, and Ingmar Weber. 2017. Automated Hate Speech Detection and the Problem of Offensive Language. *Proceedings of the International AAAI Conference on Web and Social Media*, 11(1):512–515. Number: 1.

Mai ElSherief, Caleb Ziems, David Muchlinski, Vaishnavi Anupindi, Jordyn Seybolt, Munmun De Choudhury, and Diyi Yang. 2021. Latent Hatred: A Benchmark for Understanding Implicit Hate Speech. In *Proceedings of the 2021 Conference on Empirical Methods in Natural Language Processing*, pages 345–363, Online and Punta Cana, Dominican Republic. Association for Computational Linguistics.

Komal Florio, Valerio Basile, Marco Polignano, Pierpaolo Basile, and Viviana Patti. 2020. Time of Your Hate: The Challenge of Time in Hate Speech Detection on Social Media. *Applied Sciences*, 10(12):4180. Number: 12 Publisher: Multidisciplinary Digital Publishing Institute.

Paula Fortuna and Sérgio Nunes. 2018. A Survey on Automatic Detection of Hate Speech in Text. *ACM Computing Surveys*, 51(4):85:1–85:30.

Antigoni Maria Founta, Constantinos Djouvas, Despoina Chatzakou, Ilias Leontiadis, Jeremy Blackburn, Gianluca Stringhini, Athena Vakali, Michael Sirivianos, and Nicolas Kourtellis. 2018. Large Scale Crowdsourcing and Characterization of Twitter Abusive Behavior. In *Twelfth International AAAI Conference on Web and Social Media*.

Md Saroar Jahan and Mourad Oussalah. 2021. A systematic review of Hate Speech automatic detection using Natural Language Processing. Technical Report arXiv:2106.00742, arXiv. ArXiv:2106.00742 [cs] type: article.

Prashant Kapil and Asif Ekbal. 2020. A deep neural network based multi-task learning approach to hate speech detection. *Knowledge-Based Systems*, 210:106458.

Urja Khurana, Ivar Vermeulen, Eric Nalisnick, Marloes Van Noorloos, and Antske Fokkens. 2022. Hate Speech Criteria: A Modular Approach to Task-Specific Hate Speech Definitions. In *Proceedings of the Sixth Workshop on Online Abuse and Harms (WOAH)*, pages 176–191, Seattle, Washington (Hybrid). Association for Computational Linguistics.

Eric Lavergne, Rajkumar Saini, György Kovács, and Killian Murphy. 2020. TheNorth @ HaSpeeDe 2: BERT-based Language Model Fine-tuning for Italian Hate Speech Detection. In Valerio Basile, Danilo Croce, Maria Maro, and Lucia C. Passaro, editors, *EVALITA Evaluation of NLP and Speech Tools for Italian - December 17th, 2020*, pages 142–147. Accademia University Press.

Alyssa Lees, Vinh Q. Tran, Yi Tay, Jeffrey Sorensen, Jai Gupta, Donald Metzler, and Lucy Vasserman. 2022. A New Generation of Perspective API: Efficient Multilingual Character-level Transformers. *arXiv:2202.11176 [cs]*. ArXiv: 2202.11176.

Mike Lewis, Yinhan Liu, Naman Goyal, Marjan Ghazvininejad, Abdelrahman Mohamed, Omer Levy, Veselin Stoyanov, and Luke Zettlemoyer. 2020. BART: Denoising Sequence-to-Sequence Pre-training for Natural Language Generation, Translation, and Comprehension. In *Proceedings of the 58th Annual Meeting of the Association for Computational Linguistics*, pages 7871–7880, Online. Association for Computational Linguistics.

Pengfei Liu, Weizhe Yuan, Jinlan Fu, Zhengbao Jiang, Hiroaki Hayashi, and Graham Neubig. 2021. Pre-train, Prompt, and Predict: A Systematic Survey of Prompting Methods in Natural Language Processing. *arXiv:2107.13586 [cs]*. ArXiv: 2107.13586.

Thomas Mandl, Sandip Modha, Anand Kumar M, and Bharathi Raja Chakravarthi. 2020. Overview of the HASOC Track at FIRE 2020: Hate Speech and Offensive Language Identification in Tamil, Malayalam, Hindi, English and German. In *Forum for Information Retrieval Evaluation*, pages 29–32, Hyderabad India. ACM.

Thomas Mandl, Sandip Modha, Prasenjit Majumder, Daksh Patel, Mohana Dave, Chintak Mandlia, and Aditya Patel. 2019. Overview of the HASOC Track at FIRE 2019: Hate Speech and Offensive Content Identification in Indo-European Languages. In *Proceedings of the 11th Forum for Information Retrieval Evaluation*, FIRE '19, pages 14–17, New York, NY, USA. Association for Computing Machinery. Event-place: Kolkata, India.

Ioannis Mollas, Zoe Chrysopoulou, Stamatis Karlos, and Grigorios Tsoumakas. 2022. ETHOS: a multi-label hate speech detection dataset. *Complex & Intelligent Systems*.

Zewdie Mossie and Jenq-Haur Wang. 2020. Vulnerable community identification using hate speech detection on social media. *Information Processing & Management*, 57(3):102087.

Thomas Müller, Guillermo Pérez-Torró, and Marc Franco-Salvador. 2022. Few-Shot Learning with Siamese Networks and Label Tuning. In *Proceedings of the 60th Annual Meeting of the Association for Computational Linguistics (Volume 1: Long Papers)*, pages 8532–8545, Dublin, Ireland. Association for Computational Linguistics.

Preslav Nakov, Vibha Nayak, Kyle Dent, Ameya Bhatawdekar, Sheikh Muhammad Sarwar, Momchil Hardalov, Yoan Dinkov, Dimitrina Zlatkova, Guillaume Bouchard, and Isabelle Augenstein. 2021. Detecting Abusive Language on Online Platforms: A Critical Analysis. *arXiv:2103.00153 [cs]*. ArXiv: 2103.00153.

Huy Nghiem and Fred Morstatter. 2021. "Stop Asian Hate!" : Refining Detection of Anti-Asian Hate Speech During the COVID-19 Pandemic. *arXiv:2112.02265 [cs]*. ArXiv: 2112.02265.

Debora Nozza. 2021. Exposing the limits of Zero-shot Cross-lingual Hate Speech Detection. In *Proceedings of the 59th Annual Meeting of the Association for Computational Linguistics and the 11th International Joint Conference on Natural Language Processing (Volume 2: Short Papers)*, pages 907–914, Online. Association for Computational Linguistics.

Endang Wahyu Pamungkas, Valerio Basile, and Viviana Patti. 2021. A joint learning approach with knowledge injection for zero-shot cross-lingual hate speech detection. *Information Processing & Management*, 58(4):102544.

Flor Miriam Plaza-Del-Arco, M. Dolores Molina-González, L. Alfonso Ureña-López, and María Teresa Martín-Valdivia. 2021. A Multi-Task Learning Approach to Hate Speech Detection Leveraging Sentiment Analysis. *IEEE Access*, 9:112478–112489. Conference Name: IEEE Access.

Fabio Poletto, Valerio Basile, Manuela Sanguinetti, Cristina Bosco, and Viviana Patti. 2021. Resources and benchmark corpora for hate speech detection: a systematic review. *Language Resources and Evaluation*, 55(2):477–523.

Rahul Pradhan, Ankur Chaturvedi, Aprna Tripathi, and Dilip Kumar Sharma. 2020. A Review on Offensive Language Detection. In *Advances in Data and Information Sciences*, Lecture Notes in Networks and Systems, pages 433–439, Singapore. Springer.

Colin Raffel, Noam Shazeer, Adam Roberts, Katherine Lee, Sharan Narang, Michael Matena, Yanqi Zhou, Wei Li, and Peter J. Liu. 2020. Exploring the Limits of Transfer Learning with a Unified Text-to-Text Transformer. *Journal of Machine Learning Research*, 21(140):1–67.

Paul Röttger, Bertie Vidgen, Dong Nguyen, Zeerak Waseem, Helen Margetts, and Janet Pierrehumbert. 2021. HateCheck: Functional Tests for Hate Speech Detection Models. In *Proceedings of the 59th Annual Meeting of the Association for Computational Linguistics and the 11th International Joint Conference on Natural Language Processing (Volume 1: Long Papers)*, pages 41–58, Online. Association for Computational Linguistics.

Niloofar Safi Samghabadi, Parth Patwa, Srinivas PYKL, Prerana Mukherjee, Amitava Das, and Thamar Solorio. 2020. Aggression and Misogyny Detection using BERT: A Multi-Task Approach. In *Proceedings of the Second Workshop on Trolling, Aggression and Cyberbullying*, pages 126–131, Marseille, France. European Language Resources Association (ELRA).

Punyajoy Saha, Binny Mathew, Pawan Goyal, and Animesh Mukherjee. 2018. Hateminers : Detecting Hate speech against Women. *arXiv:1812.06700 [cs]*. ArXiv: 1812.06700.

Maarten Sap, Saadia Gabriel, Lianhui Qin, Dan Jurafsky, Noah A. Smith, and Yejin Choi. 2020. Social Bias Frames: Reasoning about Social and Power Implications of Language. In *Proceedings of the 58th Annual Meeting of the Association for Computational Linguistics*, pages 5477–5490, Online. Association for Computational Linguistics.

Timo Schick, Sahana Udupa, and Hinrich Schütze. 2021. Self-Diagnosis and Self-Debiasing: A Proposal for Reducing Corpus-Based Bias in NLP. *Transactions of the Association for Computational Linguistics*, 9:1408–1424.

Lukas Stappen, Fabian Brunn, and Björn Schuller. 2020. Cross-lingual Zero- and Few-shot Hate Speech Detection Utilising Frozen Transformer Language Models and AXEL. *arXiv:2004.13850 [cs, stat]*. ArXiv: 2004.13850.

Moshe Uzan and Yaakov HaCohen-Kerner. 2021. Detecting Hate Speech Spreaders on Twitter using LSTM and BERT in English and Spanish. *CLEF 2021 – Conference and Labs of the Evaluation Forum, September 21–24, 2021, Bucharest, Romania*, CEUR Workshop Proceedings:8.

Sinong Wang, Han Fang, Madian Khabsa, Hanzi Mao, and Hao Ma. 2021. Entailment as Few-Shot Learner. *arXiv:2104.14690 [cs]*. ArXiv: 2104.14690.

Zeerak Waseem. 2016. Are You a Racist or Am I Seeing Things? Annotator Influence on Hate Speech Detection on Twitter. In *NLP+CSS@EMNLP*.

Zeerak Waseem and Dirk Hovy. 2016. Hateful Symbols or Hateful People? Predictive Features for Hate Speech Detection on Twitter. In *Proceedings of the NAACL Student Research Workshop*, pages 88–93, San Diego, California. Association for Computational Linguistics.

Adina Williams, Nikita Nangia, and Samuel Bowman. 2018. A Broad-Coverage Challenge Corpus for Sentence Understanding through Inference. In *Proceedings of the 2018 Conference of the North American Chapter of the Association for Computational Linguistics: Human Language Technologies, Volume 1 (Long Papers)*, pages 1112–1122, New Orleans, Louisiana. Association for Computational Linguistics.

Thomas Wolf, Lysandre Debut, Victor Sanh, Julien Chaumond, Clement Delangue, Anthony Moi, Pierric Cistac, Tim Rault, Remi Louf, Morgan Funtowicz, Joe Davison, Sam Shleifer, Patrick von Platen, Clara Ma, Yacine Jernite, Julien Plu, Canwen Xu, Teven Le Scao, Sylvain Gugger, Mariama Drame, Quentin Lhoest, and Alexander Rush. 2020. Transformers: State-of-the-Art Natural Language Processing. In *Proceedings of the 2020 Conference on Empirical Methods in Natural Language Processing: System Demonstrations*, pages 38–45, Online. Association for Computational Linguistics.

Wenjie Yin and Arkaitz Zubiaga. 2021. Towards generalisable hate speech detection: a review on obstacles and solutions. *PeerJ Computer Science*, 7:e598. Publisher: PeerJ Inc.

Wenpeng Yin, Jamaal Hay, and Dan Roth. 2019. Benchmarking Zero-shot Text Classification: Datasets, Evaluation and Entailment Approach. In *Proceedings of the 2019 Conference on Empirical Methods in Natural Language Processing and the 9th International Joint Conference on Natural Language Processing (EMNLP-IJCNLP)*, pages 3914–3923, Hong Kong, China. Association for Computational Linguistics.

A Zero-Shot Results: Comparing Hypotheses

Table 7, the extended version of Table 2, contains all results for comparing hypotheses for zero-shot hate speech detection on HateCheck. "average:< `expression`>" refers to the average accuracy of all hypotheses containing `expression`. The highest accuracy is in bold.

hypothesis	accuracy (%)
Containing hate speech.	74.7
Contains hate speech.	78.6
Hate speech.	72.9
Hateful.	71.8
It contains hate speech.	78.7
It is hateful.	75.0
It contains hate speech.	78.7
It is hate speech.	70.8
It is hateful.	75.0
That contains hate speech.	**79.4**
That contains hateful content.	78.0
That example contains hateful content.	77.8
That example is hate speech.	66.6
That example is hateful.	76.8
That is hateful.	66.6
That text contains hate speech.	78.8
That text contains hateful content.	78.6
That text is hate speech.	69.2
That text is hateful.	77.2
This contains hate speech.	79.1
This contains hateful content.	78.2
This example contains hate speech.	77.3
This example contains hateful content.	77.8
This example is hate speech.	67.2
This example is hateful.	77.4
This is hateful.	70.6
This text contains hate speech.	78.8
This text contains hateful content.	78.3
This text is hate speech.	69.5
This text is hateful.	78.7
average: It	74.8
average: This	75.7
average: That	74.9
average: hateful	75.8
average: hateful content	78.1
average: hate speech	74.5
average: example	74.4
average: text	76.1
average: is	73.9
average: contain	78.2
SiftNinja	33.2
BERT fine-tuned on Davidson et al. (2017)	60.2
BERT fine-tuned on Founta et al. (2018)	63.2
Google-Jigsaw	76.6

Table 7: Full evaluation of hypotheses, that claim hate speech exists in the input text, on HateCheck.

B Evaluating Supporting Hypotheses

B.1 Target Groups and Target Characteristics

Each example in HateCheck which mentions a protected group or revolves around a protected group is annotated with said group. If no group is targeted the example is annotated with an empty string. By using these annotations as labels, we can create a binary classification task for each protected group: for detecting a mention of a specific protected group x, we convert label x to 1 and all other labels (i.e. all other protected groups) to 0.

We use the same model and as in the previous zero-shot experiments for evaluation and test the performance for detecting mentions for all protected groups in HateCheck. We additionally test the detection of the supercategory *queer people* covering the two protected groups *gay people* and *transgender people* in HateCheck. When testing if a text revolves around gender, we treat both *women* and *transgender people* as positive classes and all other protected groups as negative classes. While this mapping obviously can result in incorrect labels (a text can be about gender even if another group is targeted), we assume that it holds true for examples in the HateCheck dataset.

Table 8 shows the results for detecting if *black people* are mentioned, Table 9 for mentions of *Muslims*, Table 10 for mentions of immigrants, Table 11 for mentions of *disabled people*, Table 12 for mentions of *gay people*, Table 13 for mentions of *transgender people*, Table 14 for mentions of *queer people*, and Table 16 for detecting if a text is about *gender*.

The results show that in many cases the detection of a mentioned group is surprisingly accurate. The difference in accuracy between the best performing hypothesis and the worst performing hypothesis does not exceed 12%. This is a similar range to the differences found between hypotheses when testing if a text contains hate speech (see Table 2 and Table 7). However, when looking at F_1 scores the differences are much larger, with more general terms, such as *faith* or *ethnicity* preforming worse than the specific terms *Muslims* and *black people*.

Detecting if a text revolves around gender performs worst, compared to detecting other protected groups or characteristics. This is mostly due to low precision scores. We assume that this is a consequence of sexual orientation (*gay people*) being closely associated in the embedding space with *gender* and thus leading to false positives.

B.2 Self-Directedness

Evaluating the accuracy of detecting self-directedness is difficult, because there exist no

hypothesis	accuracy (%)	↓ F_1 (%)	recall (%)	precision (%)
That example is about black people.	97.9	92.0	93.8	90.2
This example is about black people.	97.6	90.9	94.0	88.0
That text is about black people.	96.4	87.1	93.2	81.8
That is about black people.	95.8	85.0	92.5	78.7
This text is about black people.	95.2	83.6	94.4	75.0
This is about black people.	95.0	83.0	93.6	74.5
That example is about people of colour.	94.3	80.7	92.7	71.4
That example is about race.	94.0	79.8	91.3	70.9
This example is about people of colour.	93.8	79.3	92.3	69.5
That is about race.	94.6	77.5	72.6	83.1
This example is about race.	90.9	72.3	91.7	59.6
That text is about people of colour.	89.8	70.6	94.2	56.4
That example is about ethnicity.	90.5	69.8	85.3	59.1
This is about race.	88.9	67.6	89.4	54.4
That text is about race.	87.8	66.3	92.3	51.7
That is about people of colour.	87.4	65.9	93.8	50.8
This text is about race.	86.5	64.5	94.6	48.9
This text is about people of colour.	84.9	62.1	96.1	45.9
This example is about ethnicity.	85.6	62.1	91.1	47.1
This is about ethnicity.	85.4	58.1	78.4	46.2
That text is about ethnicity.	81.5	56.1	91.3	40.5
This text is about ethnicity.	80.2	55.0	93.6	38.9
This is about people of colour.	74.8	49.4	95.2	33.3
That is about ethnicity.	87.0	28.4	19.9	49.7

Table 8: Results for supporting hypotheses aimed at detecting mentions of black people. The hypotheses are sorted by macro F_1-score in descending order. Note, that some of the hypotheses listed use broader terms ("people of colour", "race", "ethnicity") that should also detect the mentions of other target groups. However, in the context of HateCheck, we can only test the detection of mentioning black people.

labels in HateCheck that could be used as a ground truth.

One possibility, that follows the motivation for introducing the FRS-method, is to treat all examples of functionality F9 ("reclaimed_slur") as self-directed and examples of all other functionalities as not self-directed. We conducted this experiment. The results are given in Table 17. However, one should keep in mind that this disregards that reclaimed slurs can be used in a not-self directed manner and that other functionalities, such as functionality F11 *non-hateful use of profanity*, might contain examples of self-directed speech.

B.3 Counterspeech

We perform a simple evaluation of the supporting hypothesis that predicts the stance of an outer text towards its quoted inner text (see Section 5.2 for an explanation) using only functionality F20 (*Denouncements of hate that quote it*) as an evaluation set. We treat stance detection here as a binary task with the labels *is_for* or *is_against*.

How these labels are mapped onto NLI labels depends on the specific hypothesis. If the hypothesis claims that the outer text supports the quoted text, then *is_for* is mapped to *entailment* and *is_against* is mapped to *contradiction*. Conversely, if the hypothesis claims that the outer text denounces the quoted text, then *is_for* is mapped to *contradiction* and *is_against* is mapped to *entailment*.

We test various formulations including the verbs "supports [X]" and "is for [X]". The results are given in Table 18. Since all examples in this category are considered hate speech, that is denounced by the outer text, the true label is always *is_against*. We only report accuracy, since there can be no false positives and true negatives, which makes precision and recall lose its usefulness.

hypothesis	accuracy (%)	$\downarrow F_1$ (%)	recall (%)	precision (%)
That example is about Muslims.	98.3	93.1	90.7	95.6
This example is about Muslims.	98.1	92.7	90.7	94.8
This text is about Muslims.	98.1	92.6	90.3	95.0
That text is about Muslims.	98.0	92.3	90.3	94.4
That example is about Muslim people.	98.0	92.0	90.7	93.4
This example is about Muslim people.	97.9	92.0	90.9	93.0
This is about Muslims.	97.8	91.6	90.7	92.4
This text is about Muslim people.	97.8	91.5	90.7	92.2
That text is about Muslim people.	97.7	91.1	90.1	92.2
This example is about religion.	97.7	90.3	83.3	98.5
This text is about religion.	97.5	89.7	83.9	96.4
This is about Muslim people.	97.3	89.6	89.9	89.3
That text is about religion.	97.5	89.5	82.9	97.3
That is about Muslims.	97.2	89.1	88.6	89.6
That example is about religion.	97.3	88.5	80.2	98.7
That is about Muslim people.	96.8	87.8	89.7	85.9
This is about religion.	96.4	84.5	74.8	97.1
This example is about faith.	95.0	78.2	69.2	89.8
This text is about faith.	95.0	78.1	69.0	90.0
That text is about faith.	94.4	74.2	62.4	91.5
That example is about faith.	93.4	68.9	56.6	88.1
This is about faith.	92.0	63.3	52.9	78.8
That is about religion.	89.6	34.5	21.1	95.3
That is about faith.	88.3	21.9	12.6	82.4

Table 9: Results for supporting hypotheses aimed at detecting mentions of Muslim people. Note, that some of the hypotheses listed use broader terms ("faith", "religion") that should detect other target groups too. However, in the context of HateCheck their applicability is restricted to Muslim people, since no other religion occurs in HateCheck.

hypothesis	accuracy (%)	$\downarrow F_1$ (%)	recall (%)	precision (%)
That example is about immigrants.	97.8	91.2	92.4	89.9
This example is about immigrants.	97.7	90.8	92.4	89.2
That is about immigrants.	97.2	88.8	89.2	88.4
That text is about immigrants.	97.0	88.6	92.2	85.2
This text is about immigrants.	96.3	86.4	93.7	80.1
This is about immigrants.	96.4	86.2	91.6	81.4
This text is about national origin.	77.7	42.2	65.4	31.1
That text is about national origin.	78.0	41.3	62.4	30.9
This is about national origin.	83.4	37.0	39.3	35.0
That example is about national origin.	81.4	30.0	32.2	28.1
This example is about national origin.	79.8	30.0	34.8	26.3
That is about national origin.	86.5	24.6	17.7	40.2

Table 10: Results for supporting hypotheses aimed at detecting mentions of immigrants.

hypothesis	accuracy (%)	$\downarrow F_1$ (%)	recall (%)	precision (%)
That example is about disabled people.	98.4	93.7	90.3	97.3
This example is about disabled people.	98.4	93.5	90.1	97.1
This text is about disabled people.	98.0	92.3	91.3	93.2
That example is about disability.	97.9	91.9	92.4	91.4
That text is about disabled people.	97.9	91.3	87.0	96.1
This example is about disability.	97.7	91.3	93.0	89.6
That is about disabled people.	97.7	90.9	87.2	94.8
This is about disabled people.	97.4	89.9	90.3	89.5
That text is about disability.	96.6	87.6	91.5	84.1
That is about disability.	96.6	86.0	80.4	92.4
This is about disability.	94.8	82.0	91.7	74.1
This text is about disability.	94.5	81.6	94.4	71.9

Table 11: Results for supporting hypotheses aimed at detecting mentions of disabled people.

hypothesis	accuracy (%)	↓ F_1 (%)	recall (%)	precision (%)
That example is about gay people.	99.1	96.7	94.2	99.4
This example is about gay people.	99.0	96.6	94.0	99.2
This text is about gay people.	98.8	95.9	92.9	99.0
This is about gay people.	98.8	95.8	92.6	99.2
That text is about gay people.	98.5	94.6	90.0	99.6
That is about gay people.	98.4	94.4	90.4	98.8

Table 12: Results for supporting hypotheses aimed at detecting mentions of gay people.

hypothesis	accuracy (%)	↓ F_1 (%)	recall (%)	precision (%)
That example is about transgender people.	99.0	95.8	92.7	99.1
That text is about transgender people.	99.0	95.6	92.2	99.3
This text is about transgender people.	98.9	95.6	92.9	98.4
This example is about transgender people.	98.9	95.4	92.2	98.8
That is about transgender people.	98.8	94.9	92.0	97.9
This is about transgender people.	98.7	94.6	92.2	97.0

Table 13: Results for supporting hypotheses aimed at detecting mentions of transgender people.

hypothesis	accuracy (%)	↓ F_1 (%)	recall (%)	precision (%)
This is about queer people.	94.3	88.6	81.3	97.5
That example is about queer people.	93.7	87.1	77.9	98.8
This example is about queer people.	93.2	85.9	76.2	98.5
This text is about queer people.	93.1	85.7	76.4	97.5
That is about queer people.	92.4	84.0	73.5	98.2
That text is about queer people.	91.7	82.3	70.8	98.4

Table 14: Results for supporting hypotheses aimed at detecting mentions of queer people, which in HateCheck corresponds to the categories *gay people* and *transgender people*.

hypothesis	accuracy (%)	↓ F_1 (%)	recall (%)	precision (%)
This example is about women.	97.2	90.2	94.1	86.6
That example is about women.	97.2	90.1	94.1	86.5
That is about women.	96.2	86.6	88.6	84.6
This text is about women.	95.9	86.1	93.9	79.5
That text is about women.	95.7	85.3	91.6	79.8
This is about women.	94.8	83.0	92.7	75.0

Table 15: Results for supporting hypotheses aimed at detecting mentions of women.

hypothesis	accuracy (%)	↓ F_1 (%)	recall (%)	precision (%)
That example is about gender.	90.0	81.8	85.8	78.2
This example is about gender.	89.0	80.5	87.0	74.9
That text is about gender.	88.4	79.6	86.8	73.5
This text is about gender.	87.9	79.3	88.9	71.5
This is about gender.	87.1	75.1	74.7	75.5
That is about gender.	81.6	52.9	39.5	79.8

Table 16: Results for supporting hypotheses aimed at detecting texts concerning gender, which in HateCheck corresponds to the categories *transgender people*, and *women*.

hypothesis	accuracy (%)	↓ F_1 (%)	recall (%)	precision (%)
That text is about myself.	97.4	38.5	37.0	40.0
This text is about myself.	96.4	33.7	42.0	28.1
That is about myself.	97.3	33.3	30.9	36.2
This is about myself.	97.0	31.3	30.9	31.6
That example is about myself.	96.2	31.2	39.5	25.8
This example is about myself.	95.9	31.1	42.0	24.6
This text is about us.	85.1	16.8	69.1	9.6
That text is about us.	89.4	16.2	46.9	9.8
That is about us.	88.3	14.8	46.9	8.8
This example is about us.	77.4	12.8	76.5	7.0
That example is about us.	75.8	12.1	76.5	6.6
This is about us.	73.9	10.3	69.1	5.6

Table 17: Results for supporting hypotheses aimed detecting if a text is self-directed.

hypothesis	accuracy (%)
This text supports [X].	100.0
This supports [X].	100.0
That supports [X].	100.0
This example supports [X].	91.9
That example supports [X].	91.9
That text supports [X].	85.5
This text is for [X].	69.4
This is for [X].	50.9
That is for [X].	46.8
That text is for [X].	38.7
This example is for [X].	18.5
That example is for [X].	0.0

Table 18: Results for supporting hypotheses aimed at detecting the stance of an outer text p_1 towards its inner, quoted text p_0. Precision, recall and F_1-score are omitted, since with only positive test examples no false positives and true negatives are possible.

Author Index

Association for Computational Linguistics
209 N. Eighth Street
Stroudsburg, Pennsylvania 18360

ISBN 978-1-7138-6197-3

CURRAN ASSOCIATES INC.
proceedings.com